MONARCHS, MURDERS & MISTRESSES

A BOOK OF ROYAL DAYS

DAVID HILLIAM

The History Press

First published in 2004
This edition first published in 2009

The History Press
The Mill, Brimscombe Port
Stroud, Gloucestershire, GL5 2QG
www.thehistorypress.co.uk

British Library Cataloguing in Publication Data.
A catalogue record for this book is available from the British Library.

ISBN 978 0 7524 5235 7

Typesetting and origination by The History Press
Printed in Great Britain

*Cover illustrations: (left) detail from Roy 15 E IV f.236 Coronation of
William I, Vol I, by Jean Batard de Wavrin, c. 1470–80, Anciennes Chroniques
d' Angleterre (15th century), (British Library, London, UK/Bridgeman Art
Library); (right) detail from* The Execution of Lady Jane Grey, 9th–18th July
1553 *(finished study) by Hippolyte Delaroche (Paul) (1797–1856) (Guildhall
Art Gallery, Corporation of London UK/Bridgeman Art Library).*

CONTENTS

PREFACE

This book presents a royal event for each day of the year, drawing on a thousand years of English history. It is an anthology of anniversaries: a book for browsers. The events vary considerably, but the overall picture shows the recurring occupational difficulties of being royal. As Henry IV so memorably sums it up in Shakespeare's *Henry IV Part II*, 'Uneasy lies the head that wears a crown.'

Kings and queens have often been remarkable and fascinating individuals. But what makes them different, and what they they all have in common, is that they are constantly placed in extraordinary situations. Even the ordinary processes of life, such as birth and death, have to be carried out in public. Charles II urbanely apologised to the crowd of onlookers for being so long in dying (see FEBRUARY 5), while the 'warming-pan' rumours attached to the birth of the Old Pretender led to official witnesses being required for every subsequent royal lying-in (see NOVEMBER 14).

But kings and queens also have to cope with situations which are astonishingly different from the humdrum events of our own lives. Some have been beheaded (see FEBRUARY 13 and MAY 19); many, including Queen Victoria, have suffered assassination attempts (see FEBRUARY 29); others have had to beat off rivals, either in battle or even by signing death-warrants for their own relatives (see FEBRUARY 1 and JULY 15). No wonder that the pressures of circumstance have led so many monarchs, even in the twentieth century, to consult soothsayers and magicians (see AUGUST 9).

Here, then, is a series of close-ups, showing how flesh-and-blood men and women have found themselves caught up in the strange webs of history.

David Hilliam

CHRONOLOGY

CHRONOLOGY

1981	Death of Victoria's last haemophilia-carrying grandchild	Jan 3
1981	Marriage of Prince Charles and Lady Diana Spencer	Jul 29
1982	Birth of Prince William	Jun 21
1982	Prince Charles welcomes troops home from the Falklands conflict	Jul 11
1984	Birth of Prince Harry	Sept 15
1986	Prince Andrew and Sarah Ferguson announce their engagement	Mar 19
1987	Princess Anne is given the title 'Princess Royal'	Jun 12
1987	'Prince charges planners with rape of Britain' (*The Times*)	Dec 3
1994	Prince Charles survives an 'attack' in Sydney, Australia	Jan 26
1997	Death of Diana, Princess of Wales	Aug 31
1999/2000	Queen Elizabeth sings *Auld Lang Syne* in the Millennium Dome at Greenwich	Dec 31
2000	Queen Elizabeth the Queen Mother celebrates her 100th birthday	Aug 4
2002	Death of Queen Elizabeth the Queen Mother	Mar 30
2005	Charles and Camilla marry at last, after a 34-year friendship	Apr 9

JANUARY 1   1651
The Scottish coronation of King Charles II

A strange and unique coronation took place on 1 January 1651, at Scone in Scotland, when Charles II was crowned King of England, Scotland, Ireland and France (at that time a traditional title). It was less than two years since his father Charles I had been executed at Whitehall. Charles II had been only eighteen at the time, and was in France when the news of his father's death had reached him. He had burst into tears when the messengers addressed him as 'Your Majesty'.

Now, in 1651, aged twenty, still uncrowned and with the parliamentarians in full power in England, Charles had come to Scotland to try to claim his kingdom as it were by the back door. His defeat at the Battle of Worcester was still nine months into the future.

The coronation at Scone was an odd affair, as the Covenanters who were offering him the crown had no belief in bishops or many of the traditional ceremonies. Archibald Campbell, Marquis of Argyll, handed him the crown and sceptre, but anointing with oil was considered too superstitious. After the coronation feast, Charles celebrated by playing a game of golf – the Scottish game which his grandfather James I had introduced into England.

1766
Death of the 'Old Pretender'

After a lifetime of disappointment, James Stuart, the 'Old Pretender', who was known by his Jacobite supporters as 'James III', died this day in Rome. On the death of his father, the exiled James II, he had become 'king' in 1701, when he was only thirteen. His reign, if it had been a real one, would have been the longest in British history (see SEPTEMBER 9). His birth was surrounded by malicious rumours that his mother, Mary of Modena, had not been pregnant at all, but had smuggled the baby into St James's Palace in a warming-pan (see JUNE 10).

Now, having spent his entire life in exile, apart from a few weeks trying to gain a foothold in Scotland (see DECEMBER 22), he died aged seventy-seven, still an honoured guest of the Pope, who had given him a pension to live on, and an old palace, the Palazzo Muti in the square of the Holy Apostles, to live in.

The Pope continued to honour him even in death, and he was given a royal funeral in St Peter's, Rome. Rather poignantly, at James's funeral a royal crown was placed on his head for the first and only time.

1877

QUEEN VICTORIA BECOMES EMPRESS OF INDIA

Disraeli notoriously pandered to Queen Victoria's vanity: 'Everyone likes flattery,' he once said, 'and when you come to royalty, you should lay it on with a trowel.' Arguably, his most lavish 'gift' to her was the title 'Empress of India'. The Royal Titles Bill, legalising this in Parliament, was passed in 1876, and Victoria officially became Empress of India on 1 January 1877. At a celebratory dinner at Windsor on this day, Disraeli toasted her for the first time as 'Your Imperial Majesty'.

Victoria was gratified not merely with this new title, but also with the thought that her own daughter Vicky, married to Crown Prince Frederick William of Germany and likely to become Empress of Germany, would thereby never out-rank her. Empresses, after all, take precedence over mere queens.

Also on this day:
1801 Act of Union with Ireland. A revised 'union jack' was introduced, incorporating the diagonal red cross of St Patrick. George III was declared to be King of Great Britain and Ireland. At the same time, he ceased to use the ancient title 'King of France'.
2007 Zara Phillips, daughter of Princess Anne and Captain Mark Phillips, was awarded an MBE for her services to equestrianism (see JUNE 12) – a unique honour for a member of the Royal Family

JANUARY 2   1649

PARLIAMENT SETS UP A SPECIAL COURT TO TRY CHARLES I FOR TREASON

The move to put Charles I on trial for treason began with the setting up of a special court consisting of about a hundred and fifty members and presided over by two Chief Justices. The reasons for this trial were outlined thus:

> Whereas it is notorious that Charles Stuart, the now King of England, not content with the many encroachments which his predecessors had made upon the people in their rights and freedoms, hath had a wicked design totally to subvert the ancient and fundamental laws and liberties of this nation, and in their place to introduce an arbitrary and tyrannical government, and that besides all other evil ways and means to bring his design to pass, he hath prosecuted it with fire and sword, levied and maintained a cruel war in the land, against the Parliament and Kingdom, whereby the country hath been miserably wasted, the public Treasure exhausted, trade decayed, thousands of people murdered and infinite other mischiefs committed. . . .

The House of Lords, meeting the next day, were reluctant to accept this and adjourned for a week. At this, the House of Commons declared that they would take full responsibility for this bill, without any further reference to the House of Lords.

1698
DESTRUCTION OF WHITEHALL BY FIRE

We can hardly begin to imagine the huge complex of buildings which formed the original 'Whitehall' from the time of Henry VIII, who took over Cardinal Wolsey's palace there. Over the next reigns this area was developed into what was at once a centre of government offices and a collection of apartments for court favourites and ministers. William III ('Dutch William') hated the place because he thought it aggravated his asthma, and so he developed 'Nottingham House' into what is now Kensington Palace.

It was on 2 January 1698 that Whitehall was destroyed. A Dutch laundress had left some clothes to dry in front of an open fire, and when these caught alight the flames immediately spread in a conflagration that lasted seventeen hours. Many parts of the palace were blown up with gunpowder to try to prevent the fire spreading, but despite all efforts, the damage was virtually total. Only the banqueting house in present-day Whitehall now remains.

It has been calculated that over a thousand royal apartments were lost, including the guard room, the wardrobe, the treasury, the privy council office, the secretary of state's office and the chapel. And all these had contained numerous relics and pictures of former kings and queens. Some 150 houses or lodgings of the nobility were also destroyed. Twelve people lost their lives in the fire, including the unfortunate laundress whose carelessness had caused it.

John Evelyn recorded the event with succinct sharpness in his diary: '2. January. Whitehall burnt: nothing but walls and ruins left.'

JANUARY 3   1981
DEATH OF VICTORIA'S LAST HAEMOPHILIA-CARRYING GRANDCHILD

Towards the end of her life Queen Victoria was affectionately known as 'the Grandmother of Europe'. She had borne nine children, almost all of whom had married into the royal houses of Europe and who had in their turn produced numerous offspring. What is known more clearly now than it was during her lifetime is that Victoria was a 'carrier' of a rare and life-threatening disease, haemophilia. Two of her daughters, Princesses Alice and Beatrice, were also carriers, and her youngest son, Prince Leopold, was a haemophiliac. He passed the disease to his daughter Alice, who was a 'carrier', and she in turn passed it to her own son Viscount Trematon, who died in 1928, aged twenty-one.

Princess Alice, who married Queen Mary's brother, Prince Alexander of Teck, was in fact the last survivor of Queen Victoria's grandchildren, dying aged ninety-seven on 3 January 1981. She was better known in her later years as the Countess of Athlone, for she and her husband had been obliged to change their German name of Teck to a more British one during the First World War, when George V assumed the name of Windsor.

The history of the royal family's haemophilia and the way that they spread it to the royal families of Europe is now well documented. Princess Alice, Countess of Athlone, bore singular personal witness to this situation, as her father, her brother and her son were all afflicted with 'Victoria's Gene'.

JANUARY 4   1642
CHARLES I ENTERS THE CHAMBER OF THE HOUSE OF COMMONS

One of the most dramatic moments in the conflict between king and Parliament took place on 4 January 1642 when King Charles I burst into the chamber of the Commons to arrest five members who in his opinion had committed treason: John Pym, John Hampden, Arthur Haslerig, Denzil Holles and William Strode.

The Commons were outraged at this, and were further appalled when Charles addressed the Speaker, telling him that parliamentary privilege did not extend to traitors, and demanded that the five MPs should be arrested. The Speaker, William Lenthall, made his famous reply: 'Your Majesty, I have ears to hear and eyes to see only as this honourable House shall command me.'

Charles was furious as he looked round in vain for the five members in question. Luckily for them, the king's arrival had been foreseen and they had all managed to escape to the City by barge.

'I see all my birds have flown,' said Charles, as he stalked out of the chamber with the MPs derisively shouting 'Privilege! Privilege!' after him as he departed.

This was the first and only time that a monarch has dared to invade the privacy of the chamber of the House of Commons, and this incident finally triggered the civil war.

JANUARY 5   1066
DEATH OF KING EDWARD THE CONFESSOR

The saintly Edward the Confessor spent the last fifteen years of his reign and a tenth of his income on building Westminster Abbey. He did not actually found it, but he transformed a small earlier church into a vast Romanesque Benedictine abbey 300ft long, with a nave of twelve bays. At last, on 28 December 1065, Holy Innocents' Day, his dream came to fruition: the new abbey was consecrated. However, by then Edward was on the brink of death; it must have been a great disappointment to him that he was too ill even to attend the consecration ceremony.

Just eight days later, on the eve of Epiphany, 5 January 1066, he passed away quietly in his nearby palace. The following day he was buried in the abbey he had worked so hard to build. It was the first burial there – indeed almost the first service there – and his bones lie there to this day.

Edward's reputation for holiness spread far and wide even in his lifetime. He was kind to his subjects, generous to the poor, reputed to have visions, and was thought to have refused to consummate his marriage to Edith, daughter of Godwin, Earl of Wessex. He became known as 'Confessor' (one who bears witness to Christ by his life) to distinguish him from King Edward the Martyr (see MARCH 18).

Perhaps his most spectacular innovation was 'touching for evil'. It was believed that his royal and holy power enabled him to cure illnesses, especially scrofula ('the King's Evil') simply by touch. It became a custom practised by English kings and queens right down to the eighteenth century and Dr Johnson was 'touched', as a child, by Queen Anne.

A widespread legend, depicted in medieval art, told how Edward had once given a gold ring to a beggar near Westminster. The man disappeared, and years later two English pilgrims from Ludlow, travelling in Syria, met an old man who revealed himself as St John the Apostle. He gave them the ring, and charged them to return it to King Edward, and to tell him that he would die in six months' time. The pilgrims did so, and it is said that Edward was buried with this very ring. The ring was later recovered, and its sapphire is now reputedly set in the State Crown, worn at the state opening of parliament.

Edward the Confessor was canonised in 1161 and for centuries he was regarded as England's patron saint.

Also on this day:

1066 The Saxon Earl Harold Godwinson, aged about forty-six, son of Godwin, Earl of Wessex, and Gytha, a cousin of King Canute, was elected to be king.

JANUARY 6   1066
HAROLD II IS CROWNED WITHIN HOURS OF THE CONFESSOR'S FUNERAL

With indecent speed and ruthless determination Harold acted immediately after Edward the Confessor's funeral to get himself elected king. Literally within hours he gathered those members of the Witan who were on hand, having already come to Westminster to attend Edward's funeral, and extracted their consent to his election as Edward's successor. Arguably, it was not a fully representative gathering, but Harold's standing was high, and he knew that there was no immediate opposition from within the Witan itself.

Again within hours he arranged for Ealdred, Archbishop of York, to prepare for his coronation. And once again the churchmen and nobles processed into the abbey, this time dressed with the finery of a jubilant occasion: the first coronation in the new abbey. It was a moment of great solemnity when Harold took up the ceremonial axe, symbol of the nation, and promised to maintain justice and peace. The ageing archbishop prayed that Harold would never fail, either in governing his people in peace, or if need be to lead his armies to victory. And then came the crowning, the anointing, the blessing.

But throughout the abbey everyone knew that this acceptance of the crown was a blasphemous denial of the sacred oath of fealty and homage which Harold had publicly sworn to Duke William of Normandy. True, it was a promise made under duress and in dubious circumstances. Many years previously Harold had been tricked into making this oath over holy relics when he was virtually held a prisoner by William after being shipwrecked on the Normandy coast. Nevertheless, a promise is a promise. Would God avenge? And perhaps more urgently, what would Duke William do now?

1540
HENRY VIII MARRIES ANNE OF CLEVES

Henry's first meeting with Anne of Cleves, on New Year's Day 1540, was a complete disaster. A nobleman who was present declared 'that he never saw his highness so marvellously astonished and abashed as on that occasion'. Henry's disappointment was intense. His immediate reaction was to demand 'that some means should be found for obviating the necessity of completing his engagement'.

Quickly a council was summoned to produce a legal objection to the marriage, and much was made of the fact that Anne had already been promised to a previous suitor, Francis of Lorraine. However, it was a trumped-up objection and although Henry roared out his displeasure to his trembling minister, Thomas Cromwell, allegedly calling Anne a 'Flander's mare' and 'Dutch cow', it became increasingly clear that he would have to go through with the match.

Poor Anne, then aged twenty-four and by no means as ill-looking as the king imagined, was subjected to numerous snubs and discourtesies. Henry refused to attend the welcoming ceremonies. However, on 5 January, when pressed for a wedding date, Henry suddenly announced that it would be the following day, the Feast of the Epiphany. And in a fit of temper, to make everything as inconvenient as possible for everybody, he fixed the time at eight o'clock in the morning!

Also on this day:

1367 Birth of the future King Richard II at Bordeaux, son of the 'Black Prince' and Joan of Kent.

1610 Investiture of Prince Henry, son of James I, as Prince of Wales.

JANUARY 7 1114
ELEVEN-YEAR-OLD MATILDA BECOMES AN EMPRESS

Henry I's daughter Matilda was aged only eight in 1110, when she was sent abroad to Germany to become engaged to the Holy Roman Emperor, Henry V. He was thirty at the time, and obviously he had to wait a little before Matilda was quite ready to marry him. For the next few years, therefore, she was given an intensive course in speaking German and acquiring the necessary skills and accomplishments to be his wife.

In 1114 Matilda was just coming up to her twelfth birthday, so the time was ripe for their marriage. Accordingly, on 7 January, a great wedding took place, attended by princes, dukes, archbishops and dignitaries from all over Europe. Matilda was now 'Empress Matilda'. If her husband had lived, Matilda would have been merely a forgotten pawn in the royal marriage-market of those days. However, when he died, Matilda was only twenty-three and still a highly valuable prize in the nuptial stakes. Her father, Henry I, gave her away for the second time, to marry Geoffrey ('The Handsome') Count of Anjou.

Empress Matilda's life was only just beginning, for she was soon to be declared heiress to the throne of England after her brother had been drowned in the White Ship disaster. And then, on her father's death, when Stephen seized the throne, she was to spend years waging bloody civil war, trying to assert her rights. Perhaps her most important legacy was a posthumous one. Her son by Geoffrey became England's Henry II, the first of the Planagenets, a dynasty that was to last for 330 years, until Henry Tudor overthrew Richard III at the Battle of Bosworth Field.

1536
CATHERINE OF ARAGON DIES

Catherine of Aragon, Henry VIII's first wife, died this day in Kimbolton Castle in Cambridgeshire, where she had been kept virtually a prisoner for the last years of her life, after Henry VIII had discarded her. Throughout this time she was in declining health, suffering from cancer: an autopsy revealed a 'black and hideous' growth on her heart. It took Henry three weeks to decide where she should be buried. After all, a public funeral in London would probably have stirred up trouble, for the dead queen was still held in great popular esteem. So, ignoring Catherine's own wishes, he chose Peterborough Cathedral, which was then the abbey church of Peterborough.

She lies there still, buried in the north-west transept – a calculated insult, for a person of her dignity should have been buried near the high altar, a point which the Spanish ambassador was quick to notice. Shortly after the funeral, some of Catherine's friends had the nerve to suggest to the king 'that it would well become his greatness to rear a stately monument to her memory'. His reply was that 'He would have to her memory one of the goodliest monuments in Christendom.'

It was an evasive reply. What it turned out to mean was that when he ordered the wholesale destruction of the monasteries, he gave special instructions that the abbey church of Peterborough should be spared, as it contained her remains. In a sense, therefore, the whole of the cathedral may be regarded as a monument to Catherine, though there is merely a brass plate on the floor to her memory.

Also on this day:
1796 Birth of Princess Charlotte, daughter of the future George IV and
Caroline of Brunswick.

JANUARY 8   1397
THE NEW QUEEN OF ENGLAND IS CROWNED, AGED EIGHT

Richard II's first queen, Anne of Bohemia, died in 1394 aged only twenty-eight, so it was only natural for him to seek another bride. But with quite extraordinary eccentricity he chose the seven-year-old Princess Isabella of Valois, daughter of Charles the Mad. He married her in November 1396 in Calais. He was twenty-nine at the time.

Obviously it was a political marriage, and Richard hoped by it to gain a permanent peace with France. Nevertheless, the marriage raised many eyebrows. When Isabella arrived in London the crowds on London Bridge trying to catch a glimpse of her, as she made her way down the Thames from Kennington to the Tower of London, were so thick that nine people were crushed to death.

Early the following year little Isabella was given a sumptuous coronation in Westminster Abbey. She had brought with her a wardrobe of astonishing richness, including a robe and mantle made of red velvet embossed with birds of goldsmiths' work, perching upon branches made of pearls and emeralds. The robe was edged with 'miniver' (white fur) and the mantle lined with ermine.

Richard was kind to Isabella, who was taken to live and grow up in Windsor Castle. However, events overtook this odd marriage and within a couple of years Richard was forced to abdicate and died in mysterious circumstances. The usurper Henry IV proposed that Isabella should marry his son, the future Henry V, but Isabella proudly refused. Eventually she was sent back to France, where she married Charles, Duke of Orleans.

Sadly, she died in childbirth, aged only twenty.

An ironic twist to this affair is that Henry eventually married Isabella's sister, Catherine of Valois, after his victory at Agincourt. She appears, rather coyly, in Shakespeare's *Henry V*. Thus two French sisters married two English kings.

JANUARY 9   1806
GEORGE III FORBIDS THE PRINCE OF WALES TO ATTEND NELSON'S FUNERAL

St Paul's Cathedral was packed to capacity on this January day in 1806 to honour England's greatest sailor, Vice-Admiral Horatio Nelson. Oddly enough, no royal representative attended his funeral, for George III did not approve of Nelson's affair with Lady Hamilton and flatly refused to allow his son, the future George IV, to go.

The funeral was an elaborate affair. Nelson's body had been taken to Greenwich aboard his old flagship, HMS *Victory*, and after lying in state in the Painted Hall of the seamen's hospital for three days, it was taken up the Thames on his barge, rowed by his own crew. The final stage of the journey through the crowded streets of London was on a funeral car shaped like a warship.

There is a curious royal connection as Nelson was finally laid to rest in the crypt of St Paul's. His tomb is surmounted by a massive sarcophagus of black marble, which had been made almost three hundred years before, on the orders of Cardinal Wolsey. It is not known whether Wolsey intended it for himself, or whether it was to be as a macabre gift for his master, Henry VIII. For centuries this sarcophagus lay unused in the tomb-house of St George's Chapel, Windsor, but on the death of Nelson it was taken out and dusted down. There was a worthy recipient for it at last.

JANUARY 10   1931
EDWARD, PRINCE OF WALES, MEETS
MRS SIMPSON FOR THE FIRST TIME

No one could have guessed that a house-party in Melton Mowbray, organised by Thelma, Lady Furness, would change the course of the English monarchy. But it was here that the heir to the throne, the future King Edward VIII, met Wallis Simpson for the first time. According to Edward himself, in his autobiography *A King's Story*, it was a cold, damp, foggy winter's weekend, and so when Wallis Simpson was introduced to him he chose to open the conversation with a remark asking whether she, as an American, was missing the comfort of central heating.

He tells how a 'mocking look came into her eyes' and her reply must have astonished him: 'I am sorry, Sir, but you have disappointed me.' She went on to say: 'Every American woman who comes to your country is always asked that same question. I had hoped for something more original from the Prince of Wales.'

It was a daring gambit. Edward moved away to talk to other guests, but he tells us that 'the echoes of the passage lingered'. The memory remained in his mind, and when he next saw her, at a function at Buckingham Palace, he recounts how 'I was struck by the grace of her carriage and the natural dignity of her movements.'

He had met his destiny.

Also on this day:
1645 William Laud, Archbishop of Canterbury and supporter of Charles I, was beheaded on Tower Hill.

JANUARY 11 1663
KING CHARLES MEETS A PRETTY QUAKER WOMAN

Samuel Pepys notes in his diary: 'January 11th. By invitation to St. James's . . . where, this morning I stood by the King arguing with a pretty Quaker woman, that delivered to him a desire of hers in writing.

'The King showed her Sir J. Minnes, as a man the fittest for her quaking religion; she modestly saying nothing till he begun seriously to discourse with her, arguing the truth of his spirit against hers; she replying still with these words, "O King !" and thou'd all along.' (That is, she used *thou* instead of *you* – equivalent of saying *tu* instead of *vous*).

This incident has no historical significance, but it is a clear indication of Charles's kind, courteous and tolerant attitude. He was quite ready to meet and talk with quite ordinary folk, and to discuss religion with them in a civilised manner. He kept his own Catholic inclinations tactfully to himself until the last moments of his life (see FEBRUARY 5) and let the ferocious bigotry of some of his predecessors become, mercifully, a thing of the past. Good manners were now seen to be important. Presbyterianism, he observed, was 'not a religion for gentlemen'.

JANUARY 12 1954
QUEEN ELIZABETH OPENS HER NEW ZEALAND PARLIAMENT

No sovereign in history has travelled further than Queen Elizabeth II in visiting her subjects. She has been particularly punctilious in travelling to the Commonwealth countries. The first and longest tour – lasting nearly six months – took place during the winter of 1953/4. During this tour, one of the many engagements the recently crowned queen undertook was to open the New Zealand parliament on this day. It was the first time a reigning monarch had done so.

Meanwhile, back in England, her English Prime Minister Sir Winston Churchill was sending her his weekly reports to which she always replied in longhand. He was the first of the ten English Prime Ministers who have so far held office during her reign (Tony Blair being the tenth). But it is not always fully realised that at any time throughout her many decades as queen she has had to deal with literally dozens of Prime Ministers of the various Commonwealth countries. Now, after more than fifty years at the job, Queen Elizabeth II must have corresponded with many many hundreds, if not thousands, of Prime Ministers.

JANUARY 13 1154
KING STEPHEN PROMISES THE THRONE TO HENRY OF ANJOU

After almost twenty years of turbulence and civil war, and following the deaths of his wife Matilda of Boulogne and their son Eustace, Stephen had lost all will and energy to continue. Deeply superstitious, he saw a sinister omen in the fact that his horse had reared three times and thrice thrown him to the earth.

He agreed to meet Henry of Anjou (the future Henry II) at Wallingford near Oxford, and there the two men ratified the agreement that Henry should be his heir. Ten months later Stephen died of a heart attack in Dover, and the Plantagenets took over. It was to be the longest line in English history, lasting 330 years, with fourteen kings.

Also on this day:
1923 The future George VI proposed to Lady Elizabeth Bowes-Lyon.

JANUARY 14 1236
MARRIAGE OF HENRY III AND ELEANOR OF PROVENCE IN CANTERBURY

Eleanor of Provence was only fourteen when she arrived in Dover to become the wife and queen of Henry III. At twenty-eight he was twice her age. Eleanor was noted for her beauty, but became extremely unpopular because of her extravagant life-style. Once she was pelted with garbage from London Bridge by the citizens of London as she was passing beneath it in her barge, and the Mayor had to rescue her and take her to St Paul's Cathedral for safety.

It is an extraordinary fact that many, if not most, kings met their future brides for the first time only hours before being married to them, and in the case of Henry and Eleanor their wedding took place almost immediately, in Canterbury, by the Archbishop, Edmund Rich. (The archbishop was canonised after his death, and St Edmund Hall at Oxford is named after him.)

1892
DEATH OF 'EDDY', SON OF THE PRINCE OF WALES

In 1892 the heir to the throne was Albert Edward, Prince of Wales and future King Edward VII. But looking into the future, *his* successor was 'Eddy' (Albert Victor, Duke of Clarence), a young man who frankly did not have the character or indeed the mental ability required in a future king. A marriage was arranged for him, and his bride was to be Princess Mary of Teck.

Eddy's sudden death from pneumonia in 1892 was perhaps something of a relief to those who feared that he would prove a liability if ever he came to the throne. However, his parents grieved deeply. As for Princess Mary, she did her duty and married Eddy's younger brother instead, and the pair ultimately became King George V and Queen Mary.

JANUARY 15 1559
CORONATION OF ELIZABETH I, FOLLOWING A SOOTHSAYER'S RECOMMENDATION

Elizabeth had implicit faith in her personal soothsayer, Doctor Dee, who was one of the most colourful characters of the time. He had been introduced to her by her favourite, Robert Dudley. Over the years she personally visited Dee at his home in Mortlake on many occasions, consulting him over all kinds of problems: toothache; the interpretation of her dreams; the appearance of a new comet; the manner of her death. And she was gratified by his prediction of the founding of 'an incomparable British Empire'.

At Robert Dudley's suggestion, she consulted Dee about the most auspicious date for her coronation, and after studying his astrological charts his reply was that if she chose Sunday January 15th, her reign would be glorious and prosperous. According to Dee's advice, therefore, preparations were made for that date, and arguably the good soothsayer was proved correct in his prognostications.

The day before, on Saturday January 14, she staged a grand and leisurely procession through crowded streets from the Tower of London to her palace at Westminster, constantly being stopped and entertained by pageants, children's choirs, loyal speeches and the ceremonial presentation of nosegays and gifts. No sovereign before or since has enjoyed such an overwhelming display of popular affection. Typical of the day's events was a 'fair child in costly apparel' who stood on a stage in Fenchurch Street declaiming:

> Welcome O queen, as much as heart can think,
> Welcome again as much as tongue can tell!
> Welcome to joyous tongues and hearts that will not shrink
> God thee preserve, we pray, and wish thee ever well!

As for Elizabeth, she lapped it all up with her natural instinct to make the most of any dramatic occasion. 'I thank my lord Mayor, his brethren, and ye all,' she declared. 'And be ye assured that I will be as good unto ye as ever queen was to a people.'

The coronation day itself was marked with equal rapture. On the way into Westminster Abbey souvenir-hunters cut up pieces of the blue carpet specially laid down for the occasion almost as soon as Elizabeth had walked over it. However, the service was marked by religious tensions. It had been difficult even to find a bishop willing to officiate, because it was known that Elizabeth was likely to steer the church into Protestantism. In the end Bishop Oglethorpe of Carlisle consented to take the service, but insisted on a full Catholic ritual. During the mass Elizabeth herself refused to be present at the elevation of the host, retiring temporarily to a nearby curtained-off pew. Such pointed gestures were keenly noted.

Thus was Elizabeth duly appointed queen (afterwards, she confided to her ladies that 'the oil was grease and smelled ill') and the banquet and subsequent festivities in Westminster Hall lasted until one o'clock the following morning.

JANUARY 16   1556
A KING OF ENGLAND BECOMES KING OF SPAIN

On this day, in an odd kind of way, a King of England became King of Spain, King of the Netherlands, King of the Spanish Dominions in Italy, and King of the New World!

It sounds like a crossword puzzle clue, and of course it has to be explained. The fact is, that on this day the Emperor Charles V abdicated in favour of his son Philip, who thereupon became Philip II of Spain. He was, at that time, married to Mary I, and although it was by then a marriage in name only officially he still held the title of King of England, though he held no power. He had gone back to Spain shortly after his marriage to Mary Tudor, hardly disguising his dislike of her.

On the death of his father, Philip ruled as king over more territory – at least, nominally – than any other monarch on earth. Indeed, according to the Treaty of Tordesillas in 1493, Spain 'owned' the whole of North and South America. So, in theory, Philip, King of England, possessed one of the most gigantic empires ever known.

When Mary died, Philip ceased to be King of England. However, on the accession of Queen Elizabeth I, Philip offered to marry her. It was an attempt to keep England Catholic. He wrote Elizabeth a number of love-letters, but she enjoyed parading them before her courtiers. And, of course, she took pleasure in refusing him, pleading scruples of conscience.

JANUARY 17   1936
KING GEORGE V WRITES IN HIS DIARY FOR THE LAST TIME

Aged seventy, the old king was at Sandringham, his favourite home, but he was far too ill for his favourite pastime, shooting game on his estate. His family and ministers recognised that it was only a matter of days before the end would come. His son, the future uncrowned King Edward VIII wrote of the 'shadowy figures that slipped in and out of my father's room as the end approached'. One was his doctor, Lord Dawson; another was the Archbishop of Canterbury, 'a noiseless spectre in black gaiters'.

On January 17 George had written the last words in his diary: 'A little snow & wind. Dawson arrived. I saw him and feel rotten.' Two days later he could sign state papers only with Lord Dawson holding the pen. Three days later, he was dead.

Standing beside the deathbed, Edward records that immediately he was kissed on the hand by his mother, Queen Mary, followed by a similar act of symbolic homage by his brother George. 'These two spontaneous gestures', he wrote, 'served to remind me, however needlessly, that I was now King.' (See JANUARY 20)

JANUARY 18   1486
HENRY VII MARRIES ELIZABETH OF YORK: THE TUDOR ROSE IS BORN

It was an important marriage, a crucial marriage. In fact, Henry had sworn to marry Elizabeth of York, daughter of Edward IV, if ever he became king. It would unite the warring factions of Lancaster and York and so act as a permanent demonstration that the Wars of the Roses were over.

No one knows who 'invented' the Tudor rose, but it became a splendid emblem of unity. Heraldically, it is a 'badge', which is a distinctive mark worn by servants, retainers and followers of royalty or nobility; it could, therefore, be used in all sorts of places as a constant reminder of who was in authority. The heraldic rose is a flower always shown with five petals, with what is known as a 'barb' between each petal and a seed, or five seeds, in the centre. The Tudor rose shows the white rose of York superimposed on the red rose of Lancaster.

King's College, Cambridge, contains countless Tudor roses. One of the stone-masons, evidently unhappy about producing so many non-religious images in a sacred building, decided to make a one-man protest. One of the most delightful carvings to be seen there is a tiny image of the Virgin Mary, hidden in the centre of a Tudor rose. It is tucked into the north-west corner, but it has to be looked for.

JANUARY 19   1419
SURRENDER OF ROUEN TO HENRY V

After his victory at Agincourt Henry V went on to harass northern France with terrifying brutality. In 1418 he laid siege to the town of Rouen, capital of Normandy. The citizens there held out for six months, with increasing numbers dying of disease and starvation. It is recorded that they were reduced to eating rats, mice and weeds while Henry's soldiers devastated the surrounding countryside, pillaging and murdering. He hanged his victims on gibbets in full view of the city walls.

Before the town finally gave in, twelve thousand old folk, women and children came out to beg for mercy, but Henry simply forced them into the ditches around the city walls to die of exposure.

On this cold January day Rouen finally surrendered and Henry entered the town on a black charger to give thanks and hear mass in the cathedral. Apparently his conscience was clear.

JANUARY 20 1382
WEDDING OF RICHARD II AND
ANNE OF BOHEMIA

This was a successful marriage, but a childless one. The wedding took place in St Stephen's Chapel, Westminster, and at the time both Richard and his bride were fifteen years old. Both had artistic, extravagant tastes in fashion and both enjoyed daringly new and exotic foods.

Anne had landed at Dover the previous month, and there seems to have been an extraordinary convulsion in the sea. The ship she had just sailed in was completely smashed up before her very eyes: by all accounts she was lucky to have survived.

Arriving at Blackheath she had a splendid welcome from the Mayor of London, and then a huge throng of lords and ladies dressed in finery accompanied her in a grand entry into London. At Cheapside a pageant of a castle with towers had been erected, with fountains of wine running down the sides. From the top of these towers pretty girls blew gold leaf into the faces of Anne and Richard, and flung counterfeit gold florins before the bride to be.

It was an auspicious occasion, and when, a few days later, Anne asked for a general pardon of prisoners, and an end to the executions following Wat Tyler's peasants' revolt, she earned immense popularity for herself, being known thereafter as 'good queen Anne'.

1936
CURIOUS CIRCUMSTANCES SURROUNDING THE
DEATH OF GEORGE V

In his last months George V, suffering from a bronchial infection, spent many weeks in Bognor, a seaside resort on the south coast, hoping that the clean sea air would improve his health. The citizens of Bognor were so proud of this honour done to their town that they sought to dignify their town's name by adding 'Regis' to it.

Sadly, shortly afterwards the king's health began to decline, and a deputation from Bognor travelled to Sandringham to make their request. The king was dying, and being pestered on his deathbed was the last straw. Rumour has it that the last words uttered by the king were 'Bugger Bognor'. Readers of the *Daily Express*, however, were told that his last words had been 'How is the Empire?' To which Stanley Baldwin, the Prime Minister, had replied 'All is well, Sire'. And the king smiled.

This story of the king's last words has now become a part of British folklore. But what is perhaps less well known is the way in which the king died. It is now on record that the king's physician actually injected a lethal dose of morphine and cocaine into the dying sovereign, partly to alleviate his suffering and partly to speed up the process of dying. It was felt that it would be far more appropriate for the announcement of the king's death to appear in the morning papers, including *The Times*, than to be relegated to the less prestigious evening papers. This act of euthanasia was, of course, kept a close secret for many years.

Also on this day:

1236 Eleanor of Provence, aged fourteen, was crowned in Westminster Abbey, six days after her marriage to Henry III (see JANUARY 14).

1936 On the death of King George V (see above), King Edward VIII, aged forty-one, succeeded to the throne.

JANUARY 21 1603
DR DEE CASTS ELIZABETH'S HOROSCOPE AND SHE LEAVES WHITEHALL FOR EVER

John Dee, alchemist and sorcerer, was one of the most interesting characters of the Tudor period. He had been imprisoned under Queen Mary, under suspicion of attempting to murder her by magic. Edward VI, however, showed him much favour and actually conferred two church livings on him. Dee claimed to have found an elixir in the ruins of Glastonbury Abbey which transmuted a piece of a warming-pan into gold.

Elizabeth I found him a fascinating individual. Throughout her life she sought his advice, even fixing the date of her coronation on his recommendation (see JANUARY 15). She visited him several times at his Mortlake home, and she made him warden of Manchester College, now well known as the home of Chetham's School of Music.

He was, therefore, a friend of long standing when he cast her horoscope in 1603 and urged her not to remain at Whitehall. She took his advice and on this day in what was to be the last year of her life she went with her court to Richmond. It is a great pity that she did not also take her courtiers' advice and dress up more warmly in the cold January weather. Instead, defying them, she wore the lightest of summer clothes and caught a severe chill. It was the beginning of the end. During the next two months her condition deteriorated, she developed infected tonsils, fell into a moody depression and died. (See MARCH 24). Dee lived on for another five years, but under James I he was not so well favoured.

He had to petition the king to let him clear himself by public trial of the slander that he was a 'caller of divels'. He died desperately poor and is buried in Mortlake.

JANUARY 22   1901
A LONG-LOST STATUE OF QUEEN VICTORIA

Queen Victoria died on this day in her beloved Osborne House, and embraced by her favourite grandchild, the German Emperor 'Kaiser Bill'.

When it was known that the Kaiser was on his way, Bertie, the future Edward VII, had sent him a telegram telling him bluntly that his presence was not required at Osborne. There was no love lost between uncle and nephew. However, ignoring the telegram completely, the Kaiser made straight for the Isle of Wight and arrived in time to witness the old queen's final hours. Not only did he cradle her as she died, but he is also reported to have taken charge of events afterwards: measuring her and helping the doctor to lift her into her coffin.

Many years before, Victoria had had an effigy of herself made by the Italian sculptor Carlo Marochetti to lie beside that of Albert. Before her death she reminded Lord Esher that this was the statue she wanted on her tomb and she indicated that it was somewhere at Windsor.

An intensive search proved utterly useless. The statue was nowhere to be found. The royal family were becoming impatient. Then an old workman came forward saying he remembered helping to brick up an entrance to a storeroom filled with old bits of rubbish way back in 1865. He vaguely remembered a white statue lying amidst all the oddments.

He showed the courtiers the bricked-up wall, and when it was pick-axed open, sure enough there was the Queen's marble statue.

Visitors to the Royal Mausoleum at Frogmore may see it there today, on top of her tomb, just as she had desired. It depicts Victoria as a young woman – still at the age she was when Albert died turning towards him forever in love.

Also on this day:

1901 On the death of Queen Victoria (see above), King Edward VII, aged fifty-nine, succeeded to the throne.

LONGEST REIGNS	
Victoria	63 years, 216 days, from 1837 to 1901
George III	59 years, 96 days, from 1760 to 1820
Henry III	56 years, 29 days, from 1216 to 1272
Elizabeth II	celebrated her Golden Jubilee in 2002
Edward III	50 years, 147 days, from 1327 to 1377
Elizabeth I	44 years, 127 days, from 1558 to 1603

JANUARY 23   1045
EDWARD THE CONFESSOR MARRIES

On 23 January, or 'ten days before Candlemas' as the *Anglo-Saxon Chronicle* puts it, King Edward 'took to wife Edith, the daughter of Earl Godwin'. The wedding took place in Bath. It was an odd marriage, with rumours that the saintly Edward was refusing to consummate it because of an oath of chastity he had made in earlier years. Whatever the truth of this, the couple had no heirs, and so this paved the way for Harold, Edith's brother, to get himself elected king after the death of the Confessor.

Edith was about fifteen years younger than Edward, and she lived on in Winchester until her own death in 1075. She had the bitter task of handing over the keys of Winchester and the royal treasury there, as the final act of surrender to William the Conqueror. She is buried in Westminster Abbey.

JANUARY 24   1327
EDWARD II BURSTS INTO TEARS AS HE IS FORCED TO ABDICATE

Edward was being held state prisoner at Kenilworth Castle when Bishop Adam Orleton of Hereford and twelve other commissioners arrived to demand his abdication. They drew themselves up in formal array to renounce their homage to the king and to receive his personal renunciation of royal dignity. It was an unprecedented event.

Bishop Orleton was the spokesman and Edward had to listen to a long harangue describing the details of the errors of his life and government.

Throughout this long speech Edward wept. Finally, it was put to him that he should be grateful that his son Edward was being chosen to succeed him, and not a stranger of non-royal blood. The king meekly agreed, and withdrew to prepare himself for the formal act of abdication.

After they had been waiting for some time, Edward reappeared, dressed completely in black. As he came among them he sank down to the floor in a deep swoon as if he were dead. The Earl of Leicester and the Bishop of Winchester came to his assistance and raised him up. However, as Orleton relentlessly pressed on with his insults Edward once more burst into a paroxysm of weeping.

Eventually the king composed himself sufficiently to speak, and told them that he was 'aware that for his many sins he was thus punished, and therefore he besought those present to have compassion upon him in his adversity'. He went on to say that he was 'grieved for having incurred the hatred of his people but glad that his eldest son was so gracious in their sight'.

With that, he surrendered to the commissioners the crown, the orb and sceptre, and other emblems of royalty for his fourteen-year-old son's coronation and investiture.

1328
THE YOUNG KING EDWARD III MARRIES PHILIPPA OF HAINAULT

Coincidentally it was exactly a year to the day after the abdication of his father that Edward III, now king, married his young bride Philippa of Hainault. He was fifteen; she was fourteen.

The wedding took place in York Minster, and the celebrations were made all the more spectacular by the arrival of many Scottish lords, coming south to conclude a peace treaty with England, which itself was about to be cemented by another marriage – that of King David II of Scotland (then aged *four*!) to Edward II's little sister Joanna (aged seven). Marriages had their uses in those days.

Also on this day:

1965 Sir Winston Churchill died, aged ninety, on the seventieth anniversary of the death of his father, Lord Randolph Churchill. Sir Winston was Elizabeth II's first Prime Minister, who had greeted her in 1952 on her return from Kenya as queen.

JANUARY 25 1533
HENRY VIII SECRETLY MARRIES HIS CONCUBINE

Anne Boleyn was never considered a beauty. Indeed with her sallow complexion, a large mole on her neck and an extra rudimentary finger on her left hand, some would have called her a witch. Indeed that was her reputation. All the same, Henry lusted after her with desperate desire. And she, on her part, by playing hard to catch, did nothing to decrease his sexual eagerness. Her nickname 'the Concubine' was in fact hardly fair, for she positively held out for marriage or nothing.

At last Henry gave in, and promised to wed her. And Anne herself gave in, too, for by the end of January 1533 she was already pregnant. The wedding Henry gave her, therefore, was a secret affair in Whitehall: obviously, the precise date was best kept obscure.

One of the royal chaplains, Dr Rowland Lee, is reported as having received a sudden command at a very early hour on St Paul's Day (January 25) to celebrate mass in a little-used turret of Whitehall. When he got to the required place, he found the king with two of the grooms of the chamber, and Anne Boleyn with her train-bearer Anne Saville, waiting for him. Immediately, he was told to perform the nuptial rite between Henry and Anne in the presence of the three witnesses.

At first he hesitated, but Henry is said to have assured him that the Pope had agreed to the divorce, and that he had a dispensation for a second marriage in his possession. The chaplain had no choice other than to comply, and when the ceremony was over, all went their several ways, silently, in the early morning darkness.

News of the marriage did not come out until about a fortnight afterwards. Even Cranmer was kept in total ignorance about it. And as for Anne's baby, the future Queen Elizabeth I, she was born just seven and a half months later.

Also on this day:
- **1308** King Edward II, aged twenty-three, married Isabella of France, in Boulogne.
- **1327** King Edward III, aged fourteen, succeeded to the throne on the abdication of his father (see JANUARY 24).

JANUARY 26 1994
PRINCE CHARLES SURVIVES AN 'ATTACK' IN SYDNEY, AUSTRALIA

January 26 is Australia Day. In 1994 Prince Charles had gone to Sydney to make a difficult speech to smooth relations between England and Australia in the face of the growing republicanism down-under. The speech was to be made in the evening, but earlier in the day Charles found himself on a dais in Darling Harbour surrounded by a huge crowd of people ready to watch him present prizes to the schoolchildren of the year.

Suddenly, out of the blue, racing towards the prince came a young man carrying what appeared to be a gun. Shots were fired. Bodyguards barged Charles out of the way. The would-be assailant tripped up and was quickly pounced upon. The excited crowd felt they were watching an assassination. In actual fact it was a student making a protest with a starting pistol. Their horror turned to fascinated admiration as the prince maintained his cool throughout the incident. Videos were shown throughout the world showing the royal *sangfroid*.

Later that day, when Charles came to make his Australia Day speech, he was given more attention and respect than perhaps otherwise would have been the case. The political background was such that he had been advised not to go to Australia at all. However, with a carefully and sensitively written speech he managed to defuse what might have been an ugly republican rebuff. He said:

> It is perhaps not surprising that there are those who would wish to see such a rapidly changing world reflected by a change in Australia's institutions. And perhaps they're right. By the very nature of things it is also not surprising that there are differing views: some people will doubtless prefer the stability of a system that had been reasonably well tried and tested over the years while others will see real advantages in doing things differently. The point I want to make here, and for everyone to be perfectly clear about, is that this is something which only you – the Australian people – can decide.

As Jonathan Dimbleby pointed out, Charles 'was very well aware that if a monarchy survives only by the consent of the people, it flourishes only with their goodwill'.

JANUARY 27   1649
KING CHARLES IS SENTENCED TO DEATH –
'FAREWELL SOVEREIGNTY!'

This was the day, three days before his execution, when Charles finally met his death sentence. There had been a long-drawn-out period of imprisonment and now the king was brought before the court convened to try him. Even then, the trial took four days before sentence was passed.

John Bradshaw, who had been elected President of the High Court of Justice, brought the proceedings to a climax as he told Charles:

> There is a contract and a bargain made between the King and his people, and your oath is taken: and certainly Sir, the bond is reciprocal: for as you are the liege lord, so they liege subjects . . . This we know now, the one tie, the one bond, is the bond of protection that is due from the sovereign: the other is the bond of subjection that is due from the subject. Sir, if this bond be once broken, farewell sovereignty!

Charles tried to interrupt, but Bradshaw was insistent: 'Sir, the charge hath called you a Tyrant, a Traitor, a Murderer, and a public enemy to the Commonwealth of England.'

Charles made repeated attempts to intervene, but the course of the trial was irresistible, concluding with the final sentence: 'That the said Charles Stuart, as a Tyrant, Traitor, Murderer and a public enemy, shall be put to death, by the severing of his head from his body.'

The guards led the king away. He had not been allowed to make a final point. But as he left Westminster Hall he managed to call out for all to hear: 'I am not suffered for to speak: expect what justice other people will have!'

JANUARY 28   1457
BIRTH OF THE FATHER (HENRY VII) . . .

Founder of the Tudor dynasty, Henry Tudor was destined to overthrow the Plantagenets at the Battle of Bosworth Field (1485). He was born in Pembroke Castle, to remarkable parents. His father was the son of Owen Tudor, personal man-servant of King Henry V, who after the death of his master had been kept on by Henry's widowed queen, Catherine of Valois. The two fell in love and married in great secrecy. Indeed they had several children before the situation was discovered. Catherine died in disgrace and Owen Tudor was thrown into Newgate Gaol, though he quickly managed to escape.

Luckily, Henry VI was prepared to be lenient and created one of their sons the 1st Earl of Richmond. The future Henry VII, then, as the 2nd Earl of Richmond, inherited a relatively new title, but he could, through his grandmother, trace an honourable royal ancestry on both sides of the Channel.

As for his mother, she was Margaret Beaufort, one of the great women of her times. She could claim Edward III as her great-great-grandfather. She was aged only thirteen when she gave birth to Henry. In later life she endowed two divinity professorships at Oxford and Cambridge; founded Christ's College and also St John's College, both in Cambridge; and she was a generous patron of William Caxton.

1547

. . . AND THE DEATH OF THE SON
(HENRY VIII)

Dying on his father's birthday, Henry VIII breathed his last in St James's Palace on this day in 1547. By this time he had grown enormous, and his ulcerous and syphilitic body stank. His capricious cruelty in the last years of his life kept everyone on tenterhooks and, as with any dictator, there must have been a widespread sense of relief at his death.

His corpse was put into a huge lead coffin and taken through the streets of London on the way to St George's Chapel, Windsor. The procession reached Syon House at twilight and there it rested overnight in the chapel. A horrific event then took place: according to a contemporary account: 'The leaden coffin being cleft by the shaking of the carriage, the pavement of the church was wetted with Henry's blood. In the morning came plumbers to solder the coffin, under whose feet was seen a dog creeping and licking up the King's blood.'

This story gained wide circulation and people remembered Friar Peto's denunciation of the king from the pulpit of Greenwich Church four years previously, in which the bold friar compared Henry with Ahab, and told him to his face 'that the dogs would, in like manner, lick his blood'.

These two lifetimes, lasting exactly ninety years, left an indelible mark on English history.

Also on this day:

1547   King Edward VI, aged nine, succeeded to the throne on the death of his father.

1689   Following the flight of James II to France, the House of Commons formally declared the throne of England to be vacant.

JANUARY 29   1536
ANNE BOLEYN INFURIATES HENRY VIII BY HAVING A MISCARRIAGE

Probably the most unfortunate miscarriage in English royal history took place on this day. According to one account, Anne Boleyn happened to enter the king's apartments unannounced and found Jane Seymour actually sitting on his knee. The pair of them were obviously keenly enjoying each other's company. The sight of this upset Anne Boleyn so much that it caused her tragic miscarriage – the still-birth of Henry's much looked-for son and heir. Anne was devastated by the loss of this 'man child' and became quite hysterical. Clearly, she knew with terrifying prescience just how furious Henry would be.

He entered her room and immediately began to upbraid her 'with the loss of his boy'.

The story continues that Anne 'with more spirit than prudence', told him that 'he had no one to blame but himself for this disappointment, which had been caused by her distress of mind about that wench, Jane Seymour'.

Henry left the room growling out that 'he would have no more boys by *her*'. Whether all this is true can never be proved, but certainly Anne never recovered her spirits, and knew that her place in the king's affections had been lost for ever. Less than sixteen weeks later she was beheaded.

Also on this day:

1121   King Henry I, aged fifty-three, married his second wife, Adela of Louvain, at Windsor.

1327   King Edward III, aged fourteen, was crowned in Westminster Abbey.

1820   King George III, aged eighty-one, died at Windsor Castle.

1820   On the death of George III, his son King George IV, aged fifty-seven, succeeded to the throne.

JANUARY 30 1649
EXECUTION OF KING CHARLES I AT WHITEHALL

Charles spent his final days at St James's Palace. On January 29 he had said goodbye to the two of his children who were still in England: the thirteen-year-old Princess Elizabeth and the little Duke of Gloucester, then aged eight. He told them to forgive their enemies, and that they should 'not grieve for him, for he should die a martyr'. He took his little son on his knee and told him 'they will cut off my head, and perhaps make thee a king: but mark what I say, you must not be a king so long as your brothers Charles and James do live. The child replied: 'I will be torn in pieces first' – a reply that gave Charles much satisfaction.

On the morning of 30 January the king walked to Whitehall to await the final summons. When at last he was taken out to the scaffold he was surprised to see how low the block was placed, no more than about 10 inches from the ground. To those round him he declared: 'I go from a corruptible to an incorruptible Crown, where no disturbance can be, no disturbance in the world.' Then he gave his insignia of the Garter to Bishop Juxon, saying, 'Remember.'

Staples had been hammered into the wooden scaffold around the block, to hold the king down in case he struggled. But these were quite unnecesssary, for he died with supreme composure and courage. He lay with his neck on the block and told the executioner, 'Stay for the sign.'

'I will, an' it please Your Majesty,' replied the executioner.

After a moment of silence the king stretched out his hands. One axe-blow was enough.

A bystander described the sound which arose from the crowd who witnessed the event: 'such a groan as I never heard before, and desire I may never hear again'.

1661
OLIVER CROMWELL'S CORPSE IS DUG UP

Exactly twelve years to the day after the execution of Charles I, Oliver Cromwell was dug up in order to suffer the same fate, posthumously.

On 1 December 1660 the House of Commons, with Charles II's approval, ordered that the remains of Cromwell, Ireton and Bradshaw should be disinterred and dragged on hurdles to Tyburn, 'there to be hanged in their coffins for some time with their faces turned towards Whitehall, and then buried under the gallows'.

The vault was opened on 30 January 1661 in the presence of the Speaker of the House of Commons and his attendants. As directed, the bodies were placed in their coffins on hurdles and dragged to Tyburn, where Marble Arch stands today. Here they were hanged on a gallows until sunset. Then they were cut down and decapitated; their heads were taken and stuck high on poles over the top of Westminster Hall. Cromwell's head remained in its place for twenty-five years.

When Henrietta Maria, Charles I's widowed queen, returned to London to visit her son Charles II, she ordered her coachman to stop so that she might get a good view of these heads over Westminster Hall.

1788
BONNIE PRINCE CHARLIE DIES IN EXILE

Aged sixty-seven, Charles Stuart – 'Bonnie Prince Charlie' – died in Rome, his birthplace. To the end he had kept a strongbox under his bed containing twelve thousand gold coins, enough to take him back to Scotland if ever his supporters should call him back.

But the call had never come.

Also on this day:

1965 Queen Elizabeth II attended the funeral of Sir Winston Churchill in St Paul's Cathedral. She was the first sovereign to attend a commoner's funeral.

JANUARY 31   1820
PRINNY BECOMES KING AND HAS TO BE BLED

After the longest reign in English history up to that time, George III died on January 29 1820. He had been king for 59 years and 96 days.

At noon on January 31 the Garter King of Arms solemnly proclaimed the accession of King George IV from the forecourt of Prinny's London palace, Carlton House. It was a brief ceremony, but the weather was bitter and the new king, who was not well, caught pleurisy and within hours he was thought to be on the brink of death.

Medical bulletins were issued twice a day, and his doctors insisted on bleeding the king until they had drawn no fewer than seven-and-a-half pints of blood from him. In those days, bleeding was thought to be the remedy for everything.

So ill was the new king that it was considered inadvisable for him even to attend his father's funeral. Instead, he travelled down to Brighton to his favourite residence, the Royal Pavilion, and there he stayed for the next two months, planning how to get rid of Caroline, his unwanted queen.

Also on this day:

1606 Guy Fawkes was hanged in the Old Palace Yard at Westminster for his part in trying to blow up King James I and the Houses of Parliament.

FEBRUARY 1   1587
ELIZABETH I STEELS HERSELF TO SIGN A DEATH WARRANT

For weeks Elizabeth put off the moment. Although she knew that her cousin, Mary, Queen of Scots, had been plotting against her, making the final decision to sign Mary's death warrant gave her many sleepless nights.

Lords and Commons were begging her to sign, but still she could not bring herself to do so. A petition presented by twenty peers and forty MPs on November 12 1586 only brought forth a promise to 'pray and consider the matter'. And when, almost a fortnight later, another petition arrived, she gave them a written reply which was almost totally meaningless:

> If I should say unto you that I mean not to grant your petition, by my faith I should say unto you more than perhaps I mean. And if I should say unto you I mean to grant your petition, I should then tell you more than is fit for you to know. I am not so void of judgement as not to see mine own peril, nor so careless as not to weigh that my life daily is in hazard. But since so many have both written and spoken against me, I pray you to accept my thankfulness, to excuse my doubtfulness, and to take in good part my answer answerless.

At last, on February 1 1587, she suddenly sent for Sir William Davison, signed the death-warrant in his presence, and told him that she wished the execution to take place as soon as possible in the Great Hall of Fotheringhay Castle.

At last a decision! And her councillors, led by Lord Burghley, acted with speed, before she could change her mind.

FEBRUARY 2   1626
CORONATION OF CHARLES I, THE 'WHITE KING'

Charles chose the date of his coronation with care: it was Candlemas – the Feast of the Purification of the Virgin Mary. He thought it would be a pretty compliment to his young fifteen-year-old wife, whose name was also Mary – Henrietta Maria.

31

However, he did not reckon on one important fact: as a fervent and ferociously determined Catholic, she would refuse to attend. She positively flew into a temper at the very thought of being crowned by a Protestant heretic! As the procession wound its way from Whitehall to Westminster Abbey, she stood watching it from a bay window in the palace gate-house, while her French ladies and attendants danced and frisked around her. Her gesture earned her everlasting unpopularity.

Meanwhile, her tiny husband (he was only 4ft 7in tall) entered Westminster Abbey dressed exquisitely in white satin, thus gaining for himself the curious nickname the 'White King'. All sorts of omens are said to have occurred during the coronation ceremony. Charles himself slipped as he went through the abbey door, and had to be supported by 'Steenie', the Duke of Buckingham. A wing of the dove on the sceptre had broken off, and a precious stone slipped out of the coronation ring. There was an embarrasssed silence at the moment when the congregation should have shouted their acclamations, and the Earl of Arundel actually had to tell everyone that they should cry out 'God save King Charles!'

But to the crowds waiting outside the abbey perhaps the most extraordinary omen of the day occurred at about two o'clock in the afternoon, while the service was being held, when the ground beneath them was shaken by a sharp and sudden earthquake.

This was no ordinary coronation.

Also on this day:

1461 The 'obstinate, bloody and decisive' Battle of Mortimer's Cross was fought and won by eighteen-year-old Edward Mortimer, Earl of March, who became King Edward IV a month later, partly as a result of this victory. At this battle Owen Tudor, grandfather of Henry VII and lover of Queen Catherine of Valois, widow of Henry V, was captured and executed in Hereford market-place.

1650 Nell Gwynne, one of Charles II's mistresses, was born in Hereford. (For a list of Charles's mistresses, see OCTOBER 9.)

FEBRUARY 3   1134
DEATH OF ROBERT CURTHOSE, AFTER TWENTY-EIGHT YEARS OF IMPRISONMENT

England might well have had a vigorous King Robert, but for the energetic opportunism of his younger brother Henry I. Robert was the eldest son of the William the Conqueror. He was nicknamed 'Curthose', which means 'short trousers', because apparently he had stocky little legs. Arguably he should have succeeded his father as King of England. However, the Conqueror divided his lands among his sons so that Robert became Duke of Normandy and William 'Rufus' became King of England. As for Henry, he was merely left with £5,000 in silver.

Robert's opportunity should have come with the death of Rufus, slain by an arrow in the New Forest. However, he was away on a crusade at the time, and so Henry I smartly took the vacant throne. Obviously, Robert was greatly put out and on his return tried to force the issue at the Battle of Tinchebray, in Normandy.

Unluckily for him, he lost. Henry seized him as his prisoner and flung him into a succession of castles: Wareham, Bristol and finally Cardiff, where he languished for the remaining twenty-eight years of his life.

On February 3 1134 he died, aged eighty, just a few months before Henry himself. He had spent the last years of his life learning Welsh, and wrote a little poem in that language about an oak tree which he could just see from the draughty window of his cell. It ends:

Oak, which has lived through storms and tempests, in the midst of
the tumult of war and the ravages of death:
Misery to the man who is not old enough to die.

Also on this day:
1014 Death of Sweyn Forkbeard, father of King Canute, at Gainsborough, Lincolnshire.
1399 Death of John of Gaunt, aged fifty-nine, father of Henry IV, in London. (See MARCH 18 for an account of his funeral.)
1954 Queen Elizabeth II visits Australia: the first reigning sovereign to go there.

FEBRUARY 4   1865
'THE QUEEN'S HIGHLAND SERVANT' TAKES UP RESIDENCE AT OSBORNE HOUSE

It was Dr Jenner, the queen's physician, who thought of inviting John Brown, the royal ghillie, to Osborne House, to assist Victoria in keeping up her riding. He had thought that having a familiar groom in attendance would be good for her, particularly as her grief at Albert's death showed no signs of abating.

Brown arrived and seized the queen's total attention from that moment until his death eighteen years later. The relationship was extraordinary. In fact, as early as 1851 Prince Albert had personally recommended Brown to be the queen's pony leader and outdoor personal attendant: he was a huge, handsome, 25-year-old red-whiskered ghillie, five years younger than the queen herself. Soon she had begun speaking with him with a freedom of manner which she would hardly have allowed herself with an English groom, say, at Windsor, and he had responded with a rough and genial humour which she had done little to check. The beginnings of a friendship had begun.

When, in 1865, Victoria looked down from her window in Osborne House and saw John Brown leading 'dear little Loch-na-gar', her Highland pony, it was reported that she smiled – for the first time since that awful night when Albert had died. Until that day, Victoria had hardly left her house, but now, with Brown to lead her, she ventured out among the trees. It was quite a while before the pair of them returned. A link with Albert had been restored.

Also this day:
1901 Funeral of Queen Victoria at the Royal Mausoleum, Frogmore, Windsor.

FEBRUARY 5   1685
CHARLES II SECRETLY BECOMES A CATHOLIC ON HIS DEATHBED

Nobody expected Charles to die when he did. After all, he was only fifty-four and still as lascivious as ever. He did not acquire his nickname 'Old Rowley' for nothing: it was the name of a lecherous old goat tethered on the green at Whitehall.

On the Sunday, February 1, Charles had been his normal self, happily chatting about his new Versailles-type palace which he was building at Winchester. However, he was certainly not himself on the Monday morning, and collapsed as his barber was about to give him his daily shave. Emetics, purgings and bleedings had no effect, and by the afternoon a vast crowd had gathered in the streets, anxiously waiting for further news.

Tension mounted throughout the next few days, and Charles himself, with his usual *sangfroid*, despite his pain, excused himself: 'I am sorry, gentlemen, for being such an unconscionable time a-dying.' It was indeed clear to all that the monarch was shortly to meet his Maker.

On the Thursday, February 5, his Catholic brother James was seen to whisper in Charles's ear, obviously offering to send for a priest. 'For God's sake, brother, do, and please lose no time,' was Charles's reply.

The king's bedroom, which had been filled with courtiers, was quickly cleared, except for a couple of trusted peers, the Earls of Bath and Feversham. James disappeared from view and soon returned with Father Huddleston, an aged priest who had helped Charles after the defeat of his army at Worcester, thirty-four years before. 'He is come to save your soul,' said James, to which the king replied 'He is very welcome.'

Then came Charles's confession, followed by extreme unction, and the final sacrament; after which the courtiers were brought back into the room again, with the king conscious and at peace. He lived until about noon the next day. Rumour was rife that he had been poisoned.

Also on this day:
1649 Charles II was proclaimed king in Edinburgh (see JANUARY 1).

FEBRUARY 6   1952
SMOKER'S LUNG CANCER KILLS GEORGE VI

The day before he died George VI had enjoyed a good day's shooting on his Sandringham estate, bagging eight hares and a wood-pigeon. Prince Charles and Princess Anne, then aged three and one, were staying with him at the time, as their parents, Princess Elizabeth and the Duke of Edinburgh, had just gone abroad, intending to make the tour of Australia which the king was too ill to undertake.

Everyone knew that the king was ill, but the end came with unexpected suddenness. The previous September he had had a cancerous lung removed, and although he was still weak, it was hoped that he was on the road to recovery. At that time, of course, the connection between smoking and lung cancer was only just beginning to be recognised. George had been a heavy smoker all his life, and now he was fifty-six.

George said prayers with his young grandchildren before they went off to bed, had dinner with the queen and Princess Margaret, and then went to bed at about ten o'clock. No one saw him die. It was a peaceful end, while he slept.

Queen Elizabeth II unveiled a memorial to her father in the Mall a few years later. Those who remember the king will know how true her tribute was:

> Much was asked of my father in personal sacrifice and endeavour, often in the face of illness; his courage in overcoming it endeared him to everyone. He shirked no task, however difficult, and to the end he never faltered in his duties to his peoples. Throughout all the strains of his public life he remained a man of warm and friendly sympathies – a man who by the simple qualities of loyalty, resolution and service won for himself such a place in the affection of us all that when he died millions mourned for him as for a true and trusted friend.

Also on this day:

1665 The future Queen Anne was born, at St James's Palace, London, the daughter of Anne Hyde and the future James II.

1685 Death of Charles II, aged fifty-four, at Whitehall Palace, London. King James II, aged fifty-one, succeeds to the throne.

1811 George, Prince of Wales, formally becomes Prince Regent, as a result of the incurable mental illness of his father.

1952 Queen Elizabeth II, aged twenty-five, succeeds to the throne on the death of her father.

FEBRUARY 7   1301
A NEW TITLE IS CREATED – 'PRINCE OF WALES'

Edward I, the great warrior-king, later dubbed the 'Hammer of the Scots', made a peace-offering to his Welsh subjects by proclaiming his only son, another Edward, 'Prince of Wales'.

A romantic legend has grown up that Edward I held up his new-born son to the Welsh people and declared 'Here is a native-born Prince of Wales who can speak no word of English!' However, this is pure fiction, as the new 'Prince of Wales' was an energetic sixteen-year-old when he was given the title. True he had been born at Caernarvon on April 25 1284, in the same year that the Welsh lost their independence with the Statute of Rhuddlan. But he had hardly been to Wales since then; and in any case, the proclamation making him Prince of Wales was made at Lincoln.

Also on this day:

1403 King Henry IV, aged thirty-six, married his second wife, Joanna of Navarre, in Winchester Cathedral.

THE TWENTY-FOUR PRINCES OF WALES

1. Edward, son of Edward I, crowned as Edward II.
2. Edward, son of Edward II, crowned as Edward III.
3. Edward, son of Edward III. Known as 'the Black Prince', he died before coming to the throne.
4. Richard, son of the Black Prince. Richard was crowned as Richard II.
5. Henry, son of Henry IV, who became crowned as Henry V.
6. Henry, son of Henry V, who became crowned as Henry VI.
7. Edward, son of Henry VI. This Prince of Wales was killed at the Battle of Tewkesbury, and so never came to the throne.
8. Edward, son of Edward IV. This Prince of Wales was never crowned, although for a while he became Edward V after the death of his father. He was one of the princes murdered in the Tower of London, probably on the orders of Richard III.
9. Edward, son of Richard III. This Prince of Wales died in 1484, and so never came to the throne.
10. Arthur, son of Henry VII. This Prince of Wales died in 1501, and the title was passed to his younger brother, Henry.
11. Henry, son of Henry VII, who became crowned as Henry VIII.
12. Edward, son of Henry VIII, crowned as Edward VI.
13. Henry, son of James I. This Prince of Wales died in 1612, and the title was passed to his younger brother Charles.
14. Charles, son of James I, who became crowned as Charles I.
15. Charles, son of Charles I, who became crowned as Charles II.
16. James, son of James II, who was exiled with his father and became known as 'James III' or the 'Old Pretender' by the Jacobites. He was the 'warming-pan baby'.
17. George, son of George I, who became crowned as George II.
18. Frederick, son of George II. This Prince of Wales died in 1751, and so never came to the throne.
19. George, son of Frederick, Prince of Wales. George became crowned as George III.
20. George, son of George III, crowned as George IV.
21. Albert Edward, son of Queen Victoria, who became crowned as Edward VII.
22. George, son of Edward VII, who became crowned as George V.
23. Edward, son of George V, who became Edward VIII, never crowned because he abdicated in 1936.
24. Charles, son of Elizabeth II. The present Prince of Wales.

FEBRUARY 8 1587
MARY, QUEEN OF SCOTS, IS BEHEADED AT FOTHERINGHAY

Nothing but a grassy mound remains nowadays to mark the site of the Great Hall of Fotheringhay Castle, but in 1587 this was the impressive scene of legalised royal murder. True, Mary did pose a threat to Elizabeth I. True, she did appear to be plotting to overthrow the Virgin Queen. Nevertheless, execution is murder, however it is authorised. Elizabeth had signed the document only days before, and her advisers were only too ready to act swiftly, in case she changed her mind.

The actual execution took place shortly after eight o'clock in the morning, witnessed by about three hundred spectators. Mary herself was calm and dignified, remarking to her attendant ladies, 'Thou hast cause rather to joy than to mourn, for now shalt thou see Mary Stuart's troubles receive their long-expected end.'

She was helped to undress down to her satin bodice and scarlet velvet petticoat, and when the executioner asked her forgiveness she granted it, saying 'I hope you shall make an end of all my troubles.' However, it took the poor man two strokes of the axe, and it was reported that the queen's lips were still moving even quarter of an hour afterwards. Then, as her head was lifted up for all to view, her cap and red wig fell off, revealing surprisingly short-cropped grey hair.

A pathetic incident then ensued. According to one account, as the executioner bent down to take off her stockings (he had orders that her body was to be stripped, so that no souvenirs should remain to be kept as relics):

> . . . he found her little dog under her coat, which, being put from thence, went and laid himself down betwixt her head and body, and being besmeared with her blood, was caused to be washed, as were other things whereon any blood was. The executioners were dismissed with fees, not having any thing that was hers. Her body, with the head, was conveyed into the great chamber by the sheriff, where it was by the chirurgeon embalmed until its interment.

Her great lead coffin was not taken for burial in Peterborough Cathedral, then still just an abbey church, until July 30 – a delay of almost six months.

FEBRUARY 9   1649
SECRET BURIAL OF THE 'WHITE KING'

Oliver Cromwell refused to allow Charles I to be buried in Westminster Abbey, although this had been the king's wish. A burial service in such a venue would surely have brought ugly crowds out on to the streets of London. It was therefore at night that the king's corpse was taken to Windsor, to be buried in the Garter Chapel of St George's Chapel. Snow began to fall as the pathetic little cortège approached the west end of St George's, and before the coffin could be taken inside the building it became totally covered with pure white snow – the colour of innocency, as it was remarked. 'So went our white king to his grave!' said his servants.

It was suddenly realised, as the coffin was about to be lowered into the vault, that no inscription had been placed on it. A band of sheet lead was found, and one of the gentlemen present cut the words CHARLES REX into the metal, and then this leaden band was wound about the coffin.

It was placed so unceremoniously in the vault that for years afterwards no one knew precisely where it was.

Also on this day:
2002   Death of Princess Margaret, sister of Queen Elizabeth II, aged 72.
    Her ashes are interred in St George's Chapel, Windsor.

FEBRUARY 10   1840
QUEEN VICTORIA MARRIES PRINCE ALBERT

'He is perfection in every way – in beauty, in everything . . . Oh, how I adore and love him!' Thus had Victoria written about her cousin Albert when they first met. At that first meeting they were both aged just twenty; she proposed to him within five days – and four months later they were married.

Considering the importance of such a wedding, it seems rather surprising that it was a very intimate family affair, taking place in the privacy of St James's Palace. Then, after a huge wedding breakfast in the newly built Buckingham Palace, the happy couple went off for a *two-day* honeymoon in Windsor Castle. Albert had wanted a much longer honeymoon, but Victoria had decided otherwise: 'You forget, my dearest love, that I am the sovereign, and that business can stop and wait for nothing.'

Nevertheless, after the wedding evening she wrote: 'I NEVER NEVER spent such an evening!!! My DEAREST DEAREST DEAR Albert sat on a footstool by my side, & his excessive love & affection gave me feelings of heavenly love & happiness, I never could have *hoped* to have felt before!'

Also on this day:

1552   Katherine Howard was imprisoned in the Tower of London (see FEBRUARY 13).

1554   Princess Elizabeth was imprisoned in the Tower of London (see MAY 22).

1557   Lord Darnley, second husband of Mary, Queen of Scots, and father of King James I of England, was murdered in Edinburgh.

FEBRUARY 11   1466
BIRTH OF ELIZABETH OF YORK, FUTURE WIFE OF HENRY VII, AND . . .

1503
DEATH OF ELIZABETH OF YORK, WIFE OF HENRY VII

Elizabeth of York was the eldest child of Edward IV and Elizabeth Woodville. Henry, Earl of Richmond, had sworn a solemn oath in Rennes Cathedral on Christmas Day in 1483, two years before the Battle of Bosworth, that if he defeated Richard III and became King of England he would marry Elizabeth of York. It was a curious way of proposing marriage! Nevertheless, when he did become king, marry her he did; and although the marriage may have seemed a somewhat calculated political move, Elizabeth and Henry enjoyed a happy and successful life together. As everyone knows, this marriage united the warring factions of the Yorkists and the Lancastrians and brought an end to the Wars of the Roses.

Elizabeth of York had an alarmingly eventful life. Her father, King Edward IV, died when she was only seventeen, and she found herself stripped of all possessions as her wicked uncle, Richard III, set about vilifying her mother and all the upstart Woodvilles. At one point she had to live in asylum for a while in Westminster Abbey, helping her mother to look after all her nine younger brothers and sisters in extremely difficult circumstances. Two of her little brothers disappeared mysteriously in the Tower of London, never to be seen again.

It was a godsend to her when Richard was defeated and her dignity was restored. It must have seemed a miracle when she found herself marrying Henry and actually becoming Queen of England.

Sadness came to her when her son Arthur died, shortly after his marriage to Catherine of Aragon. However, Elizabeth became pregnant again, and she and Henry must have been looking forward to a new addition to the family in 1503. Her second son, the future Henry VIII was still only eleven, her daughter Margaret thirteen, and Mary six.

It was a bitter blow to the family when, on her thirty-seventh birthday, Elizabeth of York died shortly after childbirth. Henry VII was devastated and lived morosely for the rest of his life. He gave her a magnificent tomb in Westminster Abbey, but her universal memorial is in virtually every household, although few people are aware of it. It is her somewhat stylised image which we see as the queen on every pack of cards.

FEBRUARY 12   1554
LORD GUILFORD DUDLEY IS BEHEADED,
FOLLOWED SHORTLY AFTER BY . . .

1554
THE EXECUTION OF LADY JANE GREY

These two teenagers, Lord Guilford Dudley and his wife Lady Jane Grey, both aged sixteen, were sent to the block within minutes of each other on this day. They were victims of plotting and manipulation by Guilford Dudley's father, the Duke of Northumberland, who was scheming to be the power behind the throne as he proclaimed Lady Jane Grey Queen of England on the death of her young kinsman, Edward VI.

Guilford Dudley was beheaded first, at about ten o'clock in the morning. He protested his innocence, but his conscience must have reminded him how much had had wanted the plot to succeed. His decapitated body was wrapped up and trundled back to the Tower on a hand-cart. It was actually pushed past the window of the room where Lady Jane Grey happened to be looking out. With horror she saw her young husband's corpse on its way to be buried in the Tower chapel. It was obvious to her that it was her turn next.

Jane had been perfectly innocent, yet totally aware of what was happening. She knew that she had no right to be queen, and had no wish to be. Nevertheless she had been forced, at times with physical intimidation, to go through with Northumberland's scheme.

She spoke briefly to the spectators standing round the block: 'I do wash my hands in innocency before God, and in the face of all you good Christian people this day.' And then, in carefully coded Protestant terms, she added: 'And now good people, *while I am alive*, I pray you assist me with your prayers.'

As she reached the block, she was blindfolded and had to grope forwards to find it. 'Where is it? Where is it? What shall I do?' she exclaimed. Someone came forward to help her find it. 'Lord, into Thy hands I commend my spirit,' she called out, just before the axe fell and the executioner roared out his accustomed phrase – 'Behold the head of a traitor!'

Also on this day:
1689 The House of Commons declared that James II had abdicated.

FEBRUARY 13   1542
THE GHOST OF KATHERINE HOWARD

On Monday, February 13, Henry VIII divested himself of his fifth wife. The same block was used for her execution that had been used almost six years previously to behead Anne Boleyn. Katherine particularly asked that it should be brought to her the night before, so that she could practise laying her head on it. So when the moment came, her end was mercifully swift.

Poor Katherine! She was a fun-loving teenager of about fifteen when she married Henry, who was thirty-three years older. The marriage lasted less than two-and-a-half years, so that Katherine was probably no more than twenty when she met her fate.

In his rage against her infidelity Henry refused even to let her plead in her own defence. But Katherine knew when the king would be at his prayers in the Chapel Royal at Hampton Court, where they were living, and it was her desperate hope to reach him in his pew and beg his forgiveness. In a state of incandescent terror she broke from her guards, flew along the great long gallery, and actually reached the chapel door, hammering on it hysterically and begging the king to see her. But the guards caught up with her and dragged her back, screaming and sobbing.

Katherine's desperate flight along the the Hampton Court gallery has been seen many times by later residents in a ghostly re-enactment of this scene. Her frantic screams have also been heard. It is as if Katherine has imprinted her agony of mind on this place for ever.

1689
A UNIQUE ROYAL DOUBLE ACT IS DECLARED: WILLIAMANMARY

The departure of James II left a curious situation in its wake. Who was officially to be the next monarch? It was a constitutional problem that had never presented itself before. Winston Churchill described it succinctly:

> Was the throne vacant? Could the throne ever be vacant? Was there a contract between the King and the people which James had broken? Had he abdicated by flight, or merely deserted? Could he be deposed by Parliament? Arising from all this, should William become Regent, governing in the name of the absent James? Should Mary become Queen in her own right? Had she not, in view of the virtual demise of the Crown, in fact already become Queen? Or should William be made sole King; or should William and Mary reign jointly; and if Mary died, should Anne forthwith succeed, or should William continue to reign alone as long as he lived?

The fact is, Mary was adamant in refusing to take the throne alone, although she was the legal heir, and William made it clear that he himself would accept nothing less than the throne. The impasse was solved on this day in 1689, when William and Mary accepted the offer made to them by the Lords and Commons to rule jointly, as king and queen regnant.

It was a unique solution. In the immortal words of *1066 and All That*: 'WilliamanMary: England Ruled by an Orange'.

FEBRUARY 14   1613
AN IMPORTANT ST VALENTINE'S DAY MARRIAGE

On the face of it, the wedding which took place on this day in 1613 between Princess Elizabeth and Frederick, Elector Palatine of the Rhine, was just another piece of minor political manoeuvring. Most people would conclude that Elizabeth, daughter of James I, would simply go overseas and hardly be heard of again.

Elizabeth, aged sixteen at the time and four years older than her brother, the future Charles I, was James's favourite. 'Bessy', as he called her, was given a most extravagant wedding in Westminster Abbey, with immensely expensive dresses and jewels on display; and this was followed by entertainments and fireworks on the Thames costing over £90,000. Incidentally, it was the first royal wedding to be celebrated according to the Book of Common Prayer.

True, Elizabeth did go away and live abroad. True, she hardly made any immediate impact on the state of Europe. Nevertheless, this marriage was ultimately of far-reaching importance to the history of our monarchy, for it was her grandson who returned to England just over a hundred years later, in 1714, to become our King George I. (See NOVEMBER 22)

Also on this day:

1317 Death of Margaret of France, second wife of Edward I, aged thirty-five. She was buried in the church of the Greyfriars in London (now destroyed).

1400 Death (possible murder) of King Richard II, aged thirty-six, at Pontefract Castle, Yorkshire.

FEBRUARY 15   1696
'DUTCH WILLIAM' ESCAPES A JACOBITE PLOT TO ASSASSINATE HIM

On Saturday, February 15, a group of conspirators under the leadership of Sir George Barclay made plans to capture and kill King William III at Turnham Green. It was known that William intended to go hunting and would return by crossing the river there, and for a moment his guards would be separated from him. This conspiracy was known as the 'Covent Garden Plot', for the conspirators met at the Piazza at Covent Garden to plan the operation.

Luckily for the king someone in the know came forward to beg him not to go out hunting that day, saying 'It was against his religion to see a murder done, without giving a warning.' The ring-leaders were soon discovered and put to death, their remains being hung up on Temple Bar.

As for William, he actually gained some popularity over the incident, and 'popery' became even more of an anathema to the public at large.

FEBRUARY 16   1952
AN EX-KING OF ENGLAND ATTENDS THE FUNERAL
OF A DEAD KING OF ENGLAND

Never before had such an event happened: a former King of England mourning the death of his successor. It was, of course, the Duke of Windsor, the former King Edward VIII, who came from his self-imposed exile in France to be at the funeral of his brother, King George VI. He came alone. The Duchess of Windsor remained behind.

All funerals are fraught with emotion, but the tensions within the royal family caused by the abdication were still raw. 'I was bloody shabbily treated,' the ex-king had said, and he vowed he would never return officially to England unless Wallis became 'Her Royal Highness'. In fact, the Duke of Windsor had made three final attempts to 'change the position' not long before the death of George VI, each time being met by a blank refusal. The brothers, Edward and George, had met face to face in 1949 at what was to be their last encounter.

At the funeral he met and spoke with his brother's widow and his niece Elizabeth, now queen. He had not seen them since 1936. But nothing he could say could change the past; nor would it change the future.

FEBRUARY 17   1461
THE LANCASTRIANS BEAT THE YORKISTS
AT ST ALBANS

The forces of the Lancastrians won the upper hand on this day at a bloody battle at St Albans – the second battle to take place there during the confusion of the Wars of the Roses. King Henry VI, virtually a puppet king, had been placed under a tree, with guards, to watch the battle. Luckily for him, the Lancastrians, led by his wife Margaret of Anjou (the 'She-Wolf of France'), won the battle for him.

But the victory was short-lived. Only six weeks later the Yorkists were to win an even bloodier battle, fought in blizzard conditions at Towton near Leeds. Henry's days as king were running out.

1937

A NEW ROYAL FAMILY MOVES INTO BUCKINGHAM PALACE

Just over two months after succeeding Edward VIII, King George and Queen Elizabeth, with their two daughters Elizabeth and Margaret, moved from their home, 145 Piccadilly, into their new official residence, Buckingham Palace. Princess Elizabeth was ten, and her younger sister seven.

Clearly a schoolroom had to be fitted up for the royal children, and the new king rejected the dismal attic where he had received lessons when staying in the palace as a boy. 'Crawfie', the princesses' governess, described it as 'the cheerless room in which he had spent many unhappy hours as a child.'

'No,' remarked the king, 'that won't do.' And a brighter, sunnier room was chosen.

Queen Elizabeth II has lived in Buckingham Palace ever since, as her working London base. But it is well known that she much prefers Windsor Castle as her weekend home.

FEBRUARY 18   1516

CATHERINE OF ARAGON GIVES BIRTH TO A DAUGHTER

No, it was not a son. 'Sons will follow,' said a hopeful Henry VIII. But the celebrations were muted. It was not Catherine's first pregnancy, – nor, indeed, her first child. She had had a stillborn daughter in 1510, less than a year after her marriage to Henry. Then a son had come twelve months later, jubilantly christened Henry, but he had lived for less than eight weeks. Then came an unnamed son in 1513, who died within days. And in 1515 yet another son, who had died shortly after birth.

Catherine had more than her fair share of disappointments, though still she was only thirty when, at last, in 1516 she gave birth at Greenwich Palace to a daughter who would survive and inherit the throne – Mary Tudor.

The birth was long and painful, with Catherine holding a sacred relic of her patron saint to help her through the ordeal. But at last at four o'clock in the morning the new princess was successfully brought into the world, and baptized Mary, after Henry's sister, the Queen of France.

Also on this day:

1478 The Duke of Clarence, brother of King Edward IV, was murdered in the Tower of London. Tradition has it that he was drowned in a barrel of malmsey wine.

FEBRUARY 19   1547
CORONATION OF EDWARD VI, AGED NINE

Poor little Edward never knew his mother, Jane Seymour, who died only a few days after his birth. But he must vaguely have known three step-mothers – one divorced, another beheaded and yet another lucky enough to survive.

The 1547 coronation celebrations were hilariously rough-and-ready, often crude by our standards. Wine actually flowed from the street conduits and on his way to Westminster the young king was stopped time after time to watch pageants, listen to trumpeters, hear choirs, and be flattered by specially written poems, such as:

> King Edward upspringeth from puerility
> And towards us bringeth joy and tranquillity;
> Our hearts may be light, and merry our cheer,
> He shall be of such might that all the world may him fear.
> Sing up, heart; sing up, heart; sing no more down,
> But joy in King Edward that weareth the crown!

The most spectacular entertainment came as the procession halted outside St Paul's, where the young king greatly enjoyed watching a Spanish acrobat glide down a tight-rope on his chest, without using hands or feet, from the top of the cathedral spire to the pavement below. Here he kissed the king's feet and then, amid cheers, he mounted his rope and climbed back up to the top again! This, of course, was *Old* St Paul's, which had an astonishingly tall spire of 520ft. (As a comparison, Salisbury's spire is a mere 404ft high.)

One of the songs sung on this occasion was *God save King Edward*, which is thought to be the earliest version of the national anthem. It began:

> King Edward, King Edward,
> God save King Edward,
> God save King Edward,
> King Edward the Sixth!
> To have the sword,
> His subjects to defend,
> His enemies to put down,
> According to right, in every town:
> And long to continue,
> In grace and virtue,
> Unto God's pleasure
> His commons to rejoice!

Also on this day:

1960 Birth of Prince Andrew, Duke of York, son of Queen Elizabeth II and the Duke of Edinburgh, in Buckingham Palace.

FEBRUARY 20   1797
NELSON IS MADE A KNIGHT

George III recognised Nelson's great services to the nation by conferring a knighthood upon him on this day. Nelson was, in fact, a close friend of George's third son William, who eventually became William IV. When they were both serving in the navy in the West Indies, William had taken part in Nelson's marriage service to Frances Nisbet, and had given the bride away.

FEBRUARY 21   1432
KING HENRY VI RECEIVES A RAPTUROUS WELCOME IN LONDON

One of the most spectacular pageants ever witnessed in London took place on this day to welcome King Henry VI on his return from France, where the previous December he had been crowned King of France at a magnificent ceremony in the Cathedral of St Denis, near Paris. Henry had, of course, already been crowned King of England, so now he was King of *both* countries. It was a moment of rejoicing and triumph.

Henry was met on Blackheath by the Mayor, Corporation and principal citizens, all dressed up in scarlet and crimson gowns trimmed with fur. A 'mighty giant with a drawn sword' welcomed him at the entrance to London Bridge, and then a bevy of beautiful girls ceremonially presented him with symbolic gifts: a Crown of Glory, a Sceptre of Might and Mercy, the Mantle of Prudence, the Shield of Faith, the Helmet of Health and the Girdle of Love and Perfect Peace. Magical wells, of Mercy, Grace and Pity, had been set up in the city and when fair damsels offered cups of clear crystal water to the king, the liquid amazingly turned to sparkling wine.

King Henry and his attendants then moved on through gaily bedecked streets to St Paul's, where the approach to the cathedral was lined with hundreds of youths in flowing white garments, holding oak branches in their hands. And then the Archbishop of Canterbury led the king inside the building to offer gifts at the shrine of St Erkenwald.

Refreshments were served at the Bishop's Palace, after which the king and his courtiers rode on to Westminster Abbey where a similar ceremony was performed at the shrine of Edward the Confessor.

All this must have been exciting and rather tiring for little King Henry VI. After all, he was only ten.

FEBRUARY 22 1511
HENRY VIII MOURNS THE DEATH OF HIS SON, PRINCE HENRY

This largely forgotten infant lived for just fifty-two days. Born on 1 January 1511 at Richmond Palace, to Catherine of Aragon and Henry VIII, the little boy died on 22 February; but for those brief weeks King Henry had what he desired above all else: *a son*.

Christened Henry, the infant was given the title Duke of Cornwall. A tremendous two-day tournament took place a month after his birth, to celebrate this great event and to give the twenty-year-old King Henry a chance to show off his joy in jousting and knocking his opponents off their horses. It was what he was good at. The City of London enjoyed bonfires, free wine, street processions and all manner of jollifications. But alas, on 22 February, everything came to naught, as the little prince died.

No one knew at the time just how important that tiny life had been. If only he had lived, perhaps the Church of England would never have come into being, and Britain would still be filled with beautiful medieval abbeys throughout the land. Arguably this death was one of the great turning-points in our history.

FEBRUARY 23 1094
RUFUS IS REBUKED FOR SODOMY BY A SAINT

Anselm, Archbishop of Canterbury, had constant confrontations with the wicked 'Red King' Rufus, mainly over the relations between church and state. But he didn't like the king's gay life-style either. In a Lenten sermon at Hastings on this day in 1094 Anselm had the courage to preach against what he considered to be the moral laxness of the king and his courtiers. Long hair, effeminate dress, gay mannerisms and homosexuality were firmly condemned.

Anselm found it wise to retire to the continent. He returned when Rufus was dead, only to find himself in conflict with Henry I, and in exile once again.

It wasn't until 1720 that Anselm's ultimate recognition came, more than six centuries after his death. As an important writer on theology, he was canonised as one of the Doctors of the Church by Pope Clement XI. Curiously enough, it was another 'King' of England who urged the Pope to do this: the Jacobite monarch, 'James III', the 'Old Pretender'. Royal recognition at last!

Also this day:
1421 Catherine of Valois, aged twenty, wife of King Henry V, was crowned Queen of England in Westminster Abbey.

FEBRUARY 24 1652
THE 'ACT OF OBLIVION'

On this day the English Parliament formally pardoned all those royalists who, perhaps, may have been considered too zealous in supporting the king. Now that King Charles I had been dead for more than three years, it was time to put the Civil War behind them. They therefore passed the 'Act of Oblivion'. Monarchy was dead.

1945
'SPIT AND POLISH ALL DAY LONG'

On February 24 1945 Princess Elizabeth at last prevailed upon her father, King George VI, to let her join one of the military services. It was only months away from the end of the war, but of course no one knew exactly when or how that would happen. Elizabeth wanted to be treated as everyone else; accordingly, on this day she joined the Auxiliary Territorial Service at Aldershot as 'No. 230873 Second Subaltern Elizabeth Alexandra Mary Windsor. Age: 18. Eyes: blue. Hair: brown. Height: 5 ft. 3 ins.' Her duties were to include vehicle maintenance, map-reading, driving in convoy, and stripping and servicing an engine. To prove her competence she drove her commanding officer from Aldershot to Buckingham Palace through the busy London afternoon traffic. Legend has it that she drove twice round Piccadilly Circus *en route*.

But she learned more than just how to strip an engine. It so happened that her aunt, the Princess Royal, who was Head of the Auxiliary Territorial Service, decided one day to carry out a tour of inspection at Aldershot, where the young princess was being trained.

When Elizabeth got back to Buckingham Palace that evening she remarked to her mother: 'Now I know what happens when you and Papa go anywhere – *Spit and polish all day long*!'

FEBRUARY 25   1308
EDWARD II'S DISASTROUS CORONATION

Edward put his gay partner, Piers Gaveston, in charge of organising his coronation. Unluckily, Gaveston's sheer incompetence led to a day of utter disaster.

Just before the ceremony, the nobles presented Edward with an ultimatum: they would refuse to attend unless Gaveston was banished from the court. Edward managed to smooth things over, but when it was discovered that Gaveston was actually going to bear the sacred crown of St Edward, the Earl of Lancaster had to be physically restrained from murdering him even within the sanctuary of Westminster Abbey. Meanwhile, outside the abbey, the crush of spectators was so uncontrolled that some people, including a well-known knight, were trodden to death.

It wasn't until after three o'clock that the ceremony was over, and then Gaveston's management of the coronation banquet was so bungled that it wasn't for hours that anyone had anything to eat. Even when the food arrived, it was so badly cooked and served that it was virtually uneatable.

Only a month before Edward had married his sixteen-year-old French bride, Isabella of France, and so the coronation was also attended by many French princes and nobles. They were so disgusted by the coronation shambles that they returned home in high dudgeon. As for Isabella, she wrote home to her father, King Philip the Bold, in abject misery.

FEBRUARY 26   1461
THE YORKISTS ENTER LONDON

Edward of York, aged nineteen, entered London on this day in 1461 at the head of his Yorkist army. Within less than a week (on March 4), he had managed to have himself proclaimed king. Four months and a few battles later, he would be crowned in Westminster Abbey. The fact that Henry VI was still alive and well did not seem much of an impediment to his royal ambition.

FEBRUARY 27   1872
VICTORIA GOES IN THANKSGIVING TO ST PAUL'S

In 1871 a huge wave of anti-royal feeling began to sweep the country. Republican clubs sprang up everywhere, and the movement to banish the royal family was fanned by speeches by Sir Charles Dilke and Joseph Chamberlain ('The republic must come'). There were riotous scenes after a large gathering in London.

Scurrilous pamphlets appeared with titles like *Mrs John Brown*, *Guelpho the Gay*, and *The Infidelities of a Prince*, as a result of the reclusive life of the queen and the scandalous life-style of the Prince of Wales. Gladstone himself noted: 'The Queen is invisible and the Prince of Wales is not respected.'

Then, at the end of the year, Edward contracted typhoid fever and in December it was believed that he was just about to die. On December 14, exactly ten years to the day since the death of Prince Albert, Victoria sat at his bedside at Sandringham, expecting the worst. Bellringers were waiting at St Paul's, ready to toll the prince's death.

Royalist sympathies were rekindled by these fears for the prince's life, and when Edward made a recovery, all republican sentiments were drowned by a surge of relief. Despite her initial reservations, Victoria actually made a public appearance on February 27 to attend a thanksgiving service in St Paul's for the prince's recovery. The streets were lined with cheering crowds, and afterwards Victoria went out on the balcony of Buckingham Palace to acknowledge the wild enthusiasm of her subjects.

Republicanism was over.

FEBRUARY 28 1155
ELEANOR OF AQUITAINE GIVES BIRTH TO A SON

This young prince, named Henry and born on this day to Eleanor of Aquitaine and Henry II, was destined to have a unique title: the 'Young King'. When he was fifteen he was actually crowned in Westminster Abbey, so that England, for a while at least, had *two* kings. It was already a French practice to crown the heir to the throne in his father's lifetime, as a safeguard to ensure a smooth transition to a new king, in case of sudden disaster.

The Young King was intended to succeed Henry II as King of England while his brother Richard (the future 'Lionheart') was to receive his mother's inheritance of Aquitaine. All these plans came to nothing, however, when the Young King died, at the age of just twenty-eight, in 1183. His death meant that Richard would take everything.

FEBRUARY 29 1216
KING JOHN STILL STRUGGLING AGAINST THE BARONS

This was a leap-year: one more day added to the year in the bitter wrangling between John and the barons. John spent the period from February 19 to March 3 in Bedford, trying to contain the barons' rebellions. As he moved about his kingdom it is said that every morning he took delight in setting fire, with his own hands, to the house that had sheltered him the preceding night.

This is probably an exaggeration or even a blatant untruth: but the very existence of such a rumour shows how unpopular he had become. He had only seven-and-a-half more months to live (see OCTOBER 18.)

1872
QUEEN VICTORIA SURVIVES THE SIXTH
ASSASSINATION ATTEMPT

It comes as a surprise to some people to find that Victoria survived no fewer than seven assassination attempts, the sixth of which happened on February 29 1872.

ASSASSINATION ATTEMPTS ON QUEEN VICTORIA	
1840 (June 10)	Would-be assassin: Edward Oxford. This event occurred as Victoria and Albert were driving up Constitution Hill. Oxford fired two pistols at her. He was later found to be insane and put in an asylum.
1842 (May 30)	Would-be assassin: John Francis. This occurred as Victoria and Albert were in a carriage driving up the Mall. Francis's gun was unloaded.
1842 (July 3)	Would-be assassin: John William Bean. He fired a pistol, but the weapon was not properly loaded.
1849 (May 19)	Would-be assassin: William Hamilton. On Constitution Hill, as Victoria was being driven to Buckingham Palace. He fired at point-blank range, but luckily the gun was not loaded.
1850 (July 27)	Would-be assassin: Robert Pate. This was hardly an assassination attempt, as Pate was armed only with a stick, but Victoria was badly shaken and suffered a black eye and facial injuries.
1872 (Feb 29)	Would-be assassin: Arthur O'Connor. He pointed a pistol at the queen as she was about to enter the garden entrance to Buckingham Palace. John Brown knocked the pistol out of O'Connor's hand, and pinned him down before guards could arrest him. Victoria gave Brown a gold medal and an annuity of £25 for this act of bravery.
1882 (March 2)	Would-be assassin: Roderick MacLean. He fired a shot at Victoria as she was leaving Windsor railway station. (See MARCH 2)

MARCH 1 1683
BIRTH OF CAROLINE OF ANSBACH, QUEEN OF GEORGE II

Caroline was the daughter of the Margrave John Frederick of Brandenburg-Ansbach, an obscure little German state, smaller than some English counties. Her father died when she was only three, and as she grew up she was moved about several courts of Europe, with enviable prospects of marriage. She turned down the Archduke of Austria by refusing to become a Catholic. Instead, she married the Protestant Prince George Augustus of Hanover.

However, when they married in Hanover in 1705, neither Caroline herself nor her husband George had any notion that one day they would become King and Queen of England. She was twenty-two at the time of their marriage, but it was to be another twenty-two years before she became queen.

Caroline proved to be a strong character, helping George positively in his royal duties: perhaps too much so, for a popular rhyme was chanted behind his back:

> You may strut, dapper George, but 'twill all be in vain,
> We know 'tis Queen Caroline, not you, that reign . . .
> Then if you would have us fall down and adore you,
> Lock up your fat spouse as your dad did before you.

(The last line refers to the fact that George I had kept his wife Sophia Dorothea locked up for the last thirty-two years of her life, for alleged adultery.)

MARCH 2 1882
QUEEN VICTORIA SURVIVES YET ANOTHER ASSASSINATION ATTEMPT

Queen Victoria survived no fewer than *seven* attempts to assassinate her (see FEBRUARY 29).

On this occasion she was leaving the railway station at Windsor and heading towards Windsor Castle in her carriage when a young man named Roderick MacLean fired a shot at her. He missed, and some Eton schoolboys who were passing by rushed at the would-be assassin, beating him up with their umbrellas.

The queen was quite calm. Later, she remarked: 'It's worth being shot at, to see how much one is loved.'

Also on this day:

1619 Death of Anne of Denmark, aged forty-five, queen of King James I, at Denmark House, Greenwich.

MARCH 3   1141
BISHOP HENRY OF BLOIS RECEIVES THE EMPRESS MATILDA

It was in the middle of a period of anarchy. Who should rule England: the Empress Matilda, who had been promised the crown by her father Henry I? Or Stephen, her cousin, who had smartly stepped in and usurped the throne in 1135?

Henry of Blois, the powerful Bishop of Winchester, played a key role in swaying opinion and gathering up supporters. But which side was he on? After all, he was Stephen's brother.

Perhaps surprisingly, on March 3 the Empress Matilda was received in great state by the bishop, her cousin, in the newly built Norman cathedral of Winchester. Obviously he was planning to support her against his own brother! And in just over a month he was proclaiming her to be 'Lady of the English', as a preliminary to being crowned in London.

But only a few weeks later Henry switched sides, and Matilda's hopes disappeared. (See SEPTEMBER 14)

MARCH 4   1894
VICTORIA'S RELIEF AS GLADSTONE RESIGNS

On this day, after four terms as Prime Minister, William Gladstone – the 'Grand Old Man' – finally resigned, much to Victoria's relief. She had made no secret of the fact that she disliked him intensely and referred to him as 'the abominable old G. Man.'

Of his final audience with the queen, four years before his death, Gladstone, then aged eighty-four, described Victoria's conversation as 'neither here nor there'. He went on: 'To speak frankly, it seemed to me that the Queen's peculiar faculty . . . of conversation had disappeared. It was a faculty, not so much the free offspring of a rich and powerful mind, as the fruit of assiduous care with long practice and much opportunity.'

Gladstone left the royal presence without thanks; indeed, with hardly a word from her. Later, she wrote saying that she would not offer him a peerage as she knew he would not accept one.

Unlike Disraeli, Gladstone never felt at ease with the queen. Once, at Osborne House, meeting her in the evening before a dinner party, he grabbed her hand and awkwardly kissed it, thinking it the proper thing to do. She glared. 'This should have been done this afternoon,' she declared.

Also this day:

1461 King Henry VI was deposed and the throne seized by nineteen-year-old Edward of York. He was to be crowned as Edward IV on June 28 later this year.

MARCH 5   1133
BIRTH OF THE FUTURE HENRY II

Son of Count Geoffrey V of Anjou and Matilda, daughter of Henry I of England, the future Henry II was born on this day at Le Mans, France. He would be only twenty when he succeeded to the throne as a result of King Stephen's death.

His mother, the Empress Matilda, who had briefly been 'Lady of the English', was still alive when Henry was crowned, but no one wanted her to succeed as queen. She had forfeited the sympathy of the barons, and had been forced to promise the succession to Henry.

MARCH 6   1052
EMMA'S QUEENLY RECORD

The *Anglo-Saxon Chronicle* records: 'In this same year [1052] on 6 March passed away the Lady-dowager, the mother of King Edward [the Confessor] and of Harthacnut: she is called Emma. Her body lies in the Old Minster [Winchester] beside King Cnut.'

Almost a thousand years later, this remarkable old lady still holds the royal record among English queens. She is the only queen to have been married to two Kings of England and to have given birth to two future Kings of England. Her first husband was Ethelred the Unready, by whom she had her son Edward the Confessor; and her second husband was Canute, by whom she had Harthacnut.

For much of her life she lived in Winchester, where she is buried. An extraordinary story is told of how in her later years, in her second widowhood, she became a close friend of Alwine, Bishop of Winchester. The friendship led to wagging tongues, and her son Edward, now king, was so upset to think that his mother was possibly leading an immoral life that he ordered her to undergo trial by ordeal – fire-walking in fact!

Accordingly, nine ploughshares were placed in the nave of the old Saxon Cathedral and heated until they were red hot. Then Emma, blindfolded and guided by two bishops, one on each side of her, stepped lightly over the heated ploughshares. Her feet were found to be unscathed, thus proving her innocence. In gratitude she gave nine manor-houses to the monks of Winchester; Bishop Alwine gave nine more manors. King Edward, her son, added another three.

Emma's remains still lie in a mortuary chest, mingled not only with those of King Canute, but also with those of the good Bishop Alwine.

Also this day:

1707   Queen Anne gives the Royal Assent to the Act of Union, uniting the two countries of England and Scotland.

MARCH 7   1827
PRINNY SAYS FAREWELL TO BRIGHTON

In his time George IV was strongly condemned for his extravagance and mocked for his eccentric tastes. Brighton's Royal Pavilion is perhaps the most extraordinary monument to his mania for the exotic. Nowadays, of course, it is one of Britain's most popular tourist attractions.

He was twenty-one when he first came on holiday to Brighton, staying at Grove House on the Steine, accompanying his uncle, the Duke of Cumberland (the 'Butcher' of Culloden). The holiday, in 1783, was to transform his life, for he enjoyed it so much that he came to Brighton regularly during the next forty-four years.

The following year he leased the same house for ten weeks, and one day during that stay he actually commuted to London, riding there and back on horseback to transact his business: ten hours in the saddle!

It was in 1787 that he started to transform an old farmhouse into the weird building which eventually became the Royal Pavilion we know today. Bit by bit he added to it, aided by John Nash, and he established his secret wife, Mrs Maria Fitzherbert, in a villa close by, later building her a new house on the Steine.

Brighton was filled with memories for Prinny, as both prince and king, but his health crumbled and his girth expanded in his later years. On 7 March 1827 he left the Royal Pavilion for the last time.

MARCH 8   1702

WILLIAM III DIES, KILLED BY A MOLE

To the huge delight of the Jacobites, William III, 'Dutch William', had a nasty fall from his horse on February 21 1702, while riding from his newly built Kensington Palace to Hampton Court. The beast had stumbled over a mole-hill. William sustained a broken collar-bone and was badly shaken. Nevertheless, after being taken on into Hampton Court Palace to have the bone reset, he refused to rest and insisted on returning to Kensington to carry on with his duties. Unfortunately, the jolting of the coach put the shoulder out again, so it had to be reset again when he got back to Kensington.

After a few days his hand had become so swollen that he had to use a stamp to sign his documents, but he stubbornly refused to give in. Surprisingly, powdered crabs' eyes, pearled julep and sal volatile had no effect, and on Sunday March 8 he died.

For decades afterwards, the supporters of the exiled Stuarts toasted 'The little gentleman in the black velvet coat' for having helped William to his early grave. He was only fifty-one.

Also on this day:

1702   On the death of King William III, Queen Anne, aged thirty-seven, succeeded to the throne.

MARCH 9   1566
MARY, QUEEN OF SCOTS, SEES HER SECRETARY STABBED TO DEATH

The murder of David Rizzio, the Scottish queen's cultured and musical secretary, had been planned to take place a few days later, but the date was brought forward because the conspirators feared that their plot had been discovered. The motives behind the murder were mixed: Lord Darnley, Mary's husband, was anxious to get rid of Rizzio, who he thought was the queen's lover; and in any case, he wanted to become king, even at the expense of losing his wife and unborn child. His companions, however, wanted to get rid of Darnley himself, and so were planning to put all the blame on him, and thus have him executed for treason.

True enough, the all-knowing Cecil, chief adviser to Queen Elizabeth I, was quite aware of what was being planned, but Elizabeth herself did not know about it until afterwards.

On the evening of March 9, Mary, Queen of Scots, was dining at Holyrood House with David Rizzio and one of her ladies when her husband, Lord Darnley, suddenly stormed into the room with his group of assassins, including Lord Ruthven. They seized Rizzio and dragged him from the table. 'Save me, my lady!' screamed Rizzio, as he literally clung to the queen's skirts. But he was completely overpowered and one of the assassins aimed his pistol at the pregnant queen's stomach while the two were separated.

Within seconds, in a neighbouring room, Rizzio received fifty-six dagger wounds and died. The young queen was only twenty-four at the time. Luckily, her pregnancy survived the shock, and in another three months she gave birth to the future King James VI of Scotland and I of England.

MARCH 10   1863
'BERTIE', THE FUTURE KING EDWARD VII, MARRIES ALIX

It was, of course, an arranged marriage. Victoria planned that Bertie should 'happen' to meet Alexandra of Schleswig-Holstein-Sonderburg-Glücksburg while visiting the cathedral in the German town of Speyer in September 1861. The future king was charmed, and when next they met, a few months later, he proposed almost immediately; she, naturally, accepted.

Victoria was still heavily in mourning, for Prince Albert had died less than fifteen months before Bertie's wedding. Indeed she declined to be formally present at the marriage service in St George's Chapel Windsor, and watched the event from the special box, known as the 'Royal Pew', which Henry VIII had built to give Catherine of Aragon a secluded view of services.

Alexandra enchanted the nation with her beauty and the marriage was popular. 'How beloved Albert would have loved her,' wrote Victoria. The following month she took the newly-weds into the Frogmore mausoleum to visit his grave: it was a solemn occasion. 'He gives you his blessing,' she announced.

Also this day:

1629 King Charles I dissolved Parliament, calling some of its members 'vipers', and declared that henceforth he would rule alone.

1964 Birth of Prince Edward, third son of Queen Elizabeth II and the Duke of Edinburgh. He was created Earl of Wessex in 1999.

MARCH 11   1830
VICTORIA PROMISES TO BE GOOD

The dramatic moment when ten-year-old Princess Victoria became aware that she was almost certain to become queen was recorded by her governess, Baroness Lehzen. She was just about to begin her history lesson for the day, and had opened her text book, Howlett's *Tables of the Kings and Queens of England*. Suddenly, she noticed that an extra page had been inserted. 'I never saw that before,' she remarked.

'No, Princess. It was not thought necessary that you should,' replied her governess.

The young princess examined the new page, which brought the line of succession up to date, showing that only her uncle William stood between the dying King George IV and herself.

'I am nearer to the throne than I thought,' she said.

Young as she was, she was quite aware of the enormous responsibilities which would come to her, and tears came to her eyes. She raised her right forefinger and uttered her famous promise: 'I will be good.'

MARCH 12   1689
EX-KING JAMES II TRIES TO REGAIN HIS KINGDOM

Having been deposed three months earlier, James was getting restless, wanting to stage a comeback. Thinking that he could gain access to his kingdom through Ireland, he landed this day at Kinsale in County Cork, on the south-western coast. With French backing and hoping for Catholic Irish support, he believed this would be the best way to oust Protestant William from the throne. At the time he landed at Kinsale William and Mary were still uncrowned (see APRIL 11) so the future was filled with possibilities.

It was not until the following year, on July 1 1690, that William finally confronted James at the Battle of the Boyne. Sadly for the Jacobite cause, James, having lost 'a spoonful of blood', was defeated and fled to Dublin.

Meeting Lady Tyrconnel there, he complained: 'Madam, your countrymen have run away.'

'Sire, your majesty seems to have won the race,' she replied.

MARCH 13   1470
EDWARD IV QUELLS A REBELLION IN STAMFORD

Henry VI had stayed as a guest in the Lincolnshire town of Stamford in 1448 and 1452. Lancastrian loyalty, therefore, was still strong here during the confused period of the Wars of the Roses.

A Lincolnshire rising against Edward IV was organised by Sir Robert Welles in March, but Edward swiftly arrived here and ruthlessly stamped it out on this day in 1470.

1781
GEORGE III AND URANUS

William Herschel discovered the planet Uranus on this day, and immediately named it *Georgium Sidus* – 'the star of George' – after King George III. Herschel had been born in Hanover, and had come to live in England in 1737, so naturally he looked to George as a likely supporter and patron.

Herschel's fame was made. The following year George appointed him to the prestigious post of Astronomer Royal, and asked him to build six new telescopes for his own private observatory at Windsor. The largest of these was 40ft long and was in fact, for a while, the biggest telescope in the world.

The final mad years of George III's reign often unfairly cloud our memory of him and make us forget that for years he was an energetic and enthusiastic patron of the arts and sciences – indeed his books formed the nucleus of the library of the British Museum.

Also on this day:

1194 King Richard I returned to England after being released from captivity in Austria. He landed at Sandwich, Kent (see APRIL 17).

MARCH 14   1708
'JAMES III' TRIES TO LAND IN SCOTLAND

When James II died in exile in 1701, Louis XIV had proclaimed his son, James Stuart, to be the new King of England – 'James III'.

Now, aged just twenty, 'James III' tried to land in the Firth of Forth to gain his kingdom – after all, he was James VIII of Scotland, too. Everything, even the weather, was against him on this attempt. The English fleet lay in readiness for him; the French convoy abandoned him, and at the last moment he was struck down by measles.

Defeated, he went back to his mother, the widowed Mary of Modena, in France.

Also on this day:

1216 King John captured Colchester Castle, held against him by rebellious barons supported by French troops.

MARCH 15   1862
VICTORIA LAYS THE FOUNDATION STONE FOR A MAUSOLEUM AT FROGMORE

Only four days after Albert's death, Victoria had gone to Frogmore and chosen a spot for a new mausoleum beyond the lake, where she decided she and Albert would eventually lie together. In fact, her mother, the Duchess of

Kent, had already been buried in a smaller mausoleum at Frogmore, so the place was of particular significance to Victoria (see MARCH 16).

Three months later, on this day, she returned here to lay the foundation stone of what was to be her final resting-place, a chapel built in the shape of a Greek cross and having a green-roofed cupola. However, it was not until 1868 that the prince's remains were taken out of the vaults at Windsor (see DECEMBER 23) and moved to Frogmore. Samuel Wilberforce, the Bishop of Oxford, performed the service. The bishop's own description of the event gives a breath of Victoria's mood:

> I am just home from the consecration of the mausoleum . . . one of the most touching scenes I ever saw, to see our Queen and the fatherless children walk in and kneel down in those solemn prayers. I had a half-hour's talk with her yesterday and nothing could be more delightful, so gentle, so affectionate, so true, so real – no touch of morbidness – quite cheerful and so kind.

Perhaps understandably, Bishop Wilberforce's well-known nickname was 'Soapy Sam'.

MARCH 16   1861
DEATH OF QUEEN VICTORIA'S MOTHER

Victoria's mother, the Duchess of Kent, died this day of cancer at Frogmore House. She was aged seventy-four, and no one ever thought that Victoria would be particularly grief-stricken. After all, one of the first acts of her reign was to move smartly out of the bedroom she had hitherto shared with her mother, and have a room to herself.

It was, therefore, something of a shock to everyone, especially Albert, to witness the violence of the grief now exhibited by Victoria. She abandoned herself to floods and floods of tears. In her diary she wrote of 'the *weeping* which day after day is my welcome friend'. Somewhat sinisterly, in view of her later life, she proudly added, 'the approval of the manner in which I have shown my grief, is quite wonderful'.

Such was the unbalanced force of her reaction that rumours were rife that her mind was unhinged, and that she was already showing symptoms of the madness of King George III, her grandfather. She was describing her mother's death as 'the sorrow of my life' and her most 'dreadful hour'.

Prince Albert tried his best to bring her back to a normal life-style, and wrote letters abroad denying that his wife was going mad. Little did either of them realise that later this same year he himself would die and Victoria's capacity for grief would be demonstrated even more unbearably.

Later, in a self-revealing letter to the Queen of Prussia after Albert's death, Victoria wrote: 'My nature is too passionate, my emotions too fervent, and I am a person who has to cling to *someone* in order to find peace and comfort.' A Scottish servant, perhaps?

Also on this day:

1485 Death of Anne Neville, queen of King Richard III, aged twenty-nine. She was buried in Westminster Abbey.

MARCH 17   1649
PARLIAMENT ABOLISHES THE MONARCHY AND THE HOUSE OF LORDS

Less than seven weeks after the execution of Charles I, an Act of Parliament was passed on this day declaring England to be a 'commonwealth and free state'. It clearly spelt out to anyone who might still have any lingering doubts about the matter that Parliament itself was now the 'supreme authority of this nation'.

This seems obvious to modern folk, but it was a revolutionary concept which to some minds at least verged on blasphemy. James I and Charles I had set great store by the notion of the 'Divine Right of Kings', and claimed that their authority was derived directly from God himself.

Abolishing the king was one thing, but abolishing the House of Lords was another. For purely practical reasons, in any country there needs to be an administrative authority – a government, senate, council, upper chamber, call it what you will. Parliament was indeed 'the original of all just power . . . being chosen by and representing the people', but something more was needed. Accordingly, a Council of State consisting of forty-one members was set up. And Oliver Cromwell was to be its Chairman.

Little did those members of parliament imagine that in just over eight years time they would be asking Oliver to become their king.

Also on this day:

1040 Death of King Harold I ('Harefoot'), son of King Canute, aged twenty-four. He was buried in St Clement Dane's, London. On the death of his half-brother, King Hardecanute, aged about twenty-one, succeeded to the throne.

MARCH 18   978
A MURDERED TEENAGE KING BECOMES
A SAINT

On this day in 978 a royal murder took place at Corfe Castle, Dorset. The deed took place when fifteen-year-old King Edward was calling on his stepmother Elfrida and his half-brother Ethelred. Tradition tells how the young king was stabbed while still in the saddle and killed as his horse dragged him along the ground. The blame, it is said, lay with his wicked stepmother, who was keen to place her own son Ethelred (the Unready) on the throne.

The subsequent story of Edward's bones is quite extraordinary. He was buried first at Wareham, near Corfe, but when miracles started to occur there he became regarded as a saint and martyr and his body was solemnly transferred to Shaftesbury Abbey. Somehow his shrine disappeared at the Reformation and it was not until the 1930s that a box containing bones was discovered in the abbey's ruins. It seemed highly likely that these were the precious relics of King Edward, saint and martyr, which had been hidden for safety by the abbey's sixteenth-century nuns.

The relics became the subject of a legal wrangle between squabbling brothers, who contested ownership, and Edward's bones remained in a cutlery box in the vaults of the Midland Bank (now the HSBC) in Woking while lawyers tried to sort out what should happen to them. Eventually they were placed in a modern shrine in Brookwood Cemetery, Surrey, where they are now looked after and venerated by a sect of the Russian Orthodox Church.

1399
THE FUNERAL OF JOHN OF GAUNT

John of Gaunt, Duke of Lancaster, son of Edward III and father of Henry IV, was one of the greatest and most powerful figures of his age. He virtually ruled England during the minority of Richard II, and his marriage to Constance, daughter of Pedro the Cruel of Castile, led him to assume the title King of Castile.

Shakespeare gave him a magnificent speech to declaim on his deathbed, describing England in ecstatic terms:

This royal throne of kings, this scepter'd isle,
This earth of majesty, this seat of Mars,
This other Eden, demi-paradise . . .
This precious stone set in the silver sea . . .
This blessed plot, this earth, this realm, this England.

He was buried on this day in Old St Paul's, next to his first wife, Blanche of Lancaster, and a superb tomb was erected there in his memory. (See AUGUST 14 for a curious sequel.)

MARCH 19 1976
PRINCESS MARGARET AND LORD SNOWDON
ANNOUNCE THEIR SEPARATION

On May 6 1960 Princess Margaret and Anthony Armstrong-Jones married in Westminster Abbey. Now, almost sixteen years later, their separation was announced, followed in due course by the inevitable divorce in June 1978.

The curious Royal Marriages Act of 1772 is still in force and prevents any members of the royal family in the line of succession to marry without first seeking the monarch's permission. Within the Church of England, divorced people are sometimes discouraged from marrying again in church. The Catholic Church prevents a couple from marrying in a Catholic church if one of the partners has a different faith. At that time, members of the royal family are prevented from marrying in a register office within Britain. Because of all this, Prince Michael of Kent married Baroness Marie-Christine von Reibniz in Vienna Town Hall.

Uneasy lie the couple who are in line to wear the crown.

1986
PRINCE ANDREW AND SARAH FERGUSON
ANNOUNCE THEIR ENGAGEMENT

And six years later, on March 18 1992, they announced their separation.

MARCH 20   1413
HENRY IV DIES 'IN JERUSALEM'

Poor Henry! His conscience pricked him throughout his reign, for having usurped the throne. He had an idea that if he went on a Crusade all might be forgiven. Indeed a soothsayer had once told Henry that he would actually die in Jerusalem. Perhaps this comforted him.

However, before he could get there, and still at the relatively early age of forty-six, he had a kind of fit while he was praying at the tomb of Edward the Confessor in Westminster Abbey. Virtually unconscious, he was taken to a room adjoining the abbey and as he rallied he asked where he was. Significantly, it was a place called the 'Jerusalem Chamber'.

According to his chronicler, he replied: 'Praise be to the Father of Heaven, for now I know I shall die in this chamber, according to the prophecy of me beforesaid that I should die in Jerusalem.'

Tradition has it that his confessor asked him to repent of his two major sins, usurping the throne and executing an archbishop, but the king refused, saying that his sons would not permit him to relinquish the throne, and that the Pope had already pardoned him for executing Archbishop Scrope.

Popular belief, however, held that Henry was already being punished for the archbishop's death, as divine retribution had smitten him with leprosy (it was probably eczema) on the day of the execution, and that Henry had been on the itch ever since.

1751
THE PRINCE OF WALES IS KILLED BY A CRICKET BALL

England should have had a King Frederick. He was the Prince of Wales, son of King George II. But alas, he was hit hard on the chest by a cricket ball while playing the newly invented game at Cliveden House, Buckinghamshire, in the summer of 1748.

The injury never healed. An abscess broke in 1751 and as a result he died prematurely, aged only forty-four, on 20 March. Instead of King Frederick, England had his son, King George III instead.

An anonymous poet wrote:

Here lies Fred,
Who was alive and is dead.
Had it been his father,
I had much rather;
Had it been his brother,
Still better than another;
Had it been his sister,
No one would have miss'd her;
Had it been the whole generation,
Still better for the nation;
But since 'tis only Fred,
Who was alive and is dead,
There's no more to be said.

His father, George II, wrote in his diary: 'I have lost my eldest son, but was glad of it.'

Also on this day:
1413 King Henry V, aged twenty-five, succeeded to the throne on the death of his father, Henry IV.

MARCH 21   1556
ARCHBISHOP CRANMER IS BURNT TO DEATH ON THE ORDERS OF QUEEN MARY

Archbishop Thomas Cranmer had declared Mary illegitimate and the marriage of her mother Catherine of Aragon to Henry VIII null and void. When she came to the throne, therefore, according to Foxe's *Book of Martyrs*, Queen Mary I 'was resolved to sacrifice him to her resentments; and she said that it was good for his own soul that he repented; but that since he had been the chief spreader of heresy over the nation it was necessary to make him a public example. Accordingly the writ was sent down to burn him, and, after some stop had been made in th execution of it, new orders came for doing it suddenly.'

Cranmer managed to write to Mary just before his death: 'On the day of your majesty's coronation you took an oath of obedience to the Pope of Rome, and at the same time you took another oath to this realm, to maintain the laws, liberties and customs of the same. . . . But I fear that there are contradictions in your oaths . . . and if your majesty ponder the two oaths diligently, I think you shall perceive you were deceived . . .'

But Mary had no compunction. The archbishop was publicly burnt, just outside Balliol College, Oxford, on this day. A cross in the middle of the road still marks the spot.

MARCH 22   1604
JAMES I INVENTS THE NAME 'GREAT BRITAIN'

Eight months after his coronation King James held his first Parliament on this day in 1604, and proposed a union of England and Scotland under his rule, with a new name: he would call it 'Great Britain.'

'What God has conjoined, let no man separate,' he declared. 'I am the husband and my whole isle is my lawful wife.'

MARCH 23   1173
HENRY II CAPTURES HIS WIFE, ELEANOR OF AQUITAINE

Eternally active, plotting, planning and scheming, Eleanor of Aquitaine was in Chinon, France, supporting her sons in their rebellion against her husband Henry II. This was the time when England had two King Henrys: father and son.

Henry the 'Young King' had been crowned three years earlier, aged fifteen, as a safeguard to ensure a smooth succession should his father die. However, the Young King was chafing at having the title but not the power. He was now eighteen, and his mother Eleanor was supporting him. She was already estranged from Henry, and he was living openly with his mistress, 'Fair Rosamund'.

Henry II moved against Eleanor and captured her on this day. She was disguised as a man and was hoping to join her three rebellious sons, Henry, Richard and John, at the French court. Henry incarcerated her in the castle at Southampton.

Also on this day:

1151 Death of Adela of Louvain, aged forty-eight, second wife of King Henry I. She was buried in Afflighem, Flanders.

MARCH 24   1603
DEATH OF QUEEN ELIZABETH I

It was an awful end, painful for the queen and embarrassing to those around her. The rheumaticky queen, aged sixty-nine, was probably suffering from tonsillitis or the flu, but with indomitable independence she refused to take any medicines, and spent days at a time on the floor lying on cushions. No one could persuade her to go to bed.

Robert Cecil, her chief advisor, begged her to listen to advice: 'Your Majesty, to content the people, you must go to bed.' But with superb pride she had put him in his place: 'Little man, the word "must" is not to be used to princes. . . . Ye know that I must die, and that makes thee so presumptuous.'

Still she refused, and asked to be helped to her feet. And for fifteen hours she stood there, silent, rigid and unmoving, while her courtiers looked on, aghast. Eventually she sank back on to her cushions and remained there for a further four days, sitting with her finger in her mouth. All in all, she had remained lying or standing in her day clothes for almost three weeks. Later, it was rumoured that her astrologer John Dee had prophesied that she would die in her bed, and this had probably been behind the queen's reluctance to give in.

On 21 March she was virtually forced into bed, and it was clear that the end was near. Archbishop Whitgift remained by her bedside for hours: she would not let him go.

The vexed question of the succession was raised, upon which she is alleged to have made some sort of sign with her hands above her head. Rightly or wrongly, this was interpreted as referring to a crown and to King James. And at about three o'clock in the early morning, the last of the Tudors died.

1953
DEATH OF QUEEN MARY

Queen Mary, consort of George V, was born in Kensington Palace, in the same room where Queen Victoria had also been born. A great-granddaughter of George III, she lived in six reigns, closely related to all six sovereigns; steeped in tradition, she was the epitome of royalty.

When Elizabeth II realised that 'her old Granny', as Mary called herself, would not live to see the coronation, a deeply touching and private little ceremony took place. Elizabeth called for the royal crown and other articles she would wear, and solemnly put them on for the old queen to see.

After a lifetime of duty, filled with crises and much personal sadness, Mary died on March 24 1953, less than three months before her grand-daughter's coronation, but knowing that the royal tradition was safe.

MARCH 25   1960
CROMWELL'S HEAD IS FINALLY LAID TO REST

The extraordinary story of Oliver Cromwell's head begins on January 30 1661, the anniversary of the execution of Charles I. It was now some months after the restoration of the monarchy, and Charles II must have felt that this anniversary of his father's death was an appropriate date to dig up the bodies of the three 'regicides', Oliver Cromwell, Henry Ireton and John Bradshaw, and make an example of them.

Accordingly their bodies were dragged to Tyburn, where Marble Arch stands today, and after being publicly hanged, their heads were hacked off and put on permanent exhibition, stuck on 20ft poles in front of Westminster Hall. Cromwell's head remained perched up on this pole for about twenty-five years, until it blew down one stormy night and was retrieved by a soldier who took it home. He was so scared by what he had done that he hid it up a chimney, not even daring to tell his wife. On his deathbed, he confessed to this gruesome theft, and when he died his widow promptly sold the head.

The head now passed through several hands: a calico printer named Dupuis; an actor named Samuel Russell, who made money by putting it on show; James Cox, a jeweller; T.M. Hughes; and finally Josiah Wilkinson, who bought it in 1814 for £230. From then on it remained in the Wilkinson family until it was finally laid to rest. The last member of the Wilkinson family to own it was an ex-military medical man, who had it examined by experts. It still had part of the wooden pole sticking out of the top of the skull. Everything pointed to its genuineness, and it was pronounced a 'moral certainty' that the head really was that of Cromwell.

Wilkinson felt that it was wrong to keep such a relic, and offered it to various authorities who declined to accept it. However, eventually 'Rab' Butler, then Home Secretary, suggested that Sidney Sussex College, Cambridge, where Oliver had been educated, might be an appropriate final resting-place.

On this day the college gave Oliver's much-travelled skull a proper burial at last. A plaque on the wall of the College Chapel notes the fact that the head is nearby, but the exact location is kept secret, perhaps for obvious reasons.

MARCH 26   1603
JAMES VI OF SCOTLAND LEARNS THAT HE IS NOW KING OF ENGLAND

Two days before, on March 24, Elizabeth I had died at Richmond Palace. In her last hours she had made a vague sign, holding her hands over her brow, and this had been interpreted as indicating James's crown, and thus signifying that she wished him to succeed her. She kept people guessing to the very end.

Lady Scrope, one of her attendant ladies, was the first to discover that the old queen had actually died. Her brother, Sir Robert Carey, was desperate to be the first to tell James that he was now King of England. According to the traditional account, Lady Scrope dropped a sapphire ring out of a window to signal Elizabeth's death. Sir Robert caught it, and immediately dashed off on a two-day gallop to Scotland. He sustained a serious fall on his way to Scotland, and arrived late at night covered in blood. James had already gone to bed, but got up when he heard of Carey's arrival.

Carey's own account continues:

I kneeled by him, and saluted him by his titles of King of England, Scotland, France and Ireland. The King gave me his hand to kiss, and bade me welcome. He asked, 'What letters I had from the privy council?' I told him 'None; yet had I brought him a blue ring from a fair lady, which I hoped would give him assurance that I reported the truth.' He took it and looked upon it, and said 'It is enough; I know by this you are a true messenger.'

Carey had hoped for a large reward for this frantic ride from London to Scotland in two days. But he was disappointed. James was too poor and too mean to do more than to make the hopeful messenger a gentleman of his bedchamber. 'And,' says Carey, that very evening I helped to take off his clothes, and stayed till he was in bed.' Reward indeed.

MARCH 27   1837
MRS FITZHERBERT, THE 'SECRET' WIFE OF GEORGE IV, DIES, AGED EIGHTY-ONE

'Prinny' – George IV – had a huge number of mistresses as well as a queen he had discarded immediately after marriage. But when he died he left the strictest instructions that he should be buried 'with whatever ornaments might be upon my person at the time of death'. This was done.

Years after the king's death, the Duke of Wellington disclosed that he had been alone with the royal corpse as it lay in its open coffin and had noticed a locket round the king's neck. He opened it, and discovered that it contained a miniature of the king's 'secret' wife, Maria Fitzherbert. (It was an open secret, but the king denied it in public (see DECEMBER 15).

Prinny had married her in great secrecy in 1785, when he was only twenty-three. Sad to say, he had discarded her too, in his final years, although he still kept up payments of a £6,000 annuity to her.

When Maria learned that the king had been buried with her portrait round his neck, 'She made no observation, but some large tears fell from her eyes.'

On this day in 1837, seven years after the king's death and fifty-one years after their marriage, Maria Fitzherbert died.

Also on this day:

1625 Death of King James I, aged fifty-nine, at Theobalds Park, Hertfordshire. His son succeeded to the throne as King Charles I, aged twenty-four.

MARCH 28 1681
CHARLES II TRICKS HIS PARLIAMENT AND THEN DISSOLVES IT

On this day Charles abruptly dissolved the Parliament he had opened just one week before. It amounted to a piece of adroit political trickery which took the MPs completely by surprise. Unusually, the Parliament had been summoned to sit in Oxford.

The knotty point at issue was the succession. Who would succeed Charles if he died? Obviously, the next in line to the throne was his brother James, but already people were alarmed that a Catholic king would bring disaster to the country. Charles had tentatively proposed a curious plan whereby his brother would be nominally king, but actual power would reside in the hands of William and Mary. A counter-proposal to this was put forward that the king's bastard son the Duke of Monmouth should be the next king. The whole matter was fraught with tension.

Charles was clearly sick of the discussion, and sprang a surprise on everyone. He was taken from Christ Church, where he was staying, in a sedan chair to the Geometry School, where the Lords were waiting for him. Following behind, hidden inside another sedan chair, were his crown and state robes. When he got to the Geometry School he dressed himself up in full regalia, necessary for dissolving Parliament, and then summoned the Commons to his presence. They had been meeting in the nearby convocation house.

To everyone's amazement, when the Commons arrived, Charles dissolved them in just one sentence. End of discussion. After enjoying a leisurely lunch, the king drove back to Windsor. A successful day's work.

MARCH 29   1461
TOWTON – THE BLOODIEST BATTLE EVER FOUGHT IN ENGLAND

By general consent the Battle of Towton, fought this day between Lancastrians and Yorkists in a blinding blizzard, was the bloodiest conflict on English soil. Edward of York, who had proclaimed himself King Edward IV earlier this month, personally led his troops in savage hand-to-hand fighting which lasted for hours in the snow.

According to Edward's own estimate, twenty-eight thousand men were killed, and at the end of the day he had utterly routed the Lancastrian forces of Henry VI, and helped to finish off the job by having the Earls of Devonshire and Wiltshire beheaded after the battle.

The saintly Henry VI did not take part. After all, it was Palm Sunday, and he did not agree with fighting on such a holy day.

1871
QUEEN VICTORIA OPENS THE ALBERT HALL

Gradually coming out of seclusion, Queen Victoria on this day opened the Royal Albert Hall, built in memory of her beloved consort. Truth to tell, it was the Prince of Wales who declared the hall open, as the queen was overcome with emotion.

She had laid the foundation stone in 1868. Originally it was to be known simply as the 'Hall of Arts and Sciences', but at the foundation-stone ceremony she suddenly announced the name it would bear: it was, she declared, to be known as 'The Royal Albert Hall of Arts and Sciences'.

The famous echo immediately made itself heard as the Bishop of London offered up his prayers: the 'Amen' reverberated again and again round the new building. Since then it has been claimed that the Albert Hall is the only place where a composer is certain to hear his work twice.

MARCH 30 1555
'BLOODY MARY' BURNS DR FERRAR, THE PROTESTANT BISHOP OF ST DAVID'S

According to Foxe's *Book of Martyrs*, 314 people were burnt or suffered other forms of death for their Protestant faith on the orders of Queen Mary. Giving details, the book records: 'There were burnt 5 bishops, 21 divines, 8 gentlemen, 84 artificers, 100 husbandmen, servants and labourers, 25 wives, 9 virgins, 2 boys and 2 infants. 64 more were persecuted for the religion, whereof 7 were whipped, 16 perished in prison and 12 were buried in dunghills.'

The burnings began on February 4, 1555, with John Rogers, a priest, at Smithfield; then on February 8 Laurence Saunders, another priest, at Coventry; then on February 9 Dr John Hooper, Bishop of Worcester and Gloucester, at Gloucester; and then followed a long list of butchers, barbers, weavers, widows, drapers, carpenters and so on, in towns and cities throughout the kingdom. The last were burned just a week before Mary herself died (see NOVEMBER 10).

On this day in 1555 it was the turn of Dr Ferrar, Bishop of St David's, to be burnt. He had been the chaplain to Edward VI's Protector, the Duke of Somerset, and had been promoted for his firm Protestant opinions. Like Cranmer, too, he had had the temerity to marry. His burning took place in the market-place at Carmarthen, where he 'most patiently sustained the torments of fire'.

2002
DEATH OF THE QUEEN MOTHER

The death of Queen Elizabeth the Queen Mother took place this day at Royal Lodge, Windsor. Born on 4 August 1900 and aged 101 at her death, she was easily the longest-lived royal in British history, her life neatly spanning the entire length of the twentieth century.

However, the Queen Mother holds the record for not only her longevity but also for her tireless energy and public service for so many decades. After the early death of her husband, King George VI, she was tempted at first to live in retirement in the Castle of Mey in Scotland, which she had just acquired. However, as her sheer *joie de vivre* returned, she settled instead at the heart of things in London, in Clarence House. Her exuberance blossomed anew and she became president, patron, colonel-in-chief or whatever, of well over three hundred organisations, giving them active support and inspiration. She became a unique institution – the 'Queen Mum'.

Following her death, it was announced that the Queen Mother would lie in state for four days in Westminster Hall, giving mourners the opportunity to file past her coffin and pay their last respects. The crowds that came exceeded all expectations. Day after day, hundreds of thousands queued for literally miles, and Westminster Hall had to be kept open throughout the nights as well as during the days. Indeed, on the Saturday before her funeral, the queue stretched from Westminster Hall right across Westminster Bridge and along the south bank for over three miles.

It will be difficult to describe the 'Queen Mum' to future generations. Her charisma was unique – even hard-bitten anti-royalists were silenced by her natural charm.

MARCH 31   1671
DEATH OF THE DUCHESS OF YORK, MOTHER OF TWO QUEENS

Before the monarchy had been restored in 1660, James, Duke of York, and the future James II, had wooed and won the voluptuous blue-eyed court beauty, Anne Hyde. That is to say, he had promised to marry her and he had managed to make her pregnant.

In 1660 this situation had become painfully embarrassing to James. Everyone knew that making a pretty woman pregnant was one thing, but to think of a royal prince marrying a mere commoner was quite out of the question: and Anne's father was merely the Lord Chancellor. Everyone was horrified to hear that James actually wanted to marry her: his mother Henrietta Maria and his sister Mary, in whose service Anne was a lady-in-waiting, and all James's friends were solidly of one mind in the matter. However, James's brother King Charles II was much more humane and positively ordered James to go through with the match.

Marry her he did, and the marriage was a success, despite James's continual philandering. Anne was a strong, intelligent woman who quickly took to her royal duties with aplomb. The child she bore shortly after their marriage died young, but she gave James two daughters who were both destined to become queens: Mary and Anne.

Perhaps even more importantly, Anne converted to the Catholic faith and she it was who encouraged James to follow her example. The results of that conversion on the subsequent history of England are incalculable. Anne Hyde's influence in this respect should never be overlooked.

Anne died on this last day of March 1671, aged thirty-four, of breast cancer, adamant that no visiting bishop should try a last-minute attempt at converting her back to Protestantism.

Her terrifying last words to James were: 'Duke, Duke, death is terrible, death is very terrible.'

APRIL 1   1204
DEATH OF ELEANOR OF AQUITAINE, QUEEN OF HENRY II

Everything about Eleanor was spectacular: she was fabulously rich, sensationally beautiful and in her youth passionately sexy. No romantic novelist could begin to imagine her long and astonishingly varied life. Perhaps some day another enterprising film producer will 'discover' Eleanor, and give us a new blockbuster of a movie about her to equal *The Lion in Winter*. It will have to be of epic proportions.

It will show her growing up in the sultry south of France, a land of troubadours and courtly love; marrying the King of France; forming her own special 'ladies' crusade'; and having romantic adventures with lovers in distant eastern lands. It will reveal how she fell in love with the heir to the throne of England, Henry of Anjou; how she jilted her royal French husband and married Henry instead, with almost indecent haste, just eight weeks later.

It will describe how she lived a passionate, extravagant life-style, bearing Henry eight children, including the future kings Richard 'Lionheart' and John; how she later became estranged from Henry; and how for sixteen years he kept her virtually as a prisoner – she was eventually released only at his death.

But all this would be a mere prelude: her life was only just beginning! At the age of sixty-seven she attained political power in her own right and became, effectively, England's ruling monarch during the long absences of her son Richard in the Holy Land. And then, when Richard was captured, she managed to raise a huge ransom in order to rescue him.

She gave Richard a second coronation; arranged and fetched a Spanish bride for him; lived well into the reign of her youngest son John; went back to live in Aquitaine; arranged further royal marriages . . .

She was a grand old lady of eighty-two when she died on April 1 1204. But alas, buried as she is in Fontevrault Abbey in France, her splendid effigy is not easily seen, and so, perhaps, her memory is not as vivid as it should be in England.

She was one of our greatest queens.

APRIL 2   1502
DEATH OF ARTHUR, PRINCE OF WALES

Prince Arthur, heir to the throne and son of Henry VII and Elizabeth of York, died this day in Ludlow Castle, probably from some form of consumption. He was only sixteen, and left a widow just a year older than himself – Catherine of Aragon. Their marriage had lasted barely six months.

Arthur's death was a devastating blow to his father, Henry VII, who had had grand designs for him. Indeed, he had carefully arranged for Arthur to be born in Winchester, the ancient capital of Wessex, and his very name was a throw-back to the legendary King Arthur and the Knights of the Round Table. Arthurian legends were much in the air at that time, for William Caxton had only recently chosen Malory's *Morte d'Arthur* as one of his first printed books.

The prince's body was taken to Worcester Cathedral for burial. It was a journey of about 25 miles across appalling country tracks. A contemporary account tells how 'It was the foulest cold, windy, and rainy day, and the worst way [road] I have seen; and in some places the car [the funeral carriage] stuck so fast in the mud, that yokes of oxen were taken to draw it out, so ill was the way.'

Arthur's death paved the way for his younger brother, the future Henry VIII, to succeed to the throne. Until then, young Henry had been destined to become Archbishop of Canterbury.

APRIL 3   1043
THE LAST CORONATION OTHER THAN IN WESTMINSTER ABBEY

On this day – Easter Sunday – Edward the Confessor was crowned in the old Saxon cathedral of Winchester. No one realised it at the time, but it was to be the last time that an English coronation would take place other than in Westminster Abbey. In 1043 Winchester was still the ancient capital of the kingdom. True, London had its importance, but Westminster simply did not exist: Edward the Confessor still had to create it.

According to legend, the Confessor had a vision in which St Peter told him to build an abbey on a deserted island, Thorney Island ('island of brambles') in the Thames, a few miles west of London. We take Westminster so much for granted today that it takes an effort of imagination to recognise that this was an oddly eccentric decision – to build what was intended to be a royal city, containing monastic buildings as well as a royal palace and courts, on a soggy marshy site well away from any other dwellings.

But the abbey itself was expressly designed for future coronations, with a central space called 'the theatre', from which radiated nave, transepts and choir to the four points of the compass. This 'theatre' would be the place of enthronement, where the greatest number of spectators could see the solemn crowning ceremonies.

The building of Westminster Abbey was to last literally until Edward's dying day. He was too ill to attend the opening, but was buried there in January 1066 (see JANUARY 5).

Also on this day:

1367 Birth of Henry Bolingbroke, future King Henry IV, at Bolingbroke Castle, Lincolnshire. He was the son of John of Gaunt and Blanche of Lancaster (see AUGUST 14).

APRIL 4   1581
QUEEN ELIZABETH I HONOURS
SIR FRANCIS DRAKE

'Is the Queen alive?' asked Francis Drake, as he landed on what is now called Drake Island, just off Plymouth, having just completed his monumental three-year journey round the world. It was, for him, the crucial question.

On learning that England still had its queen, Drake quickly sent a message to her to ask what he should do with the vast treasure he had accumulated in her name. Elizabeth took no time in replying: he was to keep £10,000 for himself and bring the rest to London as soon as possible. So, weighing anchor, he sailed up the Channel and arrived at Deptford, where the citizens of London literally danced in the streets as they heard of his extraordinary successes.

On April 4, Elizabeth went in state to visit Drake on board his *Golden Hind* and attended a celebration banquet on board. The ship was magnificently decorated with gigantic banners for the occasion, painted in gold on silk damask with the Lion of England and the Fleur de Lys of France. Visitors to Buckland Abbey, Drake's Devon home, can still see some of these banners hanging there proudly to this day.

This was the day that she honoured Drake on the quarter-deck of his own ship, by conferring a knighthood upon him. However, with consummate tact and diplomacy she handed the sword to the French Ambassador, asking him to perform the actual ceremony of dubbing. Thus she could claim that she herself had not knighted a man with a formidable reputation for international piracy.

APRIL 5   1955
QUEEN ELIZABETH II HONOURS SIR WINSTON CHURCHILL

On April 5 1955 Sir Winston Churchill had his last official audience with his sovereign. He was eighty, and had first met Elizabeth at Balmoral when she was little more than a baby. The farewell was a poignant moment for both of them. On the previous evening the queen had paid Sir Winston and Lady Churchill the unique compliment of dining with them at 10 Downing Street. It was the first time that a reigning monarch had ever visited the Prime Minister's residence.

Sir Winston had been Elizabeth's first Prime Minister, and had greeted her as Queen on her return to England when her father had died so unexpectedly. Now, on Churchill's resignation, the queen expressed her gratitude and admiration, writing to him:

It would be useless to pretend that either he [Sir Anthony Eden] or any of those successors who may one day follow him in office will ever, for me, be able to hold the place of my first Prime Minister, to whom both my husband and I owe so much and for whose wise guidance during the early years of my reign I shall always be so profoundly grateful . . .

For my part I know that in losing my constitutional adviser I gain a wise counsellor to whom I shall not look in vain for help and support in the days which lie ahead. May there be many of them.

Churchill lived on for nearly ten more years. Before the end of the century Elizabeth would experience nine more Prime Ministers: Eden, Macmillan, Douglas-Home, Wilson, Heath, Callaghan, Thatcher, Major, Blair and Brown.

APRIL 6   1199
KING RICHARD I DIES OF A GANGRENOUS ARROW-WOUND

Richard's lifestyle of constant battles, sieges and skirmishes was almost bound to lead to an early death, and he was only forty-one when he met his fate in Aquitaine. He had heard a rumour that a peasant there had been ploughing a field and had come upon a trap-door opening into a cave containing enchanted treasure: golden statues, precious vases and vast quantities of diamonds. When Richard learned that this treasure-trove had been taken into the castle of Châlus, he wasted no time. He ordered the lord of the castle to deliver it all to him or face the consequences.

In actual fact, the peasant had only turned up a pot of Roman coins, but Richard refused to believe this and set about storming the castle. By a stroke of bad luck he was hit on the shoulder by an arrow, and when his surgeon bungled the job of hacking it out the wound turned gangrenous.

The archer, a man named Bertram, was identified, and Richard asked that he should be brought before him. He asked whether he had shot him on purpose. Legend has it that the archer replied: 'Yes, tyrant, for to you I owe the deaths of my father and my brother, and my first wish was to be revenged on you.'

With impetuous generosity, Richard pardoned him, gave him a hundred shillings and set him free: then he died in agony. He was buried next to his parents in Fontevrault Abbey in France. But as for Bertram the archer, despite the king's pardon, he was flayed alive and hanged.

King John, aged thirty-one, succeeded to the throne on the death of his brother.

APRIL 7   1141
THE EMPRESS MATILDA IS DECLARED 'LADY OF THE ENGLISH'

An important declaration was made on this day in Winchester, by the formidable Bishop Henry of Blois. The Empress Matilda, daughter of Henry I and Matilda of Scotland, was formally titled 'Domina' or 'Lady of the English'. The Bishop proclaimed:

Having first, as is fit, invoked the aid of Almighty God, we elect as Lady of England and Normandy the daughter of the glorious, the rich, the good, the peaceful King Henry, and to her we promise fealty and support.

In effect the bishop was supporting Matilda, his cousin, against King Stephen, his brother, and the declaration was, at least for a few months, the equivalent of creating an alternative monarch. It was a bold and arguably treasonable act, and it wasn't long before the bishop changed his mind and swapped sides again, back to supporting Stephen. Matilda had to flee to escape his armies.

Hers was to be a short-lived 'reign', lasting only about eight months. She made herself so unpopular with her arrogance and domineering manner that she was never actually crowned. An old writer, Robert, Bishop of Bath, spoke of her haughty refusal to grant favours even to those who had helped her to become 'Domina', 'and when they bowed themselves down before her, she did not rise in return'. (See MARCH 3 and SEPTEMBER 14).

APRIL 8   1795
PRINNY BIGAMOUSLY MARRIES HIS COUSIN CAROLINE

Pressurised by Parliament and his father, Prinny finally agreed, in a fit of petulance, to marry an official wife, choosing his cousin Caroline of Brunswick virtually at random. Lord Malmesbury, sent to Brunswick to arrange the marriage, was filled with misgivings the instant he met Princess Caroline. She already had an appalling reputation for bad manners and loose morals, and now Lord Malmesbury found, to his horror, that her teeth were rotten and that she smelt abominably.

Malmesbury noted in his journal: 'I knew she wore coarse petticoats, coarse shifts, and thread stockings, and these never well washed, or changed often enough,' and he had an embarrassing conversation with her about the need for washing herself properly. True she did have one bath after this, and had a tooth extracted, which she sent to Lord Malmesbury. Not unnaturally, he found this 'nasty and indelicate'.

Malmesbury dutifully escorted her to England, where they were met by Lady Jersey, Prinny's favourite mistress. Lady Jersey quickly reported back to Prinny, so that he was fully briefed about his future bride before actually meeting her. Malmesbury describes what happened when he took Caroline into the Prince's presence.

> Caroline . . . attempted to kneel to him. He raised her (gracefully enough), and embraced her, said barely one word, turned round, retired to a distant part of the apartment, and calling me to him, said, 'Harris, I am not well; pray get me a glass of brandy' . . . and away he went.

Three days later, on April 8, the Archbishop of Canterbury married them in the Chapel Royal, St James's, pausing with heavy significance when he arrived at the point in the service asking for 'any person knowing of a lawful impediment' to speak out.

Prinny remained silent, but wept openly. He knew perfectly well, as did everyone else, that he was already married to Maria Fitzherbert.

APRIL 9 2005
CHARLES AND CAMILLA MARRY AT LAST, AFTER A 34-YEAR FRIENDSHIP

The circumstances of the marriage of Charles, Prince of Wales, to Mrs Camilla Parker-Bowles in Windsor Town Hall on this April day in 2005 were unusual and dogged with extraordinary difficulties.

Charles had met Camilla Shand, as she then was, at a Windsor polo-match in 1971, when he was only 22 and she was 23. Meeting again shortly afterwards, Camilla's flirtatious opening remark was: 'My great-grandmother and your great-great-grandfather were lovers – so what about it?'

The friendship which had begun in 1971 developed over the years, despite Camilla's marriage to Andrew Parker-Bowles and Charles's marriage to Diana Spencer. Both marriages were doomed. In 1994, in a television interview with Jonathan Dimbleby, Charles confessed that he had been unfaithful to Diana, but only after their marriage had 'irretrievably broken down.' And giving her side of the story, Diana also gave a television interview, making the unforgettable comment that 'There were three of us in this marriage, so it was a bit crowded.'

The censorious screaming newspaper headlines after both these interviews reflected the huge tide of public disapproval. However, after the royal divorce and after Diana's tragic death, there was nothing legal to prevent Charles and Camilla from marrying – except, of course, they would have to brave public opinion, and come to terms with the church's reluctance to marry a divorcee in a place of worship.

After much debate, it was decided that the couple should marry on April 8th at a civil ceremony in Windsor Castle. It was a compromise which would satisfy all objections. But then a new difficulty emerged – that if Windsor Castle were to be given the licence to be used as a place for weddings, then legally it would have to be open for further weddings by all and sundry for the next three years – a situation quite unacceptable to the Queen. As a result, quite unprecedently, as an alternative venue, the ceremony was then planned to take place in Windsor Guildhall.

Even then, a final and totally unexpected difficulty arose, for just as the wedding arrangements had been finalised for April 8th, the aged Pope John Paul II died, and his funeral was scheduled to take place on that very same day. So yet again the royal wedding plans had to be changed. Thus it was that, at last, on Saturday, 9th April, 2005, Charles and Camilla became man and wife.

Since then, it is apparent that this marriage has become increasingly accepted and welcomed both within the royal family, and by the public at large, though some parts of the tabloid press are, as ever, viciously anxious to find opportunities to make snide remarks. Sadly, this is the price of being royal in the twenty-first century.

Also on this day:

1395   Richard II orders Sheen Palace to be demolished.

1413   Coronation of King Henry V, aged twenty-five, at Westminster Abbey.

1483   Death of King Edward IV, aged forty-two, at Westminster Palace, London.

1483   King Edward V, aged twelve, succeeded to the throne on the death of his father, Edward IV. Uncrowned, he disappeared, being last seen with his brother in the Tower of London. Almost certainly he was murdered. (See APRIL 28.)

1649   Birth of the future Duke of Monmouth, son of the future King Charles II and his mistress Lucy Walter, at Rotterdam.

APRIL 10   1702
FUNERAL OF WILLIAM III

Seven years before, when his wife and joint-sovereign Mary died, William had arranged an astonishingly elaborate and costly funeral for her. During her lying in state the ceiling of Westminster Hall was hung with three hundred glass chandeliers, each with a hundred wax candles; and thousands of yards of black cloth were given away to two hundred poor old women to come as mourners. However, when William III died, his funeral is said to have cost only as many hundreds of pounds as his wife's had cost thousands.

A design for a monument to William and Mary by Sir Christopher Wren still exists, but no one ever thought of making it. Instead, a small inscription on the floor of Westminster Abbey acts as the sole reminder of his existence.

Similarly, no monument or tomb exists for any of the Stuart monarchs. The splendid figure of Elizabeth I in Westminster Abbey is the last effigy made of any king or queen of England before that of Queen Victoria in the Royal Mausoleum, Frogmore. But as this monument is so rarely on view, in effect the next royal effigy to be seen is that of Edward VII, in St George's Chapel, Windsor: made over three hundred years later than that of Elizabeth I.

APRIL 11   978
CORONATION OF ETHELRED II
('THE UNREADY') AT KINGSTON UPON THAMES

Just outside the modern town hall at Kingston upon Thames there is a massive stone which has been part of at least seven coronation ceremonies. Everyone knows about the Scottish 'Stone of Scone', upon which every English monarch has been crowned since Edward II, but this 'English Coronation Stone' at Kingston upon Thames is curiously neglected or forgotten.

Its exact function in these old Saxon coronation ceremonies is rather vague, but certain it is that many of the old Kings of Wessex were crowned on it (or perhaps near it). Today the stone stands on a modern base on which is carved the names of the Wessex kings whose coronations are connected with it: Edward the Elder, on June 8 900; Athelstan, on September 4 925; Edmund I, sometime in 940; Edred, on August 16 946; Edwy, in January 956; Edward the Martyr, in 975; and the last king to be crowned here was Ethelred the Unready, on April 11 978.

1689
CORONATION OF WILLIAM AND MARY AT
WESTMINSTER ABBEY

One of Britain's oddest coronation ceremonies took place on this same day, 711 years after Ethelred II's coronation. It was the ceremony at which William III and his wife Mary II were crowned jointly. The occasion was fraught with tension. Everyone was acutely aware that William and Mary were being crowned while Mary's father, James II, was still very much alive and anxious to stage a comeback. Indeed the Archbishop of Canterbury refused to conduct the service and several other bishops stayed away. It was left for the Bishop of London to agree to do the job.

But an extra level of tension came just as Mary was putting on her robes and getting ready to be carried in state from Whitehall to Westminster Abbey for the coronation service. At that moment news came that her father and his army had just landed in Ireland to great popular acclaim; and Mary received a letter from him furiously cursing her if she went through with the intended coronation service. James pointed out that up to this moment he had thought that she was being guided by her husband William, but she must realise that 'the act of being crowned was in her own power, and if she were crowned while he and the prince of Wales were living, the curse of an outraged father would light upon her, as well as of that God who has commanded duty to parents'.

It was against this background then, that the coronation service took place, albeit delayed two-and-a-half hours because of all this flurry. The service itself was something of a shambles, especially as there were so many absentees. An embarrassing moment came when William and Mary were ceremonially required to give alms: no one had remembered to bring any money! After a long pause, with everyone looking at everyone else, Lord Danby fished out his purse and counted out twenty guineas for the king to use. One hopes that he was reimbursed.

As the service proceeded William and Mary did everything in unison: speaking together, sitting together, kneeling together, kissing the Bible together. And it is recorded that they presented a particularly absurd spectacle when they had to carry the huge ceremonial sword together, because William was so small and Mary so large.

It was an odd beginning to a strange reign.

Also on this day:
1471   King Henry VI was deposed for the second time, and Edward IV became king for the second time.

APRIL 12   1979
QUEEN ELIZABETH II PRESENTS MAUNDY MONEY AT WINCHESTER CATHEDRAL

The ceremony of the 'Royal Maundy' takes place annually on Maundy Thursday, the day before Good Friday. The word 'maundy' comes from the Latin biblical text which begins: *Mandatum novum do vobis* ('A new commandment I give unto you, that ye love one another'). At the reading of these words on the day before Good Friday, it became the custom throughout Catholic countries for popes, bishops, kings and church dignitaries to wash the feet of poor people.

The last English king to wash people's feet was the Catholic James II. William III decided to delegate the job to his almoner, and eventually, in 1754, the foot-washing was discontinued altogether.

However, another custom, begun by Elizabeth I – that of distributing gifts of food, clothing and money – began to replace the washing of feet on Maundy Thursday. After a long gap, George V restarted the custom, and now it is the practice for the reigning monarch to distribute 'Maundy money' – a specially minted set of coins – to a group of aged, poor folk, the number of them corresponding to the sovereign's age.

Formerly, the Maundy distributions took place in Westminster Abbey, but nowadays Queen Elizabeth II has taken the custom to a different location each year, often marking some special local celebration. For example, on April 12 1979 the queen attended a special service in Winchester to commemorate the 900th anniversary of the Norman cathedral, and distributed the traditional Maundy money there. This was the same building that William the Conqueror had ordered to replace the former Saxon Old Minster, and had been the scene of Easter crownings when the early Norman kings had the habit of wearing the crown ceremonially.

Uniquely, the queen herself wrote a foreword to a book describing the history of Winchester Cathedral and published in that 900th anniversary year. She wrote: 'I am reminded that Winchester was, from the days of Alfred the Great to the Norman Conquest, the capital of the Kings of England, and that, in the new Cathedral, begun in 1079, the Conqueror's immediate successors frequently wore the crown at the Easter festival.'

APRIL 13   1951
THE STONE OF SCONE IS RETURNED TO WESTMINSTER ABBEY

The much-travelled Scottish 'Stone of Scone' was returned this day to its 'rightful' place in Westminster Abbey after some Scottish students had stolen it on Christmas Eve in 1950.

Fact and legend are inextricably mixed up in the history of this Stone. Some claim it to be the very cushion on which Jacob rested at Beth-el; and according to this legend it travelled first to Egypt, then Spain, then Ireland, eventually reaching Scotland and being used for countless Scottish coronations. It is said to have served as the throne on which St Columba crowned Aidan at Dunadd in 574. Then it moved to Dunstaffnage, north of

Oban; it may have been from here that Kenneth McAlpine moved his court and the 'Stone of Destiny' from Argyll to Scone in 843.

Whatever the distant past, at least we can be sure that Edward I, (the 'Hammer of the Scots') seized this symbolic piece of red sandstone and brought it from Scotland to London in 1296. It was put into the base of a specially made Coronation Chair, and since then every English monarch has been crowned while sitting over it (except Edward V, who was murdered, and Edward VIII, who abdicated). The only time it ever left Westminster Abbey, until the students pinched it in 1950, was when Oliver Cromwell had it taken to Westminster Hall for his inauguration as 'Protector'.

On April 13 1951, after its removal by Scottish nationalist students, the Stone was put back in the Coronation Chair, and of course it was there for Queen Elizabeth II's coronation in 1953. Today, however, it is back in Scotland, and is on view in the Great Chamber of Edinburgh Castle. It was returned there in December 1996 – precisely 700 years after its capture by Edward I.

It was carried in procession to the castle, up Edinburgh's Royal Mile, and some spectators booed when the Nation Anthem was played in St Giles Cathedral. Among the guests at that occasion were three of the students who had stolen the Stone from Westminster Abbey forty-six years previously. Dark rumours circulated that the stone which was recovered was in fact a cunning replica, and the 'real' Stone is now hidden in a secret location. Who will ever know?

APRIL 14   1471
THE BLOODY BATTLE OF BARNET

It was on Easter Sunday, April 14, that the bloody Battle of Barnet took place between the opposing forces of the Yorkists and the Lancastrians in one of the final clashes in the Wars of the Roses. Henry VI had been taken prisoner by Edward IV and he was taken captive to Barnet to watch his supporters, led by the Earl of Warwick (the 'Kingmaker'), being butchered by Edward's Yorkist troops. The three-hour battle was fought on Hadley Green, a little to the north of High Barnet. Much of the fighting took place in dense fog, adding greatly to the confusion.

The Earl of Warwick and his brother were both slain and their bodies were taken back to London to be publicly displayed outside Old St Paul's Cathedral.

Henry VI was taken back to the Tower of London. And Edward went on to win yet another battle shortly afterwards at Tewkesbury, after which he settled himself firmly on the throne without fear of further opposition.

Underground travellers to High Barnet on the Northern Line may be interested to know that the next station, Whetstone, derives its name from the number of whetstones to be found in that locality. Tradition says that the soldiers who fought in the Battle of Barnet were pleased to whet their swords and weapons there.

Also on this day:

1578 Death of James Bothwell, third husband of Mary, Queen of Scots, at a prison in Dragsholm, Denmark, where he died, insane. His gruesome remains can still be seen there.

APRIL 15   1942
GEORGE VI AWARDS THE GEORGE CROSS TO MALTA

George VI founded the George Cross in 1940 to be awarded for acts of conspicuous heroism, primarily by civilians. It is second only to the Victoria Cross, which had been instituted by Queen Victoria in 1856 to be awarded to military personnel for acts of outstanding bravery in the presence of the enemy.

The George Cross, with its inscription 'For Gallantry', filled a gap in decorations which became more and more evident during the Second World War as civilians became increasingly involved in war activities.

The remarkable steadfastness of the people of Malta during the intense bombing of the island – suffering over a thousand German and Italian air raids in the previous three months – led the king to make a unique gesture of recognition. In April 1942 he awarded his newly founded George Cross to the entire island of Malta.

In June 1943 he visited the island personally to see for himself the damage which had been done during the fourteen-month Nazi siege.

APRIL 16   1746

BONNIE PRINCE CHARLIE FLEES FROM DISASTER AT CULLODEN

The terrible Battle of Culloden, fought this day a few miles west of Inverness, saw the destruction of any hopes for a restoration of the Stuart line. It was a short, brutal, one-sided affair, lasting not much more than forty minutes. The half-starved and poorly organised clansmen were vastly outnumbered by the Hanoverian forces led by the Duke of Cumberland, second son of George II, and were quickly routed.

The sickening slaughter after the battle earned the Duke his notorious nickname, 'Butcher Cumberland'. Over two thousand men were killed in cold blood, and in the weeks that followed hundreds of fugitives were pursued without mercy. The harrowing of the glens almost annihilated the population of the Highlands.

'Bonnie Prince Charlie' himself took no personal part in the battle. He left the field with curses ringing in his ears. Even Lord Elcho, chief of his bodyguard, jeered at him for being 'a damned Italian coward'.

Charles lived for a further forty-two years. He died in Rome and is buried in St Peter's.

Also on this day:

1657   Oliver Cromwell was formally offered the crown at Whitehall but he refused to accept it.

APRIL 17   1194

RICHARD LIONHEART IS CROWNED AGAIN, IN WINCHESTER

The year 1193 had not been a happy one for King Richard I. He had been captured by Duke Leopold of Austria and handed over to the German Emperor Henry VI, who demanded a huge ransom of 150,000 marks of silver. Richard had spent thirteen miserable months in an obscure castle on the Danube while this ransom was being scraped together in England.

Shamed and humiliated, Richard was at last released and made his way to England, landing in March 1194. There were, of course, people to punish or rebuke, and people to reward and thank, but before he could do anything, it was felt that a public reaffirmation of his kingship was required.

So it was, on April 17, that Richard was formally given a second coronation in Winchester Cathedral. Hubert Walter, the new Archbishop of Canterbury, performed the service and Richard ceremonially wore his crown before the assembled barons. His formidable mother, the widowed queen Eleanor of Aquitaine, now aged seventy-two, was present to see her son's rehabilitation.

Hubert Walter had acted as Richard's adjutant during the Third Crusade and had been entrusted with the task of commanding the English contingent on its homeward voyage. On reaching Sicily he learned of the king's capture and had gone to Germany to negotiate the terms of release. It was Hubert Walter, too, who had undertaken the enormous task, with Eleanor, of raising the necessary ransom money. It took a quarter of every man's income for a whole year to raise it: pigs were killed, sheep shorn, church plate sold. Rescuing the king was a crippling economic disaster for his country.

Richard had every reason to be grateful to Hubert, and rewarded him by making him Archbishop of Canterbury. This coronation service in Winchester, then, was a moment of triumph for both men.

Also on this day:
1945 King George VI attended a memorial service for President Roosevelt in St Paul's Cathedral, London.

APRIL 18   1949
GEORGE VI LOSES AUTHORITY AS EIRE
BECOMES A REPUBLIC

The Republic of Ireland was proclaimed on this day in 1949, and formally withdrew from the Commonwealth. Thus the twenty-six counties of the new Republic no longer have any constitutional link, however tenuous, with the rest of the British Isles. By contrast, the six counties of Northern Ireland still owe allegiance to the crown.

The concept of the 'Commonwealth' was dear to George VI, as it is to his daughter, Queen Elizabeth II. The way in which various countries of the former British Empire evolved into independence, yet still share links with Britain as members of the Commonwealth, is unique in history. George VI became the first emperor in the world to renounce his title and to transfer political power back to his peoples when he ceased to be Emperor of India on August 15 1947.

Almost two years later, the proclamation of the Republic of Ireland still further diminished the role of the British monarch, which has changed constantly over the centuries.

APRIL 19   1164

HENRY II AND THOMAS BECKET ATTEND THE CONSECRATION OF READING ABBEY

In 1121 Henry II's grandfather, Henry I, had laid the foundation stone of the Abbey of St Mary and St John in Reading, and on 4 February 1136 his embalmed body had been buried before the high altar in the abbey he had founded.

However, the abbey was still not completed, and it was on this day in 1164 that Henry II attended the consecration service conducted by the problematic Archbishop Thomas Becket. Tension must have been running high between the two men, as this consecration ceremony took place only a few weeks after a resounding clash between them at Clarendon, concerning the relative authority of Church and State.

The dissolution of the monasteries under Henry VIII resulted in the destruction of so many beautiful and historic buildings, not least of which was this great Benedictine abbey at Reading, which had witnessed so many royal events in the four centuries of its existence: jousting and feastings in 1359 after John of Gaunt's wedding to Blanche of Lancaster; celebrations in 1403 after Henry IV's marriage to Joan of Navarre; an embarrassing council in 1464 at which Edward IV had to admit that he had secretly married Elizabeth Woodville. Even after the dissolution, many kings and queens came to stay in the buildings which had been spared. But the abbey's final destruction came in 1643. Sadly, this great abbey, once one of the greatest in England, is now nothing but ruins. Today, the place where Henry I's grave once stood is marked by a simple cross.

APRIL 20   1483
EDWARD IV'S CORPSE IS EXPOSED,
NUDE TO THE WAIST

Edward IV was only forty when he died, ten days after suffering a stroke. It may have been the result of pneumonia; it may have been aggravated by over-indulgence – but malicious rumours hinted at poison and foul play.

At all events, after his death on April 9, it was deemed expedient to display the king's body, after it had been disembowelled and embalmed, for general viewing. Accordingly, it was exposed, nude to the waist, for ten days, on a bier under a canopy of black cloth fringed with gold, placed in the centre of the Royal Chapel of Westminster Palace.

A vast procession of nobles, clerics and ordinary members of the public were encouraged to pass in front of the corpse, to assure themselves that the king really was dead, and that no obvious injury was visible. Then, enclosed in a leaden coffin within a casket of oak, all covered in a pall of black velvet, the body was taken first to Westminster Abbey and then, after a requiem mass, a grand cavalcade of nobility escorted the dead king to Windsor, stopping overnight at Sheen.

It is to Edward IV that we owe one of our greatest architectural glories – St George's Chapel, Windsor, so it was fitting that he should be taken there. He was the first English king to be buried in its vaults. April 20 marks the anniversary of his burial.

Also on this day:
1653   Oliver Cromwell dissolved the 'Long Parliament', which had governed during the Civil War.

APRIL 21   1509
DEATH OF HENRY VII . . .

Henry VII seemed to lose the will to live after the deaths of his son Arthur and his young wife, Elizabeth of York. He died, aged only fifty-two, in his favourite palace at Richmond. His remains were taken by river to Westminster for lying in state, then across the river to Southwark, from where he was solemnly borne across London Bridge for a service in Old St Paul's. Finally the funeral cortège wound its way along Fleet Street, the Strand and Charing Cross to take the coffin to its last resting-place in

Westminster Abbey. Henry was buried in the beautiful chapel at the far east end, which he himself had caused to be built.

On top of the coffin was stretched a life-sized effigy, dressed in robes of state. Even today, visitors to the Undercroft Museum in Westminster Abbey can see his death-mask. It is astonishingly lifelike, and when it was carefully examined in 1950 it was noticed that the grease used in taking the mould had clotted the hair on one of the eyebrows. This would suggest that it is a genuine mask, and not just a made-up face.

After the body was lowered into the vaults, the Treasurer and the Comptroller ceremonially broke their staves into the grave; and finally the Garter King of Arms proclaimed the new monarch: 'Vive le roi Henri le huitième, roi d'Angleterre et de France, et Sire d'Irland.'

1926
. . . AND SIXTEEN GENERATIONS LATER, THE BIRTH OF HIS DESCENDANT, QUEEN ELIZABETH II

The genealogy is clear: 417 years and sixteen generations later Henry VII's descendant, the future Queen Elizabeth II, was born at 17 Bruton Street, London. The street still exists, linking Berkeley Square to New Bond Street, but the actual house was destroyed during the Blitz. Of course, at the time of her birth no one imagined that one day she would be queen. Like her parents, Elizabeth was pitchforked into majesty as a result of the abdication of her uncle, Edward VIII.

At the time of that abdication the ten-year-old Princess Elizabeth was asked by her sister Margaret, then aged six: 'Does that mean that you'll have to be the next queen?'

'Yes, some day,' was the reply. 'Poor you!' gasped Margaret.

APRIL 22   1661
CHARLES II RIDES THROUGH LONDON ON THE DAY BEFORE HIS CORONATION

London went wild with excitement as it prepared to celebrate Charles II's coronation. After all, it was no ordinary coronation: after the repressions and restrictions of Oliver Cromwell's years, this restoration of the monarchy was a return to normality – a return to freedom.

The day before the coronation in Westminster Abbey, Charles II and his brother, the Duke of York (the future James II), took part in a joyful procession from the Tower of London to the royal palace at Whitehall. Samuel Pepys, who knew them both well, arranged to view the event from a good vantage-point in Cornhill. His diary records:

> Up early and made myself as fine as I could, and put on my velvet coat, the first day that I put it on, though made half a year ago. And being ready, . . . went to Mr Young's the flagmaker, in Corne-hill; and there we had a good room to ourselves, with wine and good cake, and saw the show very well. In which it is impossible to relate the glory of this day, expressed in the clothes of them that rid [rode in the procession], and their horses and horses-clothes.
>
> Among others, my Lord Sandwich's embroidery and diamonds were not ordinary among them. The Knights of the Bath was a brave sight of itself. Remarquable were the two men that represent the two Dukes of Normandy and Aquitane. The Bishops come next after Barons, which is the higher place; which makes me think that the next Parliament they will be called to the House of Lords. My Lord Monk rode bare [headed] after the King, and led in his hand a spare horse, as being Master of the Horse.
>
> The King, in a most rich embroidered suit and cloak, looked most noble. Wadlow the vintner . . . did lead a fine company of soldiers, all young comely men, in white doublets. There followed the Vice-Chamberlain, Sir G. Carteret, a Company of men all like Turkes; but I know not yet what they are for.
>
> The streets all gravelled, and the houses hung with carpets before them, made brave show, and the ladies out of the windows. So glorious was the show with gold and silver, that we were not able to look at it, our eyes at last being so much overcome. Both the King and the Duke of York took notice of us as they saw us at the window.

The next day, Pepys records that he rose at 4 a.m. to get to Westminster Abbey for the coronation itself.

Also on this day:
1509 King Henry VIII, aged eighteen, succeeded to the throne on the death of his father, King Henry VII.

APRIL 23   1661
THE CORONATION OF CHARLES II: MONARCHY IS RESTORED

Samuel Pepys, determined to see this event, managed to get into Westminster Abbey before dawn, and 'with much ado, by the favour of Mr Cooper . . . did get up into a great scaffold across the North end of the Abbey, where with a great deal of patience I sat from past four till eleven before the King come in'.

His patience was rewarded, and he was able to see the decorated abbey, the bishops in cloth-of-gold copes, the nobility in their Parliament robes, the fiddlers in red vests, and eventually the king himself, with the 'scepter and sword and wand before him'.

Three times, Pepys records, 'the King at Armes . . . proclaimed that if any one could show any reason why Charles Stewart should not be King of England, that now he should come and speak'. Of course, no one came forward, and so the Lord Chancellor proclaimed a general pardon, and silver medals were flung among the spectators. Much feasting and merriment followed the service as the king and courtiers returned to Whitehall.

'Thus did the day end with joy every where,' wrote Pepys that night, 'and blessed be God, I have not heard of any mischance to any body through it all.'

1685
THE CORONATION OF JAMES II: MONARCHY UNDER PRESSURE

Twenty-four years later to the day, Charles's brother James inherited the throne. So fiercely Catholic was he that it is believed he actually went through an earlier unofficial coronation, being anointed and crowned in private by a Catholic bishop. Louis XIV sent him a special bottle of holy oil from Rheims which was used by French kings at their own coronations.

When he was crowned in Westminster Abbey the crown simply did not fit him, and kept wobbling off his head. The fact was that James was using the same crown that his brother Charles had used, and their heads were not at all the same size! Nevertheless, the insecure crown was considered to be a most unfortunate omen for the future.

1702
THE CORONATION OF QUEEN ANNE: THE STUART LINE COMES TO AN END

Another coronation, again on St George's Day. Poor Anne! Although she was only thirty-seven, she was suffering so badly from gout that she could hardly stand upright, and had to be carried to Westminster Abbey in an open chair.

Her husband, Prince George of Denmark, was not crowned. His duty was simply to swear homage to her and to make sure, in the years ahead, that she kept on getting pregnant. It was a duty he never shirked.

Also on this day:
1016 Death of Ethelred ('The Unready'), aged about forty-eight, in London. Edmund II ('Ironside') succeeded to the throne.
1445 Marriage of Henry VI, aged twenty-three, and Margaret of Anjou, at Titchfield Abbey, Hampshire.

APRIL 24 1558
MARY, QUEEN OF SCOTS, MARRIES THE FRENCH DAUPHIN

It was a gorgeous, fantastic wedding in the Cathedral of Notre Dame in Paris, embellished with all the theatricality which her French in-laws could devise. Mary had been Queen of Scotland since she was one week old. Now she was a teenager of fifteen, marrying Francis, the thirteen-year-old Dauphin, heir to the French throne. They had been engaged to one another for ten years, and had grown up together.

Now it was deemed time for the pair to marry, and Notre Dame was specially prepared with a kind of wooden outdoor canopy as a stage, highly decorated with fleur-de-lys painted everywhere. Mary's wedding dress was a dazzling white, which, odd to relate, was traditionally the colour of mourning for the queens of France, so she was making a defiant gesture in choosing this colour. The dress had a very long train, borne by two girls, and Mary wore a diamond necklace and a golden crown studded with sapphires, rubies, pearls and a gigantic carbuncle worth more than half a million crowns.

Inside the cathedral gold carpets led to the altar, where the Archbishop of Rouen conducted the service. Heralds outside proclaimed: 'Largesse!

Largesse!' and the crowds went wild with excitement as gold and silver pieces were thrown out into their midst for them to scramble for.

But Francis was a sickly child. He became King of France the following year, (see JUNE 30), but died within months. And as for his young widow Mary, she returned to Scotland where, in time, two more weddings were in store for her.

APRIL 25 1284
BIRTH OF THE FIRST PRINCE OF WALES

Edward I's queen, Eleanor of Castile, gave birth this day in Caernarvon Castle to a son who would one day become the first Prince of Wales and then, later still, Edward II.

Tradition points to a little dark room built in the thickness of the castle walls, without a fireplace, and measuring only 12ft by 8ft, as being the place where the delivery took place, with a local Welsh nurse in attendance.

It is said that Eleanor was the first person in England to use tapestry to decorate the walls of her room, and in fact it was a duty of the grooms of her chamber to hang up this tapestry, which was always carried with the royal baggage wherever she went.

The baby was her third son. Sadly, the first two had died young. When tidings were brought to King Edward I that he had a baby son he was so delighted that he knighted the Welsh gentleman Griffith Lloyd, who had brought him such good news.

1599
BIRTH OF THE FIRST LORD PROTECTOR OF ENGLAND

The register of the church of St John the Baptist in Huntingdon has an entry, in Latin, which translates as: 'In the year of Our Lord 1599, Oliver, the son of Robert Cromwell, gentleman, and of Elizabeth his wife, born on the 25th day of April and baptised on the 29th of the same month.' Little Oliver was given his name after his rich and distinguished uncle, Sir Oliver Cromwell, who had been knighted by Queen Elizabeth.

Truth to tell, the Cromwells' proper name was Williams. They were descended from a Welsh brewer named Morgan Williams, who had married the elder sister of Thomas Cromwell, the ill-fated adviser to Henry VIII, who had lost his head after the king had found himself obliged to marry Anne of Cleves. Morgan Williams's son, Richard, had adopted the name Cromwell, as compliment to his uncle, and the name had remained in the family.

One of Oliver Cromwell's earliest memories must have been that of a huge banquet given by his uncle Oliver in his great manor known as Hinchingbrooke House in Huntingdon. It was held in honour of King James I, then on his way down to London from Scotland to be crowned as successor to Elizabeth I.

The dignitaries from Cambridge University were present to greet the new king, and a play was performed there to entertain his Scottish majesty. It is believed that the four-year-old Oliver actually took part in this.

James I was so pleased with this reception that he remarked to his host: 'Thou hast treated me better than anyone since I left Edinburgh!'

APRIL 26   1923
THE DUKE OF YORK MARRIES A COMMONER

When the Duke of York married Lady Elizabeth Bowes-Lyon in Westminster Abbey on this day in 1923 the event was seen as a major break with tradition. Despite her noble Scottish background she was a 'commoner' marrying into royalty. In fact, Elizabeth was the first commoner bride to marry the second-in-line to the throne since Anne Hyde had married the future James II (also a Duke of York at the time of his marriage) in 1660.

The happy couple would have been merely a footnote in history had it not been for the abdication of Edward VIII thirteen years later, which ultimately swept them into the line of English monarchs as King George VI and Queen Elizabeth.

Elizabeth (the future 'Queen Mum', see MARCH 30) had been extremely reluctant at first to accept the duke's proposal of marriage. She voiced her concern with clear-sighted perception, saying that she feared 'I should never again be free to think, speak or act as I really feel I should think, speak and act.' And Bertie, as the duke was known in the family, had to propose three times before she could bring herself to say 'yes'.

At the wedding ceremony there was an unforeseen delay in the procession while Elizabeth was near the entrance to the Abbey. In that pause, she impulsively laid her bouquet of white roses on the flat tombstone of the Unknown Warrior. It was a gesture deeply cherished by those who saw it.

APRIL 27   1764
MOZART, AGED EIGHT, ENTERTAINS
KING GEORGE III AND QUEEN CHARLOTTE

Little Wolfgang Amadeus Mozart was being paraded throughout the courts of Europe, and in April 1764 it was the turn of the English royal family to witness the young musical prodigy. His father Leopold and his sister Nannerl, aged twelve, had just made a rather rough sea-crossing to England during which they had all felt desperately seasick. However, just a few days later, on April 27, they were invited to play before King George III and Queen Charlotte at St James's Palace, so they quickly got themselves ready to make a good impression, decking themselves out in new clothes according to English fashions.

The presentation was a great success, and Leopold was pleased to find that King George and his wife welcomed them more warmly than they had been received in any other royal court. He noted in his diary: 'Their easy manner and friendly ways made us forget that they were King and Queen of England.'

In fact, George was only twenty-five at the time and Queen Charlotte just nineteen. Only two of their fifteen children had then been born, so it was a young court that welcomed the 'Prodigies of genius', as Wolfgang and Nannerl were called.

What really impressed Leopold Mozart was that a week later, as he was walking in St James's Park, the royal carriage passed by, and the king opened the window to greet them all personally. Leopold was astonished to be recognised.

The Mozarts were invited back to the palace again in May for a small royal family gathering at which Wolfgang played the organ and harpsichord, accompanied the queen singing, and then did some improvisations.

A plaque on the wall of 180 Ebury Street in London SW1 marks the house where the Mozarts stayed, and notes that the young Wolfgang composed his first symphony there.

APRIL 28   1483
A WICKED UNCLE LURES HIS ROYAL NEPHEW INTO
HIS PROTECTION

No one knows for sure what happened to the twelve-year-old King Edward V. Certain it was, however, that he and his younger brother Richard disappeared while staying in the Tower of London at their uncle's behest. The ugly fate of the 'Princes in the Tower' is virtually a part of English folklore.

The dark villain in this sordid episode is usually conceded to be Richard, Duke of Gloucester, and the general belief is that he had them murdered in order to place himself on the throne as Richard III – Shakespeare's notorious 'hunchback' with that unforgettable opening line: 'Now is the winter of our discontent made glorious summer by this son of York.'

Little Edward had officially become King Edward V immediately upon the death of his royal father, Edward IV. At the time, he was living in Ludlow, so of course it was necessary for him to be brought south to London as soon as possible.

It was arranged for the young king to be taken to Northampton by his household governor, Lord Rivers, and there his Uncle Richard, the Duke of Gloucester, would meet him and take him on to London.

Everything went as planned, except that when Duke Richard met up with Lord Rivers on this day in 1483 he arrested him on the spot and thereafter took personal charge of his young nephew. He accompanied him to London, placed him in the Tower, and without more ado claimed the throne for himself. The circumstantial evidence of foul play is strong, but to this day nothing can be 'proved'.

Also on this day:

1442 Birth of the future King Edward IV, in Rouen, France. He was the son of Richard, 3rd Duke of York, and Cicely, daughter of Ralph Neville, 1st Earl of Westmorland.

1603 Funeral of Queen Elizabeth I in Westminster Abbey.

APRIL 29   1559
ELIZABETH I BECOMES THE SUPREME GOVERNOR OF THE CHURCH OF ENGLAND

The Acts of Supremacy and Uniformity passed on this day were almost the first Acts of Elizabeth's reign. After the disastrous extreme Protestantism of her half-brother Edward and the even more disastrous extreme Catholicism of her half-sister Mary, the healing process of Elizabeth's twin Acts of Supremacy and Uniformity was something which England desperately needed. It was a triumph of compromise and commonsense.

The Book of Common Prayer was restored; the mass was forbidden; the English language was to be used in church services; ornaments and vestments were to be subject to the queen's own discretion; and everyone over sixteen was required to attend church on Sundays.

Catholics and Calvinists were critical, but this middle road essentially outlawed extremists, and set a standard of gentle level-headedness which captured the essence of the English temperament. Elizabeth needed a firm, diplomatic archbishop, and chose Matthew Parker. 'I would rather go to prison than accept,' was his reaction. Nevertheless, he bowed to the queen's wishes. His claim to later fame was his nickname, 'Nosey'.

APRIL 30   1662
BIRTH OF THE FUTURE QUEEN MARY II TO A TUB-WOMAN'S DAUGHTER

According to widespread belief, Anne Hyde's mother was a 'tub-woman' – that is, a woman employed to carry out beer from a brewhouse. The story goes that she was a good-looking girl and the brewer took a fancy to her and married her. He died soon after, leaving her a large fortune.

The lucky young widow went to one Mr Hyde, an up-and-coming lawyer, to ask how to manage her affairs, and he promptly married her himself. Mr Hyde rose high in his profession; so high, in fact, that he became Lord Chancellor and Earl of Clarendon. And from this marriage came a daughter, Anne.

It was just at the time of the Restoration that the future James II, brother of Charles, managed to make Anne pregnant. These were days when princes did not marry commoners, and although both Anne's father and James's mother, Henrietta Maria, were shocked at the thought of a marriage between them, Charles told his brother that he had to go through with it.

The marriage was successful, though James was frequently unfaithful. Among their children were two girls, both of whom were destined to become queens in their own right: Mary II, wife of William III, and Queen Anne.

Anne Hyde never lived to see her husband crowned, so was never a queen herself. She died in 1671, aged thirty-four, when her little daughters, Mary and Anne, were only nine and six. Sadly, Mary, born this day in 1662, died childless aged only thirty-two.

MAY 1   1464
KING EDWARD IV MARRIES A COMMONER IN GREAT SECRECY

Edward IV, aged just twenty-two, had been on the throne for just over a year when he fell desperately in love with Elizabeth Woodville, the ravishing blonde widow of Sir John Grey. He married her on this day at the manor of Grafton Regis, Northants. The story goes that Elizabeth wanted to ask the young king to intervene in restoring some land to her sons. She waited by a tree, later known as the Queen's Oak, in the forest of Whittlebury, and when the king came by on his way to hunt deer, she stepped out and dared to accost him. Edward was captivated.

Parliament, courtiers, nobles and church leaders were kept completely in the dark about this marriage, and it wasn't until mid-September, at a council at Reading, that the king confessed to what he had done. On this occasion, when the new queen was presented as a royal *fait-accompli*, she wore a tall crown of golden filigree studded with gems, and her flaxen hair streamed down her back almost to her feet.

Beautiful though Elizabeth was, Edward's brother Richard always considered her an upstart *parvenue*, and as soon as he came to the throne as Richard III he treated her with contempt and she had to find accommodation for herself well away from the court, suffering the indignity of being called 'Dame Grey, lately calling herself Queen of England'.

Also on this day:

1118 Death of Matilda of Scotland, aged thirty-eight, first wife of Henry I. She was buried in Westminster Abbey.

1625 King Charles I, aged twenty-four, married Henrietta Maria, sister of King Louis XIII of France, by proxy, in Notre Dame, Paris.

1851 Queen Victoria opened the Great Exhibition, organised by Albert, in the Crystal Palace, Hyde Park, London.

MAY 2   1536
ANNE BOLEYN IS ARRESTED AND TAKEN
TO THE TOWER OF LONDON

May Day saw the last appearance of Anne Boleyn as a royal queen. There were lively and splendid May Day celebrations at Greenwich, with feastings and joustings. King Henry VIII and Anne attended this unusually elaborate event, at which Anne's brother, Lord Rochford, was the principal challenger and her friend Henry Norris was one of the defenders.

All seemed to be going well, when the king suddenly got up angrily from his seat and stalked out of the royal balcony, followed by a handful of his attendants. He did not even bother to say farewell to his wife. In fact, it was the last time he saw her.

The whole tournament broke up in confusion: Lord Rochford and Norris were arrested as they tried to leave. Gossipy tradition tells us that Anne dropped a handkerchief, and this, somehow, was picked up rather meaningfully by Norris. The fact is, the king suddenly decided to take umbrage and caused confusion to everyone by leaving in a thundercloud of displeasure.

The next day, May 2, witnessed the sequel to all this, when Anne herself was arrested at Greenwich and taken by boat up the Thames to the Tower of London. She was distraught and hysterical. 'Do I go into a dungeon?' she asked the Lieutenant of the Tower. 'No, Madam,' he replied, 'to your own lodging, where you lay at your coronation.' But the memory of this was too much for her, and she burst out with uncontrollable weeping followed by wild laughter.

'I am the king's true wedded wife,' she said. 'Do you know wherefore I am here?'

But there was no answer. Later, she would hear that she was being accused of adultery with several partners, of having sex with her brother (incest was punishable by being burnt at the stake), and finally of plotting to kill the king. Facing such accusations, and with Henry pulling the strings, she knew full well what the verdict would be.

MAY 3   1060
EDWARD THE CONFESSOR ATTENDS THE
DEDICATION OF WALTHAM ABBEY

Waltham Abbey was an important royal foundation. The first founder was Tovi, Canute's standard-bearer, who is said to have built it to house a miraculous cross found at Montacute, near Yeovil in Somerset. This cross had such amazing powers that Harold Godwinson (later King Harold) swore that it had cured him of an attack of paralysis. Harold was so grateful that at some considerable personal expense he rebuilt the abbey on a much grander scale, and on May 3 1060 King Edward the Confessor attended the dedication of this new building.

Waltham Abbey meant a lot to Harold. He went there to pray before the Battle of Hastings, and it is said that he saw a sorrowful Christ bow over him from the crucifix over the altar. Harold's body is believed to have been taken to Waltham Abbey for burial after his defeat.

On May 3 1060, however, the Saxon world was still intact and this ceremony was a joyful one, with the presence of the king and Earl Harold making it an event of royal significance.

Also on this day:

1152   Death of Matilda of Boulogne, aged about forty-nine, wife of King Stephen. She was buried in Faversham Abbey.

MAY 4   1471
BATTLE OF TEWKESBURY:
THE PRINCE OF WALES IS KILLED

It was a tough and ferocious Edward IV who put all his determined force into beating the Lancastrians at the Battle of Tewkesbury. After this he was undisputed king, especially after he had tidied up the situation by having Henry VI murdered in the Tower a couple of weeks later.

Edward, the seventeen-year-old Prince of Wales, was killed either during the battle or just afterwards. One version of his death tells how he was captured while trying to escape from the battlefield into Tewkesbury Abbey. According to this account, the victorious King Edward IV confronted the young Prince of Wales and asked him how he dared to oppose him, whereupon the youngster boldly told him: 'To recover my father's crown and mine own inheritance.' Edward slapped him in the face with his iron gauntlet, as a signal for his attendants to stab the prince to death.

This young prince, the only child of Henry VI, usually makes only two appearances in the history books, marking his birth and his death. He was born during his father's strange eighteen-month mental blackout; when the king finally came to his senses he had to be introduced to his baby son, then fifteen months old, and told what his name was.

The prince's second appearance in the history books is concerned with his death at Tewkesbury. What a sad, short life! It has to be recorded, however, that he did marry, shortly before the Battle of Tewkesbury, in August 1470. He was seventeen, and his bride, Anne of Warwick, just fourteen. Anne's widowhood did not last long, for she married Richard of Gloucester the following year, and ultimately, though briefly, became Queen of England.

Also on this day:
1689 The former King James II, returning from exile, was proclaimed king again, in Dublin.

MAY 5   1640
KING CHARLES I DISSOLVES PARLIAMENT

After ruling by himself without Parliament for eleven years, on 13 April 1640 Charles summoned the first Parliament to sit since 1629. But it was immediately clear that he was on a collision course with his MPs. They were led by John Pym, who now spoke fearlessly against the king's arbitrary rule and illegal taxation. Eventually, after three weeks of wrangling, and when it became increasingly obvious that Parliament would not submit to his will, Charles abruptly dismissed them all.

After a session of only twenty-one days, this came to be known as the 'Short Parliament'.

1646
KING CHARLES I IS TAKEN PRISONER

After his defeat at Naseby in June 1645 Charles fled back to his stronghold at Oxford. Early the following year it was clear that the parliamentarian forces were closing in on him; so, without telling anyone where he was going, Charles escaped from Oxford on April 27, accompanied by just two gentlemen. He was disguised as their servant, with his hair and beard closely trimmed. Someone called out 'Farewell, Harry!' as he rode over Magdalen Bridge.

At last, six years to the day after dismissing the 'Short Parliament', and having suffered defeat after defeat in the Civil War, Charles arrived at the Scottish army's camp at Newark on 5 May. He hoped that he would be treated as an honoured guest – but he was wrong. From this day on until his execution he was at the mercy of his captors.

Also on this day:
1695 Funeral of Queen Mary II in Westminster Abbey.

MAY 6   1910
EDWARD VII DIES, AS PREDICTED BY HIS FORTUNE-TELLER

It was perfectly obvious to everyone that 'Bertie' (as the future Edward VII was known), would have to wait a long time before he became king, as his mother, Queen Victoria had been so young when she came to the throne. When he was fifty-two, and perhaps feeling somewhat frustrated, he called in a famous fortune-teller who called himself 'Cheiro' to ask about the future. Cheiro told Edward that he would live to be sixty-nine.

Edward was a ripe 59-year-old when at last, in 1901, on the death of the old queen, arrangements were made for his coronation to take place on 25 June. Preparations were in place, rehearsals completed, decorations put up and Westminster Abbey made ready for the great event. Then, the day before, it was announced that Edward was seriously ill with appendicitis. Surgery was still a primitive affair and it was more than likely that the future king was on his deathbed.

Astonishingly, the Princess of Wales (due to be crowned as Queen Alexandra) suddenly remembered the prophecy. Cheiro himself came and reminded Edward of his prediction, assuring him that he would be crowned after all. Then, at Edward's request, Cheiro solemnly chose the most propitious date for the coronation – August 9. It seems almost unbelievable that a monarch in the twentieth century should consult a soothsayer like this, mirroring Elizabeth I, who had been advised by her astrologer, Dr Dee, to choose January 15 for her own coronation in 1559.

So Edward and Alexandra were duly crowned on August 9 and Edward went on to reign for almost ten years.

On May 6 1910 he died. He was sixty-eight. Cheiro almost got it right.

Also on this day:
1910 King George V, aged forty-four, succeeded to the throne on the death of his father, Edward VII.
1935 King George V and Queen Mary celebrated their Silver Jubilee, and attended a thanksgiving service in St Paul's Cathedral, London.
1960 Marriage of Princess Margaret and Anthony Armstrong-Jones in Westminster Abbey.

MAY 7   1718
DEATH IN EXILE OF MARY OF MODENA, QUEEN OF JAMES II

Sixteen years after the death of the exiled James II, his widowed queen, Mary of Modena, died at St Germain, just outside Paris. Fifty people crowded into her room to see her die. (Death was a public event in those days, especially for royals.) She was in her sixtieth year, and exactly half her life had been spent in exile. She had been just thirty when she had had to flee so dramatically from England, disguised as an Italian washer-woman and carrying her little new-born baby in a bundle of laundry.

She died in poverty. She and James were obliged to live on an allowance made to them by Louis XIV, but, as the Duc de St Simon wrote, out of the 600,000 livres allowed her annually by the King of France, she devoted the whole to support the destitute Jacobites with whom St Germain was crowded.'

With macabre precision Mary bequeathed her heart to the monastery of Chaillot; her brain and intestines to the Scotch College, to be deposited in the chapel of St Andrew in Paris; and her body to remain unburied in the Convent of St Marie de Chaillot until her son, or his descendants, should be restored to the throne of England. She gave firm directions that when the Jacobites came back into power, her body should be taken back to England for burial in Westminster Abbey.

But her remains are still in Chaillot.

Also on this day:
1625 Funeral of King James I in Westminster Abbey.

MAY 8   1945
WINSTON CHURCHILL AND THE ROYAL FAMILY CELEBRATE VE DAY

No one who was present will ever forget that day, or the celebrations that night: it was Victory in Europe Day, after the great struggle to overcome the Nazi horrors of Hitler's war. True, the war in Asia was not yet won, but the relief felt by everybody on VE Day was overwhelming.

Naturally, Buckingham Palace was the focal point of the celebrations in London, and King George and Queen Elizabeth, together with the two Princesses, Elizabeth and Margaret, came out on to the balcony to wave at the cheering crowds. Churchill, of course, came too, with the broadest of smiles. He was the hero of the nation, though he was soon to be dismissed from office at the polls. Political life is never predictable.

As evening came, the princesses slipped out of the palace and joined the crowd, looking up at their parents on the balcony. Did anyone recognise them? It must have been a moment of intense freedom for the two teenage girls.

At the end of the day, George VI's mind turned to his daughters and their disciplined life during the war, sharing rationing and bombing with all the other Londoners. The last words he wrote in his diary that night were: 'Poor darlings, they have never had any fun yet.'

Also on this day:
1657 Oliver Cromwell, urged to accept the title of 'King of England, Scotland and Ireland', refused the crown for a second time.

MAY 9   1927
THE DUKE OF YORK OPENS PARLIAMENT HOUSE IN CANBERRA

On May 9 1901 the first Australian Federal Parliament had met in Melbourne. Twenty-six years later, to the day, the Duke of York – the future George VI – came to Australia to open a new Parliament House in Australia's new purpose-built capital city, Canberra. He had left Elizabeth, his little baby daughter behind; after all, she was less than a year old.

Only a few years before, the land here had been virgin territory – a vast tract of undeveloped limestone plains spreading out from the foot of the Australian Alps. However, such was the rivalry between Melbourne and Sydney in their wish to be the home of the Federal Parliament that a brand-new capital seemed to be the only answer.

A competition for Canberra's design was held in 1911, and a young American architect, Walter Burley Griffin, was chosen. It was to be a State Capital to accommodate about 25,000 people. Construction began in 1913.

Visitors to the beautiful city of Canberra are amazed at the vast scope of its design and marvel at what has been created in the middle of nowhere. Even now, in the twenty-first century, there is still much to be done to finish this enormous project. However, the huge artificial lake and the gigantic scale of today's modern city – now with half a million inhabitants and growing fast – is one of the finest sights in the world.

In 1979 another design competition was held, this time for a new Parliament House. Once again, the Americans won, and the present building with its towering flagpole is the work of the New York firm, Mitchell, Guirgola & Thorp.

MAY 10   1536
ANNE BOLEYN IS CHARGED WITH
HIGH TREASON

Poor Anne! When she was arrested on May 2 and taken as a prisoner to the Tower of London she literally had no idea what she was being accused of. From her room in the Tower she wrote to Henry VIII:

> Your grace's displeasure and my imprisonment are things so strange unto me, that what to write, or what to excuse, I am altogether ignorant. . . . To speak a truth, never a prince had wife more loyal in all duty, and in all true affection, than you have ever found in Anne Bulen – with which name and place I could willingly have contented myself, if God and your grace's pleasure had so been pleased.
>
> Try me, good king, but let me have a lawful trial, and let not my sworn enemies sit as my accusers and as my judges; yea, let me receive an open trial, for my truth shall fear no open shames.
>
> But if you have already determined of me, and that not only my death, but an infamous slander must bring you the joying of your desired happiness, then I desire of God that he will pardon your great sin herein.

My last and only request shall be, that myself may only bear the burden of your grace's displeasure, and that it may not touch the innocent souls of those poor gentlemen, who, as I understand, are likewise in strait imprisonment for my sake.

From my doleful prison in the Tower, the 6th of May

Ann Bulen.

But Henry had indeed already made up his mind, and was impatient to marry his new love, Jane Seymour. Accordingly, on May 10 an indictment for high treason was brought by the grand jury of Westminster 'against the lady Anne, queen of England; George Boleyn, Viscount Rochford; Henry Norris, groom of the stole; Sir Francis Weston and William Brereton, gentlemen of the privy-chamber; and Mark Smeaton, a performer on musical instruments – a person specified as of low degree, promoted for his skill to be a groom of the chambers.'

All but one refused, even under torture, to make false confessions of adultery. However, Mark Smeaton could not hold out against being 'grievously racked'. His wretched signature sealed the fate of them all – including Anne Boleyn herself.

MAY 11   973
THE FIRST CORONATION AT WHICH A KING IS ANOINTED TAKES PLACE IN BATH ABBEY

Bath Abbey witnessed one of the most important ceremonies ever to take place in England on this day in 973, Whit Sunday: the coronation of the Saxon King, Edgar the Peaceful.

Edgar had already been on the throne for thirty years, during which time he had brought peace and unity to the country; and he had made a point of strengthening the Church, founding forty religious houses and encouraging learning and culture. Edgar was a great and successful king, all the more powerful for having good advisers, St Dunstan, Archbishop of Canterbury, and St Oswald, Archbishop of York.

In 973 he decided to make a great and symbolic gesture – to be solemnly crowned and anointed king – and he chose Bath Abbey as the venue for this historic moment in the chronicle of English monarchy. The previous year Oswald had gone to Rome and had obtained the Pope's permission, for anointing was a papal privilege, not granted to every king, and until now there had been no precedent for anointing a king of all England.

Hence it was that Edgar's was the very first anointing-ceremony of an English king. It was a splendid affair, with massed choirs of abbots, abbesses, monks and nuns. Dunstan and Oswald jointly crowned him, and the words 'Zadok the priest and Nathan the prophet' were chanted – words which have been heard at every coronation since. This service, devised by Archbishop Dunstan, has been the model for English coronations now for a thousand years.

In honour of this event, a 'King of Bath' was ceremonially elected on the anniversary – a piece of folk-history which lasted into the eighteenth century. The last 'King of Bath' was 'Beau' Nash, the dandified arbiter of taste and fashion there for fifty-six years.

Also on this day:
1068 Matilda of Flanders, wife of William the Conqueror, was crowned queen in the Old Saxon Cathedral at Winchester.
1509 Funeral of King Henry VII in his own chapel at Westminster Abbey.

MAY 12   1937
GEORGE VI AND ELIZABETH ARE ANOINTED KING AND QUEEN

Almost a thousand years after Edgar's coronation (see MAY 11), this day in 1937 saw a repetition of what was, in essence, the same service that Archbishop Dunstan had devised in 973. In the intervening years Handel had produced his magnificent setting of 'Zadok the Priest'; Edward I had captured the Stone of Scone and put it in a special Coronation Chair; and thirty-one generations had borne the responsibilities of the crown, with varying degrees of success. George VI could point to a clear genealogical descent from Edgar.

It was to be the last coronation service without the presence of television cameras, although forty newsreel cameramen, all in full evening dress, had taken a record of the event. The Archbishop of Canterbury, Dr Lang, had vetoed television, which was then still in its infancy, because he did not like the risk of showing anything which perhaps might go wrong. Newsreel footage was safer – it could be censored. In the event the only shot which was cut was a close-up of old Queen Mary surreptitiously wiping away her tears.

The date, May 12, had been booked months in advance; the venue was indisputably predictable; the regalia was ready; the order of service was immutable. The only difference was that it was George VI who was crowned on this occasion, and not his brother Edward VIII.

The abdication had been a mere hiccup in the line of monarchy.

Also on this day:

1191 Marriage of King Richard I ('Lionheart') and Berengaria of Navarre, daughter of King Sancho VI of Navarre, at the Chapel of St George, Limassol, Cyprus.

1343 King Edward III invested his son Edward (the 'Black Prince') as Prince of Wales.

MAY 13   1662
CHARLES II MEETS AND MARRIES HIS BRIDE

It is astonishing how many former kings met their brides for the first time only days before marrying them. Everyone knows about Charles II's mistresses, but relatively few can remember who was his queen. However, on this day the 23-year-old Catherine of Braganza arrived at Portsmouth from Lisbon. The king travelled down from London to meet her a week later, and on 21 May they were married.

There were two ceremonies, both in Portsmouth. The first was a secret Roman Catholic marriage, and the second a public Protestant service at the Great Chamber of the Governor's House. They stayed for another six days there, and then Catherine accompanied Charles back to London – and his mistresses.

Not speaking English, suffering ill-health, and submitting to the humiliations heaped on her by her husband, the unfortunate Catherine is probably one of the least-known English queens. After Charles's death she went back to live out her days in her home country, and is buried in Lisbon.

Also on this day:

878 Probable date of the Battle of Edington, at which Alfred the Great won a resounding victory over the Danish army led by Guthrum.

1568 Mary, Queen of Scots, was defeated at Langside near Glasgow by the Regent Moray. Three days later she crossed the Solway and became Elizabeth I's prisoner. She was successively held at Carlisle, Bolton, Tutbury, Wingfield, Coventry, Tutbury again, Chatsworth, Sheffield, Buxton, Chartley and Fotheringhay. (See FEBRUARY 8.)

1945 George VI and Queen Elizabeth attended a thanksgiving service in St Paul's Cathedral to celebrate victory in Europe at the end of the Second World War.

MAY 14   1264
HENRY III LOSES THE BATTLE OF LEWES

This was Simon de Montfort's day of triumph, when he fought King Henry III and his son Edward (the future Edward I, 'Hammer of the Scots') and captured them both, putting them in separate prisons.

The site of the battle was between Offham and Lewes, on the grassy slopes of Offham Hill, near the present racecourse. For years afterwards the townsfolk of Lewes were digging the remains of the king's knights out of the mud of the nearby River Ouse, some with their swords still in their hands.

Simon de Montfort, Earl of Leicester and Henry III's own brother-in-law (he had married the king's youngest sister), became virtually King of England for the next fifteen months. Perhaps it would be fairer to call him 'president', or 'protector', for he tried to establish what was in effect the first English Parliament, and he might well have succeeded in this if young Prince Edward had not managed to escape from his clutches. Having rescued his father King Henry, he defeated and killed Simon at the Battle of Evesham the following year (see AUGUST 4).

Simon de Montfort's political experiment led directly to the establishment of a similar Parliament set up by Edward in 1295 when he became king, and all subsequent English parliaments have been developments based on this. We owe much to this rebel baron, whose memory is still very much alive in Leicester, where a famous concert hall and a university are named after him.

MAY 15   1567
MARY, QUEEN OF SCOTS, MARRIES FOR THE THIRD TIME

Just three months after the murder of her second husband, Lord Darnley, Mary married her 'lover' James Hepburn, Earl of Bothwell, in the great hall at Holyrood Palace.

Superstitious folklore, dating back to Roman times, dictated that marriages should be avoided during May, as this was the month when the spirits of the dead were honoured. Someone actually dared to put a notice over the gates of the palace, quoting lines from the Latin poet Ovid: *mense malas maio nubere vulgus ait*, or as the Scottish peasantry would say, 'Marry in May and regret it for ay'.

And Mary surely must have bitterly regretted this day. No one knows the precise details of the circumstances leading up to this apparently forced marriage. Did Bothwell rape her beforehand? Was she a willing partner? Or was she too physically and mentally exhausted or disturbed to put up any resistance?

The wedding itself was a Protestant affair, a fact which in itself shows how little say Mary can have had in the arrangements. And after the wedding the sheer lack of ceremony, festive celebrations, presents, or anything to suggest a happy or regal event makes it clear that Mary was now being taken into Bothwell's brutal captivity. The next month would probably be the worst in poor Mary's pathetic life.

MAY 16 1659
'IDLE DICK' DISAPPEARS

Richard Cromwell, Oliver's son and successor as 'Lord Protector II', found it impossible to continue in office and simply gave up on this day in 1659, without any formal declaration of resignation. His departure brought England to a state of chaos, and left a dangerous power-vacuum. Arguably, his disappearance triggered the thought in many people's minds: 'Why not bring back the king now?'

We have to be sorry for poor Richard – 'Idle Dick' – for inheriting what was virtually an impossible task. He had to contend with numerous factions, both in the army and in Parliament, and the treasury was bankrupt. His father Oliver had ruled by force of his dominant personality, having earned the respect of the army; but Richard had no friends, no power-base and no experience. He was quite out of his depth.

Richard fled to the continent, first to Paris and then to Italy, where he lived under the name John Clark. His long-suffering wife never saw him again, and he did not return to England until the reign of William and Mary, and then he lived in Chelsea.

A story is told about a court ceremonial in 1709, presided over by Queen Anne. Amid the throng of onlookers was an old man of eighty-three, dressed as a poor countryman. 'Have you ever seen such a sight before?' asked someone, rather patronisingly. 'Never since I sat in her chair,' came the surprising reply . . . it was 'Idle Dick' himself.

Also on this day:
1911   King George V unveiled the Victoria Memorial in front of Buckingham
          Palace, in the presence of the German Kaiser, Victoria's 'favourite grandchild'.

MAY 17   1220
YOUNG KING HENRY III HAS A SECOND CORONATION

At the relatively mature age of twelve, Henry was crowned in Westminster Abbey by Stephen Langton, the Archbishop of Canterbury. This was the ninth coronation to take place in Westminster Abbey, and the occasion must have meant a great deal to the young king, with his religious fervour and his deep reverence for the abbey's founder, Edward the Confessor. Although Henry III never became especially popular or successful in political or military terms, his patronage of the arts puts him in a different league from most other medieval kings. During his reign he greatly enlarged and beautified Westminster Abbey, so that this coronation in 1220 was the last to take place in the much smaller original building of the Confessor.

In fact, Henry had already been crowned, on 28 October 1216, in a hasty ceremony in Gloucester Cathedral, on the death of his father King John. He had been nine at the time.

Also on this day:
1768   Birth of Caroline, second daughter of Charles, Duke of Brunswick, future wife of King George IV (see APRIL 8).

MAY 18   1152
ELEANOR OF AQUITAINE MARRIES THE FUTURE HENRY II

Eleanor was thirty-two and Henry nineteen when they married on this day in the cathedral of Saint-Pierre at Poitiers, at a wedding service which was, according to contemporary writers, 'without the pomp and ceremony that befitted their rank'.

However, for Eleanor it must have been a relief to have divorced her husband, Louis VII of France, for it was a union which had given her little pleasure. Now, just eight weeks after that divorce, she was marrying the energetic and lusty young Henry Plantagenet, Count of Anjou, who was soon to become King Henry II of England.

The Plantagenet descendants of Eleanor and Henry were to rule for the next three centuries. They had more than thirty grandchildren, and Eleanor had even more grandchildren than Henry, through her first marriage to Louis. As most of these descendants married into many continental royal families, Eleanor of Aquitaine may well be called the 'Grandmother of Europe' – long before Queen Victoria was popularly given that well-known 'title'.

MAY 19   1536
ANNE BOLEYN IS BEHEADED AT THE TOWER OF LONDON

The enormity of this deed still silences today's tourists as they gather round the spot where Anne Boleyn, Henry's VIII's second queen, was so brutally executed.

She had risen at two o'clock that morning and had spent the early hours with her priest, Father Thirlwall, making her final confession and hearing three Masses. Then, after breakfast, for which, understandably, she had little appetite, she called in her attendants to take leave of them, after which she again spent time in prayer until eleven o'clock.

It was then time to lead her to the scaffold, constructed close beside the church of St Peter ad Vincula, and here she met the executioner, specially brought over from Calais. He was dressed in a tight-fitting suit of black and wore a half-mask over the upper part of his face. He was an expert in using his sword for special assignments such as this.

Anne carried a handkerchief and a small prayer-book bound in solid gold. Several hundred spectators were watching as she mounted the scaffold, which stood about five feet above the ground, surrounded by a low rail and covered with straw. Then she took a final leave of her women, gave the prayer-book to one of them, and made a short speech in which she declared her innocence and begged all those present to pray for her. Her last words were: 'Mother of God! pray for me. Lord Jesus! receive my soul.'

The moment had come for her ermine cloak and head-dress to be removed, and then Mistress Lee, one of her ladies, bound her eyes with a white linen handkerchief and she was led to the block. She immediately knelt down and laid her head on it.

The executioner had concealed his sword in the straw, but as he took it out of its hiding-place he tricked her by saying 'Bring me the sword,' to an assistant on the other side. Anne instinctively moved her head in the direction he intended, and this gave him the perfect opportunity to sever her head with just one savage blow.

The crowd moved away. Mistress Lee lifted the severed head, covered it with a cloth and laid it in an old arrow chest, since no one had remembered to bring a proper coffin for her. Other women helped her to lift Anne's body into the chest, and then, when the lid had been fastened, it was taken into the vault under the high altar.

Father Thirlwall pronounced a blessing over the chest, and all was over.

Also on this day:

1935   Sir Thomas More, beheaded on the orders of King Henry VIII four hundred years before, on July 6 1535, was canonised by the Roman Catholic Church and became a saint.

MAY 20 1910
EDWARD VII IS BURIED WITH GREAT POMP – AND CAESAR TAKES PRECEDENCE

The funeral of King Edward VII marked the end of an era. His mother, Queen Victoria, had died just over nine years before and her passing, at the end of the century, had itself seemed like the end of an age. Never again would so many royal mourners gather together. The crowned heads of Europe who came to this magnificent event little suspected that within a few years the First World War would erupt and the map of Europe would change for ever.

Edward died unexpectedly, after only a few days of bronchial illness. Popular grief was intense, and a quarter of a million people filed past the king's coffin as he lay in state in Westminster Hall between May 7 and May 19. The Kaiser himself came to pray beside it.

Then, in brilliant sunshine on May 20 the streets of London were packed to see the vast funeral procession move slowly from Westminster to Paddington station, on its way to Windsor. The German Emperor and eight kings followed the gun-carriage bearing the coffin: the new King George V, and the crowned heads of Belgium, Bulgaria, Denmark, Greece, Norway, Portugal and Spain. Also present were the Archduke Francis Ferdinand of Austria-Hungary, the Dowager Empress Marie Feodorovna of Russia, ex-President Theodore Roosevelt of the United States, and hundreds of other royal and distinguished mourners from around the world.

King Edward VII had been a keen observer of protocol, and it would have amused him to know that taking precedence over all these royal dignitaries, and first to follow after his gun-carriage, walked his bewildered little fox-terrier, Caesar.

Visitors to St George's Chapel, Windsor, can see Caesar still lying at Edward's feet, carved as part of his magnificent white marble effigy.

Also on this day:

1867   Queen Victoria laid the first stone of a 'Hall of Arts and Sciences' in Kensington, and announced that it would be called the 'Royal Albert Hall'.

MAY 21   1471
THE MURDER OF KING HENRY VI

The memory of King Henry VI is kept alive on this day, the anniversary of his death in the Wakefield Tower of the Tower of London. Henry was taken there as prisoner after the Battle of Tewkesbury (see MAY 4).

Precise details of his death are understandably vague, but tradition tells how the king was violently murdered while kneeling at prayer, and a tablet on the floor of the oratory in the Wakefield Tower marks the spot where he is believed to have fallen. It is possible that the assassin was Richard, Duke of Gloucester, the younger brother of the usurping King Edward IV.

Henry, who was passionately interested in religion and education, was a gentle, peace-loving, cultured monarch who was totally out of place in the crude violence of the Wars of the Roses. History has been less than kind to him, but he is remembered with gratitude and respect by Eton College and King's College, Cambridge, the two important institutions he founded.

Today, on the anniversary of his murder, representatives from these two establishments come to the Tower of London and, in a quiet and private little ceremony, place flowers on the spot where he was killed: white lilies for Eton College and white roses for King's College, Cambridge.

A similar ceremony takes place in St George's Chapel, Windsor, just before Evensong on the eve of this anniversary (20 May), with lilies and roses, and in recent years members of the Henry VI Society have brought yellow roses too, in memory of the fact that during his lifetime Henry was awarded the Papal Golden Rose by Pope Eugenius, for his services to religion and scholarship.

If it had not been for the Reformation, King Henry might well have become a saint. All the preparations were in hand for his canonisation, and Henry VII had built his 'Henry VII's Chapel' as an extension of Westminster Abbey especially to receive the saintly king's remains.

Also on this day:

1553   Marriage of Lady Jane Grey, aged fifteen, and Lord Guilford Dudley, fourth son of John Dudley, Duke of Northumberland, at Durham House, London. (See JULY 10.)

MAY 22   1554
MARY I RELEASES ELIZABETH FROM THE TOWER OF LONDON

The three months when her half-sister imprisoned her in the Tower of London were the worst in Elizabeth's life. Later, when she was queen, she told Parliament: 'I stood in danger of my life; my sister was so incensed against me.'

In fact, Mary was quite certain that Elizabeth was implicated in Sir Thomas Wyatt's rebellion, which was a protest against her plan to marry Philip of Spain. Indeed she continued to be convinced of Elizabeth's guilt even after she released her without charge on this day in 1554. As for Elizabeth, she was so traumatised by her imprisonment that even years after the event she was constantly giving thanks to God for her deliverance.

But Elizabeth's release from the Tower of London was no return to freedom. She was packed off to the royal palace at Woodstock with an escort of a hundred guardsmen, and when she arrived there sixty soldiers were on guard all day and forty kept watch within the building at night.

In her frustration and misery Elizabeth is believed to have scratched a sad little couplet with a diamond on a pane of glass in the window of her room there:

> Much suspected, of me
> Nothing proved can be,
>> Quoth Elizabeth, prisoner.

Also on this day:

1455   The first Battle of St Albans was fought, effectively beginning the Wars of the Roses. It was a Yorkist victory and King Henry VI was captured, receiving a slight arrow-wound in the neck. Oddly, his opponents went down on bended knee to kiss Henry's hand after the battle. Though captured, he was still king! (See FEBRUARY 17.)

1762   King George III and Queen Charlotte first moved into Buckingham House, later to be greatly enlarged as Buckingham Palace.

MAY 23   1533
ARCHBISHOP CRANMER DECLARES HENRY VIII'S MARRIAGE NULL AND VOID

Although Henry VIII and Anne Boleyn had been married in January 1533, and by May Anne was more than five months pregnant, Henry's first marriage, to Catherine of Aragon, had still not been annulled. Anne was due to be crowned on 1 June, so Henry needed to get the divorce proceedings wrapped up quickly.

The ever-compliant Archbishop Thomas Cranmer was pressed into service, and he demanded that Catherine attend an ecclesiastical court at Dunstable in Bedfordshire – well away from London and about 6 miles from Ampthill, where she was then living.

Catherine flatly refused to acknowledge the existence of this court and failed to appear. Henry was not present either, as he was too busy preparing Anne Boleyn's coronation. Hence it was that Cranmer, in front of just two notaries in the Lady Chapel of Dunstable Priory, solemnly declared Catherine to be contumacious; that her marriage to Henry was null and void; and that both Henry and Catherine were henceforth free to marry elsewhere if they chose. Thus Henry's long-drawn-out 'Great Matter' was concluded.

Just one week later Cranmer dutifully crowned the pregnant Anne Boleyn in Westminster Abbey.

Also on this day:

1125 Death of the Holy Roman Emperor, Henry V, first husband of Matilda, daughter of King Henry I and later nominated as his heir. It was through this marriage that she became known as the 'Empress Matilda', and it was through Henry's death that she became free to marry Count Geoffrey IV of Anjou, thus becoming the mother of the long line of Plantagenet monarchs.

MAY 24   1819
BIRTH OF THE FUTURE QUEEN VICTORIA

At 4.15 in the morning the future Queen Victoria was born on this day in Kensington Palace. She was the only legitimate child of George III's fourth son, the Duke of Kent. With fulsome congratulation, the Duchess of

Coburg, mother of the future Prince Albert, wrote to Victoria's mother: 'The rays of the sun are scorching at the height to which she may one day attain. It is only by the blessing of God that all the fine qualities He has put into her soul can be kept pure and untarnished. May God bless and protect our little darling.'

We take Victoria's name for granted, but it was a near thing. Only three days after she was born, her christening took place in Kensington Palace. A font was specially brought over from the Tower of London. Prinny, the future King George IV, was present to witness the baptism of his niece.

'Name this child,' said the Archbishop of Canterbury, Dr Sutton.

'Alexandrina,' replied her father, the Duke of Kent, naming her after the Emperor of Russia, who was her godfather, though he was not present at the christening.

Prinny immediately vetoed this choice.

'Charlotte?' 'Augusta?' 'Elizabeth?'

But Prinny ruled out all these names. Clearly, he was in charge of the event. By now, Victoria's mother, the Duchess of Kent, was in tears. Prinny was moved to make a suggestion. 'Give her the mother's name also, then, but it cannot precede that of the emperor,' he decreed.

Thus, the infant princess and future queen was finally christened Alexandrina Victoria. As a child, she was always known as 'Drina'.

Also on this day:

1659 Final resignation of Richard Cromwell, son and successor of Oliver Cromwell.

MAY 25 1962
QUEEN ELIZABETH II ATTENDS
THE CONSECRATION SERVICE OF THE
NEW COVENTRY CATHEDRAL

On the night of Thursday November 14 1940 Coventry suffered the longest air-raid of any one night on any British city during the Second World War. The old cathedral was utterly destroyed by fire-bombs. Less than forty hours afterwards, on November 16, King George VI visited the city to see for himself the terrible devastation which the German bombers had wrought.

On this day in 1962, nearly twenty-two years after that dreadful night, his daughter Elizabeth II came to Coventry to attend the consecration of a beautiful new cathedral designed by Basil Spence. The design of the new cathedral had been the subject of an open competition, and when the assessors awarded the commission to Basil Spence they declared: 'We not only feel that it is the best design submitted, but that it is the one which shows that the author has qualities of spirit and imagination of the highest order.'

The consecration was a moving occasion. Inside the cathedral sat a congregation of 2,300, while another 2,000 were seated in special stands in the ruins of the old cathedral (which lie alongside the new building). No fewer than twelve archbishops were present, as well as the bishops, deans and provosts of every diocese in the British Isles. As the queen entered the new Coventry Cathedral, Parry's famous anthem was sung. Its words, 'I was glad when they said unto me we will go into the house of the Lord,' were poignantly appropriate.

MAY 26   1867
BIRTH OF PRINCESS VICTORIA MARY AUGUSTA LOUISE OLGA PAULINE CLAUDINE AGNES

The princess whose full name is such a mouthful is far better known to us as Queen Mary, consort of George V and grandmother to Queen Elizabeth II. In her earlier days she was known as Princess Mary of Teck, and she was royally connected, being a great-granddaughter of George III and a great-niece of George IV and William IV.

Originally she had been engaged to 'Eddy', Duke of Clarence and Avondale, who was the eldest son of the future Edward VII. It would have been embarrassing to say so openly, but in fact Eddy was a distinct liability to the monarchy, being intellectually retarded. It was fortunate for Princess Mary that Eddy died of pneumonia in 1892, just six weeks before the wedding was due to take place.

Queen Victoria quickly got to work on the situation and suggested that Princess Mary might marry Eddy's younger brother George instead; accordingly, the following year, on July 6 1893, the wedding took place in the Chapel Royal, St James's Palace. It may have seemed a somewhat calculated union, but in fact it was a happy, solid marriage and the couple were to have six children, including the future Edward VIII and George VI.

Princess Mary, the future Queen Mary, was born this day in Kensington Palace in the same room in which Queen Victoria had been born almost exactly fifty-two years before (see MAY 24).

Also on this day:

946 Murder of King Edmund I, aged twenty-five, at Pucklechurch, Gloucestershire. He was stabbed to death by Leofa, an outlawed thief. His brother Edred, aged twenty-three, succeeded to the throne.

1465 Coronation of Elizabeth Woodville, wife of Edward IV (see MAY 1) in Westminster Abbey.

MAY 27   1199
KING JOHN IS CROWNED

Seven weeks after the death of his brother Richard the Lionheart, John finally achieved the power and prestige he had always craved. He was the youngest of Henry II's eight children and his fifth son. Originally, his father had given wealth and lands to all his older brothers but nothing to him, so his nickname about court until this moment had been 'Lackland'.

But now, aged thirty-two, John had everything: all his brothers were now dead, so legally he could claim the crown. In reality, John's nephew, Arthur of Brittany had a better claim to the throne, but this did not deter John. Rumour has it that John personally murdered him.

On this day in 1199 the Archbishop of Canterbury, Hubert Walter, who had formerly been one of Richard's fighting companions in the Holy Land, crowned John in Westminster Abbey. John's wife, his cousin Isabella of Gloucester, however, did not attend. He was just about to divorce her on grounds of 'consanguinity' – always a useful excuse, if it could be accepted by the Church. What it meant was that he had got his hands on her wealth and so had no further use for her. Meanwhile, he had his eye on a nubile fourteen-year-old, Isabella of Angoulême.

Eyebrows were raised when John did not take Communion after the coronation. It was, perhaps, a sign of the state of his soul . . .

MAY 28 1972
DEATH OF THE DUKE OF WINDSOR, FORMER KING OF ENGLAND

Just eight days before he died, the duke's niece Queen Elizabeth and his great-nephew Prince Charles visited him in his house in the Bois de Boulogne, on the outskirts of Paris. It was a mansion blazoned with royal coats of arms, hung with banners, and with servants dressed in royal livery. Even in France, the duke did not wish to forget his regal past.

Everyone knew that he was on the brink of death, suffering from cancer of the throat, and it was doubtful whether he would even survive until the visit. The British Ambassador in Paris had instructed the duke's physician that the ex-king could die before the visit, or indeed after the visit, but in no circumstances should he die while the visit was actually taking place.

The queen and Prince Charles were greeted by the Duchess of Windsor and then they were ushered up into the royal sickroom. Of course, no one knows what passed between uncle and niece, but it must have been a moment fraught with emotion.

When the Duke did die on this day in 1972, at the age of seventy-seven, his remains were brought back to London and he was buried in the Royal Burial Ground at Frogmore, Windsor. As a child he had played in the garden nearby.

Also on this day:

1660 Birth of the future King George I in Osnabrück, Hanover.

1982 Pope John Paul II visited Queen Elizabeth II in Buckingham Palace and spent thirty-five minutes alone with her. He was the first Pope to visit England since Henry VIII broke off relations with Rome.

MAY 29 1660
RESTORATION OF THE MONARCHY: CHARLES RETURNS IN TRIUMPH

The restoration of the monarchy was a unique event. No other king has ever returned from years of exile to such a rapturous welcome as Charles was given on this day in 1660 – coincidentally his thirtieth birthday. After the Commonwealth and the Protectorate there was an almost tangible yearning in England to return to a stable monarchy and crowds turned out in their thousands to see the king as he travelled by easy stages from Dover, where he had landed a few days before.

As an eye-witness, John Evelyn went into ecstasies over the day's events as the king was formally welcomed at Blackheath. In his diary he records:

> . . . the triumph of above 20,000 horse and foote brandishing their swords and shouting with inexpressible joy: the wayes strew'd with flowers; the bells ringing, the streetes hung with tapestry, fountains running with wine; the Mayor, Aldermen, and all the Companies in their liveries, chaines of gold, and banners: Lords and nobles clad in cloth of silver and gold and velvet: the windows and balconies well set with ladies: trumpets, music, and myriads of people flocking, even from Rochester, so they were seven hours in passing the City even from two in the afternoon till nine at night.

As Evelyn stood in the Strand he felt moved to say that he could but thank God that he had seen such a sight as the world had not seen 'since the return of the Jews from the Babylonish captivity'.

Later that night there were fireworks over the Thames, which was so crowded with boats and barges that 'you could have walked across it'.

Also on this day:

1630 Birth of the future King Charles II, son of King Charles and Henrietta Maria, at St James's Palace, London.

1982 Prince Charles met the Pope in Canterbury.

MAY 30   1536
HENRY VIII'S THIRD MARRIAGE:
JANE SEYMOUR BECOMES QUEEN

Popular legend has it that on the morning of May 19, the day of Anne Boleyn's execution, King Henry waited under an oak tree on the highest point of Richmond Hill, waiting for a gun-signal from the Tower, to announce that his second queen's head was properly severed. When he heard the gun's booming in the morning air, the king is then alleged to have shouted triumphantly: 'Ha, ha! the deed is done. Uncouple the hounds and away!' – whereupon he headed west with all speed towards Wolf Hall in Wiltshire, where Jane Seymour was waiting for him.

Whether or not this scene took place, the fact is that on May 30, just a few days after Anne's execution, Henry and Jane were married quietly at Whitehall Palace, in the Queen's Closet. Archbishop Cranmer had thoughtfully granted a dispensation for the king to marry Jane Seymour 'without publication of banns', and had signed this on the day of Anne Boleyn's death.

Chapuys, the Spanish Ambassador, wrote back to Spain, describing Jane 'as no great beauty, of middle stature: so fair one might almost call her pale. She is twenty-five years old. I leave you to judge, whether, being English and having long frequented this court, she is likely to have any scruples.'

Also on this day:
1445 Margaret of Anjou, wife of King Henry VI, was crowned queen in Westminster Abbey (see APRIL 23).
1842 Second assassination attempt on Queen Victoria (see FEBRUARY 29).

MAY 31   1246
ISABELLA OF ANGOULÊME DIES IN A 'SECRET CHAMBER' AT FONTEVRAULT

Before she married King John (she had no choice in the matter), Isabella of Angoulême had been hoping to marry her lover, Hugh de Lusignan, in France. She must have been quite relieved when John died, rather suddenly, sixteen years later. She was only about thirty, so she went back to her home in Angoulême and married Hugh, who was still waiting for her. It was a happy marriage, and Isabella and Hugh had three sons and several daughters before 1244, when suddenly, out of the blue, she was accused of plotting to poison the King of France!

Isabella, perhaps wisely, made no attempt to defend herself. She simply fled to Fontevrault Abbey and sought sanctuary there in a 'secret chamber'.

Poor Isabella! She died on this day in 1246, still in hiding, aged about sixty, and was buried according to her own wishes in an open cemetery there.

Many years later, her son Henry III, whom she had crowned rather hastily in Gloucester Cathedral thirty years before (see OCTOBER 28) with one of her own golden collars, visited Fontevrault and was horrified to see that his mother's remains were lying in such a humble grave. He ordered her to be moved inside the abbey church, to lie alongside his other ancestors.

She lies there still, with a splendid effigy, the last of the four English kings and queens to be buried there. The other three are Henry II, Eleanor of Aquitaine and Richard I.

Also on this day:

902 Coronation of Edward the Elder, son of Alfred the Great, at Kingston upon Thames.

JUNE 1   1533
CORONATION OF ANNE BOLEYN

Archbishop Cranmer had hastened back from Dunstable (see MAY 23) once more to do Henry's bidding, and on June 1 1533 he officiated at one of the most splendid and colourful events of the reign – the coronation of 'the Concubine', Anne Boleyn.

A contemporary account describes Anne arriving at Westminster Abbey 'in a chariot upholstered in white and gold, and drawn by white palfreys. Her long black hair streamed down her back and was wreathed with a diadem of rubies. She wore a surcoat of silver tissue, and a mantle of the same lined with ermine. A canopy of cloth-of-gold was borne over her by four knights on foot. After came seven great ladies, riding on palfreys, in crimson velvet trimmed with cloth-of-gold, and two chariots covered with red cloth-of-gold. Fourteen other Court ladies followed with thirty of their waiting-maids on horseback.' It was a gorgeous event, as Henry intended it to be, and it was followed by a sumptuous banquet in Westminster Hall.

None of Henry's other future wives were given coronations. Anne alone had this moment of triumph: in fact she was probably crowned with the uniquely precious St Edward's Crown – the only occasion on which any consort has been accorded with such a privilege. It was the pinnacle of her success. However, she noted with shrewd observation that during the coronation procession she had seen 'many caps on heads'. In other words, there were few cheers and few hats raised in her honour.

JUNE 2   1953
CORONATION OF ELIZABETH II

Thousands of British families bought their first television set to watch the coronation of their new young queen on this day. Elizabeth II had acceded to the throne aged twenty-five – the same age as Elizabeth I – and there was a marvellous sense of expectancy in the air as the nation seemed to be on the brink of a new Elizabethan Age. At the beginning of the twenty-first century it isn't easy for younger people to imagine the youthful glamour of the new sovereign in 1953.

Uniquely, this first televised coronation brought the event into ordinary homes. But few realised at the time that this was the queen's personal wish, directly opposed to the combined advice of Winston Churchill, the entire Cabinet and the Archbishop of Canterbury. They were surprised at her firmness, but had to bow to her wishes.

Today, we take it for granted that royal events will appear on our screens, but in 1953 television coverage was an unthinkable intrusion into the almost mystical world of royalty. One of the archbishop's objections had been that the television programme would be seen in pubs, and it was quite likely that some men would fail to take their hats off.

Elizabeth I had complained about the oil used to anoint her (see JANUARY 15). Since then, a special formula had been concocted, originally made for Charles I, which included musk, sesame, jasmine, cinnamon, roses, orange flowers, civet and ambergris. The custom was to mix up plenty of this so as to last for several coronations, but it was discovered that the mixture made up for Edward VIII and then used in 1937 for George VI had been destroyed in the Blitz.

The firm of pharmacists who had made up this esoteric oil had gone out of business, but luckily someone was found who had kept a little of the original as a royal keepsake. A heroic chemist, J.D. Jamieson, gave up smoking for a month in order to improve his sense of smell, and then set about making up the requisite potion, following the recipe that was used for Charles I.

Also on this day:

1129 Marriage of the Empress Matilda to Geoffrey IV ('The Handsome'), Count of Anjou, subsequently the parents of the future Henry II.

1420 Marriage of Henry V, aged thirty-two, and Catherine of Valois, daughter of King Charles VI of France, at St John's Church, Troyes, France.

JUNE 3   1937
MARRIAGE OF THE DUKE OF WINDSOR AND MRS SIMPSON

Ex-King Edward VIII and Bessie Wallis Simpson (née Warfield) were married on this day in the drawing-room at the Château de Candé, Monts, near Tours, France. It was the home of Charles Bédaux, a French-born naturalised American friend. No member of the royal family was present.

There were in fact two ceremonies. The first was a civil ceremony conducted, according to the *Daily Mirror*, by 'the plump, gay little French doctor, M. Mercier, Mayor of Monts, with a bristling moustache and tricolour sash round his waist'. According to the *Mirror*'s report, the Duke replied 'Oui, in a firm voice' when the mayor asked 'Do you consent to take Mrs Wallis Warfield as your wife?'

The second ceremony, a religious one, followed, this time in the music room, where an old oak chest served as an altar. The service was conducted by the Revd Anderson Jardine, vicar of St Paul's Church, Darlington. As the duke entered, the organist Marcel Dupré played martial music; the new duchess promised to obey the duke; the best man, Major E.D. Metcalfe, handed over the Welsh gold wedding ring which Wallis had temporarily removed from her finger so that it could be placed on it for a second time.

In order to spell out legally and precisely how the new duke and duchess should be styled, it had been announced in London on May 28 that: 'The king has been pleased by Letters Patent under the Great Seal of the Realm bearing date the 27 May 1937 to declare that the Duke of Windsor shall . . . be entitled to hold and enjoy for himself only the title style or attribute of Royal Highness so however that his wife and descendants if any shall not hold the said title style or attribute.' This was a bitter blow for the Duke, who writhed with anger to his dying day that his wife did not enjoy the title Royal Highness. In private, to his friends, he continued to refer to Wallis as 'Her Royal Highness' and expected them to do the same, but everyone knew that this was a pathetic pretence.

Also on this day:

1865 Birth of the future King George V, son of the future King Edward VII and the future Queen Alexandra, in Marlborough House, London. (It will be noted, therefore, that June 3 was a curiously insensitive date for the Duke of Windsor to choose for his wedding to Wallis Simpson.)

JUNE 4 1561
QUEEN ELIZABETH SEES OLD ST PAUL'S
IN FLAMES

According to a contemporary account, 'Between one and two of the clock at afternoon, was seen a marvellous great fire of lightning, and immediately ensued a terrible hideous crack of thunder, such as seldom hath been heard

. . . For divers persons . . . being in the fields near adjoining to ye City, affirmed, that they saw a long and a spear-pointed flame of fire run through the top of the broach or spire of Paul's steeple from the east westward . . . Between four and five of the clock a smoke was espied, to break out under the bowl of the said shaft of Paul's.'

The magnificent 520ft spire of Old St Paul's had been struck by lightning, and was quickly destroyed in the ensuing fire. From her palace at Greenwich Queen Elizabeth could see the smoke and flames across the meadows, and 'As soon as the rage of the fire was espied by her majesty and others in the court, of the pityful inclination and love that her gracious highness did bear to ye said church, and the city, sent to assist my Lord Mayor for the suppressing of the fire.'

Sadly, the roof was also badly damaged, and the lead was melted. The queen contributed generously to the repair bill by giving a thousand marks and timber worth another thousand. But although the roof was made good, the spire was never rebuilt.

Fifteen years later Elizabeth was still demanding to know what the Lord Mayor was doing about the spire. Rather menacingly, she added that if his reply did not please her she 'would have the Mayor and six of the best of his brethren before her upon the very next Sunday following, though she were then in a progress and some distance from London'.

But despite this, no real progress was made. The spire had gone for ever, and the cathedral itself was to last less than a century more before the Great Fire of London destroyed it completely.

Also on this day:

1738   Birth of the future King George III, grandson of King George II, in Norfolk House, St James's Square. He was the son of Frederick and Augusta, Prince and Princess of Wales.

JUNE 5   1625
CHARLES I, ON HIS WAY TO MEET HIS BRIDE, SUFFERS A SAD EVENT

The young Charles I, just twenty-four years old, had succeeded to the throne only two months before, and now he was on the way to Dover to see his new wife, Henrietta Maria, for the first time. They were already married, for a proxy had stood in for Charles at their first wedding, in

Notre Dame in Paris a month before. However, he had never actually met Maria, who was just fifteen at the time, and he must have been looking forward to marrying her in person, at a magnificent second wedding ceremony due to take place in Canterbury Cathedral on June 13.

Everything must have seemed perfect for the new king. He had decided to take the choristers of the Chapel Royal with him, as he knew their choir-master, the brilliant new organist of Westminster Abbey, Orlando Gibbons, would make the wedding service even more memorable. As a composer of anthems, hymns and madrigals Gibbons was probably the country's foremost musician. *The Silver Swan* is one of the most beautiful madrigals ever written.

But no one could have expected the sudden death of Orlando Gibbons while the royal party was in Canterbury. He died of some kind of fit, or possibly a heart-attack, aged only forty-two. He was buried in the cathedral, while the king and his courtiers, no doubt deeply shocked, proceeded on their way to Dover.

Also on this day:
1972 Burial of the Duke of Windsor, former King Edward VIII, at Frogmore, Windsor.

JUNE 6   1405
HENRY IV MEETS THE REBELLIOUS ARCHBISHOP SCROPE

The usurper King Henry IV was never comfortably secure on the throne, and throughout his reign he was threatened by plots and rebellions. When he had clear evidence of a conspiracy led by Archbishop Scrope of York he hastened to the archbishop's palace at Bishopsthorpe on this day in 1405, to confront him. Two days later, Scrope was summarily executed at Clementhorpe, less than a mile from his minster, for plotting treason.

The whole situation must have been highly stressful for the king, for that very afternoon, as he was on horseback, he suffered from a kind of stroke: 'It seemed to him he had felt an actual blow.' Henry almost fell to the ground in pain, and for the rest of his life he never quite recovered from this seizure. He also suffered from 'leprosy' – probably some form of eczema – and these health problems were popularly attributed to the vengeance of God, seeking retribution for the archbishop's murder.

Henry himself was somewhat superstitious, and wondered whether a visit to Jerusalem would help to relieve him of his itchy guilt.

JUNE 7   1967
THE DUKE AND DUCHESS OF WINDSOR ARE INVITED TO LONDON

In 1967 it was decided to put a plaque on the wall of Marlborough House to commemorate the centenary of the birth of Queen Mary, consort of George V and grandmother of Elizabeth II. Queen Mary had lived in Marlborough House for the last seventeen years of her life, after the death of King George.

Accordingly, a select group of royals were present to witness the unveiling. It was not a world-shattering event, but to everyone's surprise the Duke and Duchess of Windsor were invited to join the group. Obviously it was only courteous to extend the invitation to them as Queen Mary was, after all, the duke's mother.

But what made this event so special was that it was the first time that the queen and the queen mother had met the Duke and Duchess of Windsor in public since the abdication in December 1936 – thirty years before.

The duchess did not curtsey to the queen, but made a slight bow. She shook hands with the queen mother.

The ice had been broken at last. Briefly.

Also on this day:

1494 Death of Anne of Bohemia, aged twenty-eight, first wife of King Richard II. She was buried in Westminster Abbey.

1967 Queen Elizabeth II knighted Francis Chichester at Greenwich for his solo circumnavigation of the world in *Gipsy Moth IV*.

JUNE 8   1042
HARDECANUTE DIES 'WITH A HORRIBLE CONVULSION'

Hardecanute, the son of King Canute, was hated for his severe taxation and feared for his ruthless cruelty to those who opposed him. He devastated the city of Worcester and the surrounding countryside as a reprisal for the murder of two of his tax-collectors.

He lasted two years on the throne and was only about twenty-three when he died. A report on his reign in the *Anglo-Saxon Chronicle* succinctly summed him up: 'He never did anything worthy of a king while he reigned.'

On this day in 1042, the *Chronicle* continues, 'Hardecanute died as he stood at his drink and he suddenly fell to the ground with a horrible convulsion; and those who were near thereto took hold of him, but he never spoke again, and died on 8 June.'

He was at a wedding feast in Lambeth, getting drunk as usual, and the sheer suddenness of his convulsions convinced everyone that he had been poisoned. Of course, nothing could be proved, but murder was the only credible explanation. He was succeeded by a totally different character, his half-brother the saintly Edward the Confessor, aged about thirty-nine.

Also on this day:

1376 Death of the 'Black Prince', Prince of Wales and heir to the throne, in the Palace of Westminster. The succession passed to his son, the future Richard II.

JUNE 9   1908
EDWARD VII MEETS HIS NEPHEW, TSAR NICHOLAS OF RUSSIA

One of Edward VII's unique contributions to international harmony was his habit of visiting heads of state and fellow-monarchs throughout Europe. Out of this came the famous 'Entente Cordiale', which improved British relations with France. But this was only the start of his energetic programme of visits. He met the German Kaiser on many occasions unofficially, but made state visits to see him in 1904 and 1909; he visited Vienna in 1903, Spain in 1907, Russia in 1908, the Mediterranean in 1905, Greece in 1906 and the Scandinavian states in 1908. And of course he entertained foreign royalty on a lavish scale in Windsor and London.

On this day in 1908 it was the turn of Russia, and Edward was the first British monarch to meet a reigning Tsar on Russian territory. It was on board the royal yacht, the *Victoria and Albert*, as it anchored at the Russian city of Reval. Relations were cordial, and the Tsar 'affectionately' greeted his uncle and aunt, Edward and Alexandra.

Sir Frederick Ponsonby, accompanying the royal party, recorded that 'the king as usual made a most impressive speech proposing the health of the Emperor'. The king was an excellent linguist and superb extempore speech-maker: he was in his element on occasions such as these.

To provide evening entertainment a steamer carrying a local choral society came alongside the yacht to serenade the two monarchs. As there were dangerous 'nihilists' about, the head of the Russian police had given orders that all the singers were to be strip-searched before being allowed to go on board.

JUNE 10   1688
BIRTH OF THE OLD PRETENDER . . . AND THE WARMING-PAN LEGEND

Mary of Modena, wife of James II, went into labour this day, Trinity Sunday, in 1688. Her Protestant ladies-in-waiting had gone to church and Mary had to summon them back urgently to St James's Palace when she realised that she was about to give birth. Mrs Margaret Dawson, one of these ladies, who had been present at many royal births, arrived first and found the twenty-year-old queen cold and trembling and asking for a single bed to be made ready in the next room.

Old Mrs Dawson knew that the quilts were not properly aired, so she persuaded Mary to go back to her own double-bed while she prepared the single bed which the queen had asked for. Thus began the preposterous 'warming-pan rumour' (see NOVEMBER 14), in which it was alleged that the queen had not been pregnant at all, and that a baby boy had been secretly smuggled into the royal bed-chamber in order to grow up and become a Catholic king!

Later, Mrs Dawson testified on oath to the Privy Council that she had personally seen coals of fire in the warming-pan when it was brought into the bedroom. But the rumour died hard, despite the fact that sixty-seven people, including the dowager queen Catherine of Braganza, had witnessed the actual birth.

The 'Old Pretender's' life, from birth to death, was something of a disaster.

Also on this day:

1840   First attempt to assassinate Queen Victoria (see FEBRUARY 29).

1921   Birth of Prince Philip, only son of Prince Andrew of Greece and Princess Alice, great-grand-daughter of Queen Victoria, on the island of Corfu.

JUNE 11   1685
THE DUKE OF MONMOUTH LANDS AT
LYME REGIS

James, Duke of Monmouth, was the bastard son of Charles II's first love, Lucy Walter, 'beautiful, bold and brown, but insipid'. Charles was always indulgent to him, the first of his many bastards.

In attempting to seize the throne after the sudden death of his father, the 36-year-old Duke of Monmouth probably considered that he was merely asserting his Protestant rights. At all events, on this day in 1685 he arrived with three boats crammed with arms and ammunition at the little port of Lyme Regis in Dorset, to try his luck.

It was a foolhardy enterprise, but when news of his arrival spread around the area plenty of young men sprang to his aid and he quickly began forming them into four regiments: the duke's own regiment, the Red Regiment; and then a White Regiment; a Green Regiment; and a Blue Regiment. There was also the artillery (four small cannon).

Enthusiasm he may have had in plenty, but his plans ran into serious difficulties. He desperately lacked horses, and sent out men to scour the countryside for them. Then two of his three ships, still carrying ammunition, were captured. And finally he lacked provisions. The duke was worried about feeding his growing army until his chaplain, the Revd Robert Ferguson, came up with an ingenious temporary solution. Ferguson told the duke that he would provide subsistence for one day for the entire army if only he would give him command of it for one minute.

The puzzled duke agreed, whereupon the chaplain declared that the following day would be observed as a solemn fast, to ensure the success of the enterprise!

Also on this day:

1183   Death of Henry 'The Young King', son and heir of King Henry II, aged twenty-eight, at Limoges, France. He was buried in Le Mans Cathedral.

1509   Marriage of King Henry VIII, aged eighteen, to his first wife, Catherine of Aragon, daughter of King Ferdinand II and Queen Isabella of Spain, at the Chapel of the Observant Friars, London.

1727   Death of King George I, aged sixty-seven, at Osnabrück, Hanover. He was buried first at the Leineschlosskirche, Hanover, and then reburied at the Herrenhausen Palace during the Second World War.

1727   King George II, aged forty-three, succeeded to the throne on the death of his father.

JUNE 12   1987
PRINCESS ANNE IS GIVEN THE TITLE
'PRINCESS ROYAL'

Just as the eldest son of a reigning monarch is given the title 'Prince of Wales', so the eldest daughter is given the title 'Princess Royal'. There is one significant difference, however, in that the title remains with the recipient for life, no matter how many other sovereigns or eldest daughters may come along. Furthermore, the title is in the personal gift of the sovereign, and does not come automatically.

The previous holder of the style (technically it is not a 'title') had been Princess Mary, Countess of Harewood, daughter of George V, who had died in 1965. The style therefore lay in abeyance for twenty-two years, until Queen Elizabeth decided that the time was right to honour Anne for her tireless work for so many charities, especially through her role as President of the Save the Children Fund. As a sportswoman too, Anne had won personal tributes, being voted BBC Television Sports Personality of the Year in 1971, having previously won the European three-day eventing championships. (It is worth recording that Princess Anne's daughter, Zara Phillips, also won the BBC Sports Personality of the Year trophy in 2006 – 35 years later).

Anne is only the seventh Princess Royal. The previous Princesses of Wales were: Mary (1631–60), eldest daughter of Charles I and mother of the future William III; Anne (1709–59), eldest daughter of George II; Charlotte (1766–1828) daughter of George III; Victoria (1840–1901), daughter of Queen Victoria; Louise (1867–1931), daughter of Edward VII; and Mary (1897–1965), daughter of George V.

JUNE 13   1842
QUEEN VICTORIA'S FIRST JOURNEY BY TRAIN

Victoria and Albert were both twenty-three when they made this controversial and daring trip on the new invention, the railway train. They travelled all the way from Slough to Paddington station. They rode in a luxurious royal saloon supplied by the Great Western Railway, and Brunel himself rode on the footplate to make sure that everything would go well. Victoria was excited and delighted, remarking that this new form of travel was 'free from dust and crowd and heat'. She even wrote to her uncle, King Leopold of Belgium, the following day, saying 'I am quite charmed by it.'

Railways were still in their infancy, and the queen was criticised for risking her life by daring to make the trip, but she ignored her critics, and shortly afterwards a branch line was built from Slough to Windsor. This royal patronage helped to popularise the railways at a time when many people were still highly suspicious of them. The Duke of Wellington was deeply prejudiced against trains, having witnessed the death of the former colonial secretary, William Huskisson, at the opening of the Liverpool & Manchester Railway. Huskisson had been struck by a train just as he was crossing the tracks to greet the duke.

Also on this day:

1625 King Charles I, aged twenty-four, married Henrietta Maria in Canterbury Cathedral (see MAY 1 and JUNE 15).

JUNE 14   1645
CHARLES I MEETS DISASTER AT THE BATTLE OF NASEBY

During the battle Charles I realised with horror that his infantry was in grave difficulties and he tried to intervene personally with his reserve horseguards. He was just about to lead a charge when the Earl of Carnwath seized the reins of the king's horse, shouting, 'Will you go upon your death?'

It was a moment of would-be bravery, but the king's apparent indecision sent fear through his ranks. The royalist forces collapsed and by lunchtime the battle was over. Not only was Charles's army in ruins but his royal baggage was captured, which included all his correspondence and about £100,000 in gold, silver and jewels. Charles was never able to raise another army. This was his final military defeat.

There is an obelisk on the B4036 near the village of Naseby, placed there in 1823, with an inscription remarking that the battle provided 'a useful lesson to British kings never to exceed the bounds of their prerogative'.

Also on this day:

1170 Coronation of Henry 'The Young King', aged fifteen, second son of King Henry II and Eleanor of Aquitaine, in Westminster Abbey, during the lifetime of his father. Henry II was still very much alive, and so for thirteen years, until the Young King died (see JUNE 11), England had *two* King Henry's!

1381 King Richard II, aged just fourteen, rode out alone to confront the rebels of the 'Peasants' Revolt' at Mile End. His courage defused an ugly situation (see JUNE 15).

JUNE 15   1215
KING JOHN SETS HIS SEAL TO MAGNA CARTA

Runnymede, where John put his seal to Magna Carta, is on the south bank of the River Thames, about three miles south-east of Windsor. There is nothing to be seen there dating from that time, but in 1957 the American Bar Association built a memorial to the occasion, and there is a memorial to President John Kennedy nearby, dedicated by Queen Elizabeth II in 1965. The inscription reads: 'This acre of English ground was given to the United States of America by the people of Britain in memory of John F. Kennedy.'

Throughout the centuries King John has been regarded as the archetypal 'Bad King'. Here, without comment, is a nineteenth-century account of John's reactions to having been forced to bow to the will of the barons:

After signing Magna Charta at Runnymede, King John retired in a rage to his fortress at Windsor, the scene of many of his secret murders. Here he gave way to tempests of personal fury, resembling his father's bursts of passion; he execrated his birth, and seizing sticks and clubs, vented his maniacal feelings by biting and gnawing them, and then breaking them in pieces.

Giving an example of John's unpleasant habits, the writer went on to describe the way in which, when travelling about his kingdom, 'the king every morning took delight in firing, with his own hands, the house that had sheltered him the preceding night'.

Also on this day:
1330 Birth of Prince Edward, later to be known as the 'Black Prince', son of Edward III and Philippa of Hainault, at the old palace of Woodstock.
1381 King Richard II met the rebellious mob at Smithfield, led by Wat Tyler. On this famous occasion the boy-king challenged the rebels by saying: 'Sirs, will you shoot your king? I am your captain. Follow me.' Once again his courage saved the day.

JUNE 16   1644
QUEEN HENRIETTA MARIA HAS HER NINTH CHILD

However much she may have deserved her fate, we have to feel sorry for Henrietta Maria during the Civil War. It was nineteen years since she had arrived as a giggly teenager to marry Charles I, and now she was aged thirty-four, already with eight children and about to give birth to her ninth. Meanwhile the country was torn asunder in civil strife and after the battles of Edgehill, Newbury and Marston Moor, the royalists were in deep trouble.

Having no clear idea of her husband's whereabouts, Henrietta had decided to go to Exeter, where she knew she had friends, for her confinement, and so in these difficult circumstances, on June 16 she gave birth to her ninth child, another daughter.

Unluckily for her, within less than a fortnight a parliamentarian army led by the Earl of Essex arrived and laid siege to the city. Henrietta, still weak, begged for safe leave to go to Bath, but she got short shrift from Essex, who curtly sent back his answer that 'It was his intention to escort her majesty to London, where her presence was required to answer to Parliament for having levied war in England.'

This was the last straw for Henrietta, and in desperation she planned her escape. Taking just two servants and her confessor, and leaving behind her new-born baby, she slipped through the parliamentarian troops surrounding Exeter, hid for a couple of days in a farm hut, and then pressed on, hoping to reach Plymouth. However, on reaching Falmouth she decided to take advantage of a Dutch ship there to make an immediate crossing to France.

Meanwhile, King Charles, thinking she was still in Exeter, fought his way there and entered the city in triumph only days after his queen had sailed for France. He had missed her by days, and never saw her again. Perhaps it was some consolation for Charles to see his new little daughter, but sadly it was to be the first and only time. He had her christened Henrietta Anne, after her mother. Later, to her older brother, Charles II, she was his darling 'Minette'.

JUNE 17   1239
A COMET MARKS THE BIRTH OF THE FUTURE EDWARD I

The birth of a son and heir on this day to Henry III and Eleanor of Provence was a matter of great celebration, and given Henry's deep veneration for

Edward the Confessor it was only to be expected that he would give his son the resounding name of Edward. The child was born at Westminster Palace.

The birth coincided with the appearance of a comet. Appparently, it grew bigger every night with flames before it and a huge tail behind, and it reached its greatest altitude just at the moment when Eleanor gave birth. Of course, the phenomenon had to have a meaning, and the court astrologers shrewdly predicted that the flames which went before the comet gave promise of a brilliant future for the new prince. However, they also claimed that the long tail behind it signified great calamity for the prince's successor.

JUNE 18 1066
WILLIAM THE CONQUEROR GIVES HIS DAUGHTER TO A NUNNERY

William was making his invasion plans throughout the fateful year of 1066, not merely by preparing his expedition force and all its necessary equipment, but also in other rather more subtle ways. For example, he had sent to Rome asking for the benediction of the Pope, hoping that the Holy Father would grant him a papal banner. He must have been pleased when the banner was actually forthcoming. He also shrewdly made treaties with other European rulers, just in case they decided to back Harold when it came to the crunch.

But perhaps his most extraordinary act, as a living sacrifice to God, was to give his seven-year-old daughter Cecily to become a nun in the abbey of La Trinité at Caen on this day in 1066, just four months before his planned invasion of England. God, surely, would approve of such a pious act. Both William and his wife Matilda were united in making this offering of their child to God's service.

It was an important and solemn ceremony attended by bishops, abbots and all the nobility of Normandy; and the proceedings were conducted by the Archbishop of Rouen. Everyone knew what William was intending to do, and the significance of the occasion.

The gift of Cecily as a nun came at the dedication of Matilda's abbey. William and Matilda, having married as cousins, had incurred the displeasure of the Pope, and had each been required to build an abbey as a penance. Both abbeys still exist in Caen today: after their deaths William was buried in his 'Abbaye aux Hommes' and Matilda was buried in her 'Abbaye aux Dames'.

No one knows whether Cecily's life was a happy one, but she certainly played her part in ensuring the success of the Norman Conquest.

Also on this day:
1633 King Charles I was crowned King of Scotland, in Holyrood House, Edinburgh.
1815 The battle of Waterloo was fought, at which Napoleon was defeated by troops led by the future Duke of Wellington (See JUNE 20).
1896 Birth of Wallis, the future Duchess of Windsor, in Blue Ridge Summit, Pennsylvania, USA.

JUNE 19   1566
MARY, QUEEN OF SCOTS, GIVES BIRTH TO THE FUTURE KING JAMES VI AND I

Visitors to Edinburgh Castle can see the tiny, bleak room in which the 'wisest fool in Christendom' was born. It was only three months after Mary had witnessed the death of her secretary, David Rizzio (see MARCH 9), and she decided that Edinburgh Castle was a much safer place than Holyrood House in which to have her baby.

It was a difficult birth, and superstitious attempts were made to transfer the birth-pangs to one of Mary's companions, Lady Reres, who lay in a nearby bed hoping to help the queen by attracting the pains to herself by witchcraft. Unfortunately for Mary, however, the magic did not seem to work, and Mary 'began to wish she had never been married'.

After many hours the infant prince was born, with a caul over his face, a circumstance filled with superstitious significance: it was thought in Scotland that a caul gave protection against the Evil Eye, and bestowed the power of second sight. Any child born with a caul was thought to grow up with the gifts of an orator.

Edinburgh was filled with jubilation when the birth of James was announced, and it is recorded that five hundred bonfires were lit, and the booming sounds of the castle's artillery filled the air.

James, of course, was directly in line to the English throne, and posed yet further threat to Elizabeth, should she not marry and produce a child herself. When she learned of the birth, Elizabeth was later said to have burst out with jealousy: 'Alack, the Queen of Scots is lighter of a bonny son, and I am but of barren stock.'

JUNE 20   1685
A SECOND JAMES II IS DECLARED AT TAUNTON

James Scott, Duke of Monmouth, reached the pinnacle of his ambition on this day in the market-place of Taunton, in Somerset, when he was declared to be 'James II' – ignoring the fact that there was already a James II on the throne. A man from Bristol named Tilly read out a proclamation at the market cross:

> Whereas upon the decease of our Sovereign Lord King Charles the Second . . . the right of succession to the Crown . . . did legally descend and devolve upon the most illustrious and high-born Prince, James, Duke of Monmouth, son and heir-apparent of the said King Charles the Second; but James, Duke of York (taking advantage of the absence of the said James, Duke of Monmouth, beyond the seas) did first cause the said King to be poisoned and immediately thereon did usurp and invade the Crown and doth continue to do so. We, therefore, the noblemen, gentlemen and commoners here assembled . . . for the deliverance of the Kingdom from popery, tyranny and oppression, do recognise, publish and proclaim the said high and mighty Prince, James, Duke of Monmouth, our lawful and rightful sovereign and King, by the name of James the Second.

Thus, in an odd kind of way, for a few weeks England had *two* King James IIs!

The new monarch immediately proceeded to display his royalty by 'touching' sufferers for the King's Evil, and allowed his 'subjects' to show their loyalty by kissing his hands on bended knee.

Also on this day:

1837 Death of King William IV, aged seventy-one, at Windsor Castle. He had desperately wanted to celebrate another anniversary of Waterloo and had begged his doctors to 'try if you cannot tinker me up to last over that date'. He just managed it – see JUNE 18.

JUNE 21   1982
BIRTH OF PRINCE WILLIAM

Prince William, the first son of Prince Charles and Princess Diana, was born on this day in St Mary's Hospital, Paddington, at 9.03 p.m. He weighed 7lb 10oz (3.5kg) and according to Prince Charles he had 'a wisp of fair hair, sort of blondish, and blue eyes'. And he was named William Arthur Philip Louis.

If tradition is allowed to take place, Prince William will ascend the throne in due course as King William V, on the death of his father, the future Charles III.

Also on this day:
1377 Death of King Edward III, aged sixty-five, in Sheen Palace (later rebuilt as Richmond Palace).

THE PRESENT ORDER OF SUCCESSION

After the death of Queen Elizabeth II the order of succession is as follows:

1.	Prince Charles (born November 14 1948)
2.	Prince William (born June 21 1982)
3.	Prince Henry (born September 15 1984)
4.	Prince Andrew (born February 19 1960)
5.	Princess Beatrice (born August 8 1988)
6.	Princess Eugenie (born March 23 1990)
7.	Prince Edward (born March 10 1964)
8.	Lady Louise Windsor (born November 8 2003)
9.	Princess Anne (born August 15 1950)
10.	Peter Phillips (born November 15 1977)
11.	Zara Phillips (born May 15 1981)
12.	Viscount Linley (born November 3 1961)

The list continues on and on, but the further it goes the more liable it becomes to change with deaths and births. A great advantage in having a clear line of succession is that there is never any doubt and never any gap. The new sovereign is deemed to have succeeded to the throne the moment his or her predecessor has died: 'The king is dead – Long live the king!'

JUNE 22   1897
QUEEN VICTORIA CELEBRATES HER DIAMOND JUBILEE

Queen Victoria's reign was the longest in British history: 63 years and 216 days. By the time she died the vast majority of her subjects could remember no other monarch on the throne, and the awe and veneration she enjoyed as the 'Grandmother of Europe' was immense. Towards the end of her reign she celebrated two jubilees: the Golden Jubilee in 1887 and the Diamond Jubilee in 1897. These public demonstrations of loyalty were unique, reflecting the mystique enjoyed by the queen at the turn of the century.

Whereas the Golden Jubilee had been an international affair, with great pomp of visiting emperors, kings and queens, the Diamond Jubilee was a more domestic occasion, with representatives of the British Empire joining the dignitaries of the 'mother country'.

This was the day to celebrate Victoria's sixty years. The queen rode in an open carriage through the streets of London, including the poorest areas, acknowledging the cheers. One of the most impressive scenes of the day took place on the steps *outside* St Paul's Cathedral, where the entire royal family joined other guests of honour for an outdoor service. Many notables, including a hundred bishops, stood on the cathedral's steps and under the huge portico.

Luckily the day was brilliantly sunny and the queen sat in her carriage at the foot of the steps to take part in this great Service of Thanksgiving. There is a plaque on the steps leading up to the cathedral, marking this memorable occasion.

Also on this day:
1377   King Richard II, aged ten, succeeded to the throne on the death of his grandfather, Edward III.
1911   Coronation of King George V and Queen Mary in Westminster Abbey.

JUNE 23   1503
PRINCE HENRY IS BETROTHED TO HIS WIDOWED SISTER-IN-LAW

Prince Arthur had died in April 1502, and his widow Catherine of Aragon was naturally expecting to go back home to Spain. For their part,

Catherine's parents, Ferdinand and Isabella of Spain, not only wanted their daughter back, but also the dowry they had given at the time of her marriage, and the revenues from Cornwall, Chester and Wales, which had been given to Catherine as Princess of Wales.

However, Henry VII was most unwilling to let such a valuable political pawn slip away from him, and made immediate proposals to her parents that she should marry his younger son Henry. The agreement by which this marriage should take place was signed this day in 1503. Of course, the Pope's agreement had still to be obtained, but this, no doubt, would come later . . .

Meanwhile, young Henry still had some growing up to do. He was not quite twelve.

Also on this day:

1894 Birth of the future King Edward VIII (later Duke of Windsor), son of the future King George V and Queen Mary, at White Lodge, Richmond Park, Surrey.

JUNE 24   1348
KING EDWARD III FOUNDS THE MOST NOBLE ORDER OF THE GARTER

King Edward III had vowed to establish an Order of Knighthood after the style of King Arthur's legendary Knights of the Round Table, and after the resounding victory over the French at Crécy in 1346 he decided that the time was right to fulfil that vow. On this day in 1348 the first official ceremony of this new Order of the Garter was held at Windsor. It was a part of the celebrations held to mark the successful birth of Queen Philippa's sixth son, William.

The traditional tale is that some time before this, at a court ball, the Countess of Salisbury dropped her garter, and this was picked up by the king. As the onlookers were raising their eyebrows, the king put the garter round his own knee, saying '*Honi soit qui mal y pense*' ('evil be to him who evil thinks'). But no one will ever know the precise details of this tale.

Yet the Order of the Garter is the oldest surviving order of chivalry in Europe, and was founded in honour of the Holy Trinity, the Blessed Virgin Mary, St George and St Edward the Confessor. Its chapel is St George's, Windsor, where the banners of the current holders of the Order are always on display.

Awards of the Garter are always the personal choice of the sovereign. Sir Winston Churchill received the Order from Queen Elizabeth II in 1953 as one of the first acts of her reign.

Also on this day:

1291 Death of Eleanor of Provence, wife of Henry III, aged sixty-nine. She died and was buried at a nunnery in Amesbury, Wiltshire.

1509 Coronation of King Henry VIII, aged eighteen, and Catherine of Aragon, in Westminster Abbey.

JUNE 25   1857
ALBERT IS OFFICIALLY CREATED PRINCE CONSORT

It comes as a surprise to find that Victoria's beloved Albert was not in fact given the title of Prince Consort until they had been married over seventeen years. In the early years of their marriage Victoria jealously kept all official affairs away from Albert. 'I am the husband, not the master in the house,' he complained.

Then, one day, as she was being driven up Constitution Hill, Victoria was shot at by a feeble-minded youth (see FEBRUARY 29). The pistol's bullet missed, but Victoria recognised how vulnerable she was without a properly appointed Regent, and she began to allow Albert more and more influence in state business: he gradually became her private secretary, household major-domo and political adviser.

At last, many years later, and well after the success of the Great Exhibition, Victoria personally appointed Albert to be Prince Consort. Quite apart from being a reward for his energetic services for so many years, this title also enabled him to assume a proper place in the the matter of precedence. This mattered enormously to the queen, for she did not like the thought that the growing Prince of Wales was treated as a more important prince than his father.

Sadly, Albert was to enjoy his increased status only four-and-a-half years before his death in 1861.

Also on this day:

1483 King Edward V, aged twelve, was deposed and the crown seized by his uncle Richard, Duke of York, on the following day; he thus became Richard III.

JUNE 26   1830
DEATH OF GEORGE IV

Those who saw George IV in the last weeks of his life were aghast at his gluttony and lethargy. One eye-witness wrote: 'The king leads a most extraordinary life. He never gets up till six in the afternoon. They come to him and open the window-curtains at six or seven in the morning; he breakfasts in bed, does whatever business he can be brought to transact in bed too; he reads every newspaper quite through, dozes three or four hours, gets up in time for dinner, and goes to bed between ten and eleven.' His body became vast; he hated exercise; he loathed fresh air; all he wanted to do was doze and drink himself into oblivion.

Tales of his capacity for eating and drinking were bandied about. The Duke of Wellington wrote to a friend that the king's breakfast the previous day had been 'a Pidgeon and Beef Steak Pye of which he eat two Pigeons and three Beefsteaks. Three parts of a Bottle of Mozelle, a Glass of Dry Champagne, two Glasses of Port & a Glass of Brandy! He had taken Laudanum the night before and again before this breakfast, again last night and again this Morning!'

No constitution could withstand the onslaughts which George IV flung upon himself, and he died at Windsor aged sixty-seven, of a ruptured blood vessel in the stomach and cirrhosis of the liver. He was succeeded by his brother, King William IV, aged sixty-four.

Sir Wathen Waller, the king's physician, was with him in his final moments and afterwards wrote that 'he took my hand in his and I felt him instantly press it harder than usual and he looked at me with an eager eye and exclaimed, "My dear boy, this is Death!"'

Also on this day:
1657 Oliver Cromwell was inaugurated as Lord Protector for the second time.

JUNE 27   1743
THE LAST ENGLISH KING TO TAKE PART IN A BATTLE – GEORGE II

Although it sounds improbable for a 59-year-old Hanoverian monarch to lead an army to victory, this is what happened at the Battle of Dettingen, fought this day in 1743.

George II assumed command of a 40,000-strong army, composed of British, Hanoverian, Hessian and Austrian troops. They were fighting against the French in the war over the Austrian succession. The king's personal baggage train was enormous, comprising 13 carriages, 54 carts, 35 wagons and 662 horses. He was accompanied on this military expedition by his son William, Duke of Cumberland, who was shortly to gain the opprobrious nickname 'Butcher' for his brutality to the Scots at Culloden.

Both the king and his son displayed great bravery, and George personally encouraged his troops saying: 'Now, boys, now for the honour of England; fire and behave bravely and the French will soon run!'

The French did run, and George achieved popularity as never before. Handel even wrote some special music, composing his *Dettingen Te Deum* in honour of the occasion.

JUNE 28 1838
QUEEN VICTORIA'S OWN ACCOUNT OF HER CORONATION

After the elderly ugly uncle-kings, the arrival on the throne of a vivacious teenage girl was certainly a reversal of fortune for the British monarchy. Victoria was only eighteen when she succeeded to the throne, and nineteen at her coronation.

Victoria's diaries throughout her life are so vivid that her own account of the occasion cannot be bettered. After the enthronement, homage and communion, she describes what happened:

> I then again descended from the Throne, and repaired with all the Peers bearing the Regalia, my Ladies and Train-bearers, to St Edward's Chapel, as it is called; but which, as Lord Melbourne said, was more unlike a Chapel than anything he had ever seen; for, what was called an Altar was covered with sandwiches, bottles of wine, &c.
>
> The Archbishop came in and ought to have delivered the Orb to me, but I had already got it. There we waited for some minutes; Lord Melbourne took a glass of wine, for he seemed completely tired; the Procession being formed, I replaced my Crown (which I had taken off for a few minutes) took the Orb in my left hand and the Sceptre in my right, and thus loaded proceeded through the Abbey, which resounded with cheers, to the first Robing-room . . .

And here we waited for at least an hour, with *all* my ladies and train-bearers; the Princesses went away about half an hour before I did; the Archbishop had put the ring on the wrong finger (actually it had been made for the wrong finger, the fifth instead of the fourth), and the consequence was that I had the greatest difficulty to take it off again – which I at last did with great pain.

At about ½ p. 4 I re-entered my carriage, the Crown on my head and Sceptre and Orb in my hand, and we proceeded the same way as we came – the crowds if possible having increased. The enthusiasm, affection and loyalty was really touching, and I shall ever remember this day as the proudest of my life. I came home at a little after 6 – really not feeling tired.

Also on this day:

1461   Coronation of King Edward IV, aged eighteen, in Westminster Abbey, after he had seized the throne from Henry VI.

1491   Birth of the future King Henry VIII at Greenwich Palace, London, son of King Henry VII and Elizabeth of York.

JUNE 29   1509
DEATH OF THE LAST LANCASTRIAN, MARGARET BEAUFORT

Margaret Beaufort, Countess of Richmond, was a formidable old lady with royal Lancastrian blood in her veins. She was the great-granddaughter of John of Gaunt, so when Henry VI was murdered she was arguably the next in line to the throne. However, her son, the future Henry VII, was more than ready to take up the crown on her behalf: she provided his legitimate excuse to become king.

She was only twelve when she married Edmund Tudor, Earl of Richmond, and thirteen when she gave birth to the future Henry VII. She was widowed just a year later and made two further marriages. She was a great-great-grand-daughter of the great Plantagenet King Edward III and grandmother of the great Tudor King Henry VIII. She lived to see her grandson Henry and Catherine of Aragon crowned, and died just five days later.

But apart from being so royally connected, Margaret's contribution to English history goes much deeper, as she founded two Cambridge colleges, St John's and Christ's; endowed two divinity professorships, at Oxford and

Cambridge; supported William Caxton in setting up his printing-press; and became the first woman in England to achieve success as an author in print.

The passing of Margaret Beaufort marked the end of an era. Without actually using the title, she was one of the greatest of all queen mothers.

JUNE 30   1559

NOSTRADAMUS IS PROVED CORRECT AND MARY, QUEEN OF SCOTS, BECOMES QUEEN OF FRANCE

Nostradamus did not predict that Mary would become Queen of France, but he certainly predicted the circumstances which led to her coming to the French throne. In four famous lines of curiously allusive verse Nostradamus prophesied that the King of France would be killed in a duel, specifically describing that he would be wounded in the eye and die a 'cruel death'.

The actual prophecy was among 353 predictions which he published in 1555, four years before the event took place, and it was the talk of European courts. Henri II of France was fond of jousting and his queen, Catherine de' Medici, was so worried about the prediction that she summoned Nostradamus to Paris to explain exactly what he meant.

It was his habit to produce his prophecies in succinct, often obscure, four-line verses, and the one which had so perturbed the queen went like this:

> Le lyon ieune le vieux surmontera,
> En champ bellique par singulier duelle:
> Dans caige d'or les yeux luy creuera,
> Deux classes une, puis, mourir, mort cruelle.

Translated, this has been rendered as:

> The young lion will overcome the old,
> in a field of combat in a single fight.
> He will pierce his eyes in a golden cage,
> two wounds in one, he then dies a cruel death.

On this day in 1559 Henri II sustained a mortal injury in a freak jousting accident. He had been challenging Gabriel, Comte de Montgomery, son of the Captain of his Scottish Guard, and as both men had a lion on their coat of arms, there was a 'young lion' (Montgomery, aged about twenty-eight) against an 'old lion' (the king himself, aged forty).

On the third bout Montgomery's lance broke and a splinter pierced the king's gilt helmet (the 'golden cage') and entered his face and brain just above the eye. It was recorded that he had also received a second wound in the throat. The king died in agony on July 10.

This particular prophecy made Nostradamus famous throughout Europe. It had been known about for years, dreaded by the Queen of France, and now dramatically and publicly fulfilled. Henri was succeeded by his fifteen-year-old son, Francis, who was already married to Mary, Queen of Scots. Thus Mary, aged seventeen, now became Queen of France as well as of Scotland. And rather ominously for Elizabeth I, she also flaunted the royal arms of England.

JULY 1 1969
CHARLES IS INVESTED AS PRINCE OF WALES

Although the title 'Prince of Wales' is invariably given to the eldest son of the monarch, it is not a title which comes automatically at birth. The title is bestowed at a time deemed appropriate.

When Elizabeth II became queen in 1952, Charles was not quite four. Nevertheless the townsfolk of Caernarvon petitioned her to create her son Prince of Wales. At that time Elizabeth considered Charles too young, and it was not until he was aged ten, and a schoolboy at Cheam, that she felt that the time was ripe for him to receive the title. She announced to the people of Wales that: 'When he is grown up, I will present him to you at Caernarvon.' Even so, the actual investiture ceremony did not take place until July 1 1969, when Charles was twenty.

By now, this was the television age, and the photogenic ceremony in the grounds of Caernarvon Castle was staged with an eye for a huge television audience by the Earl of Snowdon, then still married to Princess Margaret. Hence the investiture took place on a Plexiglas rostrum with ultra-modern designs of such symbols as the Prince of Wales feathers.

Welsh Nationalists, although a minority, were fiercely opposed to the event and elaborate precautions were put in place against possible attacks, and a boom was stretched across the water approach to Caernarvon Castle. Two would-be bombers did in fact inadvertently blow themselves up early on the morning of the investiture. But in the event, the royal occasion passed off triumphantly.

Charles had gained popularity in Wales by learning the language and had made a speech in Welsh only a few weeks earlier. He is the twenty-fourth Prince of Wales since the title was created in 1301, but is probably the only one to have taken the trouble to familiarise himself with its difficult language. (See FEBRUARY 7.)

Also on this day:

1690 King William III defeated the former King James II at the Battle of the Boyne, near Drogheda in County Louth, Ireland. William sustained a slight bullet wound in the shoulder; James, after the battle, fled to France.

1961 Birth of Lady Diana, future Princess of Wales, at Park House, Sandringham, Norfolk. She was the daughter of John, 8th Earl of Spencer.

JULY 2 1644
ROYALIST DEFEAT AT THE BATTLE OF MARSTON MOOR

Charles I must have sensed that ultimate defeat was a distinct possibility after the overwhelming defeat of his troops on this day at the Battle of Marston Moor. It was the first of Cromwell's major victories, and at midnight, when fighting ceased, more than four thousand royalists and their allies lay dead on the battlefield.

Prince Rupert, who was leading the king's troops, had just successfully relieved the city of York, which was being beseiged. As he confronted Cromwell's troops at Marston Moor it was so late in the day that he thought it was too late to give battle, and dismissed his men so as to allow them to eat. This was a fatal mistake, and Cromwell seized the initiative. 'God made them as stubble to our swords,' said Cromwell.

Marston Moor is about eight miles west of York, and a model of the battle can be seen in York Museum.

JULY 3 1872
THE ALBERT MEMORIAL GOES ON VIEW TO THE PUBLIC

George Gilbert Scott's design for 'a kind of ciborium to protect a statue of the Prince' won the approval of Queen Victoria, who monitored the undertaking with close interest. She came privately to view the almost-complete memorial on July 1 but made no comment. Her satisfaction, however, was expressed by the fact that she knighted Scott for his effort.

The hoardings were taken down on July 3, and on this day the public were allowed to wander round and form their opinions of this unique work, 175ft high and costing £120,000. Rather surprisingly, there was no official opening ceremony. The 14ft tall statue of Prince Albert, however, was not yet in place, and the public had to wait another four years before this great bronze statue was erected. Covered in gold, it depicted Albert seated and holding a catalogue of the Great Exhibition in his hand. The sculptor was John Foley, an Irish artist, whose other works include the statues of Edmund Burke and Oliver Goldsmith at Trinity College, Dublin.

The statue was stripped of its gilt during the war, lest it should become a landmark for enemy aircraft. It was regilded and unveiled again in 1998 and has now once again become the magnificent memorial that Victoria had wished it to be. Floodlit at night it is one of the great sights of London, though critics have damned it down the decades.

Also on this day:

1816 Death of Mrs Dorothy Jordan, aged fifty-five. She was the long-time partner of the future King William IV and mother of his ten illegitimate children. She died in poverty at St Cloud, France.

1842 Shots were fired at Queen Victoria (see FEBRUARY 29).

JULY 4   1776
GEORGE III AND THE AMERICAN DECLARATION OF INDEPENDENCE

In 1776 George III had been king for sixteen years: King of Great Britain and Ireland; King of the thirteen colonies of America; King of the West Indies; King of Canada. Later in his long reign he would become King of Sierra Leone, Gambia, New South Wales, parts of India, Ceylon (Sri Lanka), Malacca, Singapore, Java, Cape Colony, Gibraltar, Corsica, Malta, the Ionian Islands, and Minorca. He was also the Elector of Hanover, and until January 1 1801 he kept up the royal tradition that he was still King of France.

It came hard, therefore, on July 4 1776, when in Philadelphia the Declaration of Independence boldly stated that 'the history of the present King of Great Britain is a history of repeated injuries and usurpations, all having in direct object the establishment of an absolute tyranny over these states'. His former American subjects went on to describe George III himself as 'totally unfit to be the ruler of a free people'.

As events unfolded, and with a growing sense of failure, George sat down to write a draft of abdication, so humiliated was he by this act of defiance. What concerned him most was the possibility that this declaration of independence would be followed by similar declarations by all the rest of his colonies. The abdication never occurred, but it is a measure of the stress felt by the king at this time.

It says much for George that a few years later, on June 1 1785, he received the first American Ambassador, John Adams, at the Court of St James's. 'I was the last to consent to the separation,' he told Adams, 'but the separation having been made and having become inevitable, I have always said, as I say now, that I would be the first to meet the friendship of the United States as an independent power.'

Also on this day:

1394 Death of Mary de Bohun, aged about twenty-six; she was the first wife of the future Henry IV and mother of the future Henry V. She was buried in the church of St Mary de Castro, Leicester. Her remains were later removed to Trinity Hospital, Leicester, where her somewhat damaged effigy is to be seen.

JULY 5   1441
HENRY VI LAYS THE FOUNDATION STONE
OF A NEW SCHOOL AT ETON

Henry's great gifts to England were his two complementary educational establishments: Eton College (the College Roiall of Our Ladie of Eton), within sight of his castle at Windsor; and King's College (the College Roiall of Our Ladie and St Nicholas, of Cambridge). The young king was not yet twenty when he laid the foundation stone of Eton College on this day in 1441. He personally drew up the statutes, making sure that all ten Fellows were to be skilled in plainsong, and at least one of the ten clerks should be able to play the organ.

As for the disciplinary regulations, it was decreed that 'the Fellows, Chaplains, Clerks, Scholars and Choristers are forbidden to grow long hair or a beard, or wear peaked shoes, or red, green, or white hose; they shall not carry swords, long knives or other arms or frequent taverns or playhouses; they shall not keep among themselves or in the College, hounds, nets, ferrets, sparrow-hawks, or goshawks for sport, or a monkey, a bear, a fox, a hart, a hind, a doe, or a badger, or any other strange beast that would be unprofitable or dangerous to the College; there shall be no jumping or wrestling, or throwing of stones or balls in the Church, the Cloister, or the Hall, lest damage be done to the walls or windows; there shall be no disputing, rivalries, factions, scurrilous talk, or invidious comparisons in College.'

Henry, it would seem, was much more fitted to be a headmaster than a king.

JULY 6   1685
THE LAST BATTLE ON ENGLISH SOIL: MONMOUTH IS DEFEATED AT SEDGEMOOR

It was a foregone conclusion. The Duke of Monmouth, King Charles's bastard son, was no match for the king's experienced troops, commanded by the Earl of Feversham and John Churchill, the future Duke of Marlborough. After a night of confused fighting Monmouth stripped off his armour and galloped off into the early morning mists, leaving his ragged followers to be hacked to pieces.

Adam Wheeler, a drummer of the Wiltshire Militia, wrote an inventory of the rebel prisoners as they were rounded up and taken into the nearby Weston Zoyland Church: it makes pathetic reading. He listed:

- 53, tied together
- 32, tied together
- 2, wounded in their legs, crawling upon the ground on their hands and knees to Weston Church
- 37, many tied and pinnacled together
- 1, alone, being naked, only his drawers on
- 1, more running, being forced along by two horsemen with blows and riding close after him
- 47, most tied together, such of them as had a good coat or anything worth the pilling were fairly stripped of it.

The full total came to 238. Drummer Wheeler concludes:

The last was very remarkable and to be admired; for being shot through the shoulder and wounded in the belly, he lay on his back in the sun stripped naked for the space of ten or eleven hours, in that scorching hot day to the admiration of all the spectators. As he lay, a great crowd of soldiers came about him and reproached him, called him:

'Thou Monmouth Dog, how long have you been with your King Monmouth?' His answer was, that if he had breath, he would tell them.

Afterwards he was pitied and they opened round about him, and gave him more liberty of the air, and there was one soldier that gave him a pair of drawers to cover his nakedness.

Afterwards, having a long stick in his hand, he walked feebly to Weston Church, where he died that night, with two wounded men more.

As for the wretched Duke of Monmouth, he was found in a ditch a few miles from present-day Bournemouth, miserably hiding beneath ferns and bracken.

Also on this day:

1189 Death of King Henry II, aged fifty-five, at Chinon, France. He was buried at Fontevrault.

1483 Coronation of King Richard III, aged thirty, at Westminster Abbey.

1534 Sir Thomas More was beheaded on Tower Hill for refusing to accept King Henry VIII as Head of the English Church.

1553 Death of King Edward VI, aged fifteen, at Greenwich Palace, London.

1660 King Charles II, recently restored to the throne, resumed the practice begun by Edward the Confessor, of 'touching for evil'.

1893 Marriage of the future King George V, aged twenty-eight, and Princess Mary of Teck, only daughter of Francis, Duke of Teck, at St James's Palace, London.

JULY 7   1789
GEORGE III TAKES A DIP IN THE SEA AT WEYMOUTH

'Mad King George' badly needed a holiday in 1789 to help restore his failing health. His brother, the Duke of Gloucester, had taken a house on the seafront a few years previously, so the king decided that Gloucester Lodge would be just the place for a ten-week break. It was comfortably well away from the London crowds.

Accordingly, King George and Queen Charlotte, with Princesses Charlotte, Augusta and Elizabeth, set off for their Dorset holiday on June 24, and their journey down to the West Country was the occasion of great displays of loyalty in the towns *en route*. Arriving at Weymouth, the royal family walked along the promenade after their evening meal, and the king remarked, 'I never enjoyed a sight so pleasing.'

In the weeks which followed, the king and queen behaved just like any parents on holiday with their children: going on boat-trips, visiting nearby towns such as Sherborne, Milton Abbey and Lulworth, attending amateur entertainments in Weymouth, watching pony racing on the sands, and above all, bathing in the sea. Everywhere the king went he was cheered wildly. Loyalty knew no bounds.

The first royal dip took place on July 7. Fanny Burney recorded the event: 'A machine follows the royal one into the sea, filled with fiddlers, who play "God Save the King", as His Majesty takes his plunge.' Queen Charlotte did not share the king's enthusiasm, coming back from one boat-trip 'very wet and bedraggled'. However, George came back to Weymouth twelve times between 1789 and 1805, staying for weeks at a time. Of course, the reputation of Weymouth and sea-bathing in general was greatly enhanced. Arguably, the development of the seaside holiday industry was the result of this visit.

Significantly, this first royal holiday to Weymouth coincided exactly with the fall of the Bastille in Paris. In fact, as the French prison was being stormed on July 14, King George was enjoying a boat-trip off Portland Bill.

Also on this day:

1307   Death of King Edward I, aged sixty-eight, at Burgh-by-Sands, near
       Carlisle. King Edward II, aged twenty-three, succeeded his father on the
       throne.

JULY 8   1376
EDWARD, THE BLACK PRINCE, IS EXORCISED
ON HIS DEATHBED

Nowadays, in our multi-racial society, young people may well be confused and misled by the curious nickname of the 'Black Prince'. In fact he was one of the greatest of all the many Princes of Wales who died before inheriting the throne. His name refers to the black armour he used to wear.

Prince Edward, born in 1330, was the son of Edward III. His military skill was phenomenal: at the age of sixteen he commanded the right wing at the Battle of Crécy, contributing to a great English victory over the French. Ten years later he won another resounding victory at Poitiers. It was said of him that he went against no army that he did not conquer, and he attacked no city that he did not take. But he coupled his military prowess with great magnanimity to those he conquered. He was, in effect, the epitome of a 'verray, parfit, gentil knight' as described by his near-contemporary, Geoffrey Chaucer.

Ill-health struck him down in mid-life. It is certain that if he had lived he would have been a magnificent king, a worthy successor to his father Edward III. But some form of wasting disease, probably cancer, killed him just before his forty-sixth birthday, and his death triggered off the troublesome period in English history occasioned by the weakness of his son, Richard II, who came to the throne aged only ten.

In his last hours the Black Prince was annoyed to be visited by Sir Richard Strong, who had offended him in the past, and he told him angrily to leave the room. The fit of temper was too much for him and he sank back in exhaustion, clearly on the brink of death. The Bishop of Bangor was appalled. He felt that Edward would die in sin if he could not bring himself to forgive his enemies, so he begged the prince to pardon Strong. 'I will,' was the reply: but this was not good enough for the bishop, who asked him to rephrase the response. Again and again the prince replied 'I will', and remained adamant in refusing a clear statement.

'An evil spirit holds his tongue – we must drive it away, or he will die in his sins,' declared the good bishop, and proceeded to sprinkle holy water in the four corners of the room, commanding the Evil One to depart.

It is reported that the Black Prince gave in without a struggle, offered up a prayer of forgiveness, and gave up the ghost. He lay in state in Westminster for four months and then, such was the veneration paid to him, he was taken to be buried in 'the most sacred spot in England' – beside the tomb of Thomas Becket in Canterbury Cathedral.

Also on this day:

975   Death of King Edgar, aged about thirty-two. He was buried at Glastonbury Abbey, Somerset. King Edward, later to be known as 'Edward the Martyr', aged about twelve, succeeded to the throne on the death of his father.

1492 Death of Elizabeth Woodville, aged about fifty-five, widow of King Edward IV, in Bermondsey Abbey. She was buried in St George's Chapel, Windsor.

JULY 9   1437
DEATH OF HENRY IV'S WIDOW,
THE 'WITCH QUEEN'

Joanna of Navarre outlived her husband Henry IV by twenty-four years, suffering strange and unpleasant treatment from her stepson Henry V, who caused her to be imprisoned more than four years for being a witch!

Henry V believed that she was trafficking with the powers of darkness to kill him; her accuser was her confessor, John Randolf, a Minorite friar.

Henry ordered that Joanna should be stripped of all she possessed: lands, property, money, furniture, even clothes, and then she was put in close confinement, first at Leeds Castle and then at Pevensey Castle. She was never given any opportunity to speak in her own defence.

The actual details of John Randolf's accusation are not known, for it is recorded that when he was discussing matters with the priest of St Peter's ad Vincula, the good priest decided to end his conversation with Randolf once and for all by strangling him.

Henry's motive for treating his royal stepmother in such a manner was probably simply to increase his revenue for his French wars; however, eventually his conscience must have pricked him, for he gave orders that she should be released and given five or six dresses in recompense.

Happily, Joanna lived out the rest of her life in regal comfort, and was accorded love and respect by her stepgrandson, Henry VI. She died on this day in 1427 and her body was taken to Canterbury Cathedral, where tourists can still see her beautiful effigy beside that of her husband Henry IV.

However, the accusation of sorcery still hung faintly about her, and earned her the title of the 'Witch Queen' at Havering Bower, where she lived.

JULY 10   1553
LADY JANE GREY IS PROCLAIMED QUEEN

The fifteen-year-old Jane was horrified to be told that she was to be queen. She knew with absolute clarity that she was being cruelly manipulated and that she had no right to accept what was being offered. On this day, her father-in-law, the Duke of Northumberland, and her own parents summoned her to the Chamber of State and led her to her place on a dais beneath the royal canopy.

After a preamble the duke declared: 'His Majesty [i.e. the newly deceased Edward VI] hath named Your Grace as the heir to the crown of England. . . . Therefore you should cheerfully take upon you the name, title and estates of Queen of England, France and Ireland, with all the royalties and pre-eminences to the same belonging; receiving at our hands the first-fruits of our humble duty – now tendered to you upon our knees – which shortly will be paid to you by the rest of the kingdom.'

Jane was stupefied. She broke down and sobbed. Then she made one final attempt to extricate herself from this nightmare. Her reply was memorable: 'The crown is not my right, and pleaseth me not. The Lady Mary is the rightful heir.'

She prayed to God for guidance, but as none came, she decided that this was tacit permission to accept the crown. 'If what hath been given to me is lawfully mine, may Thy Divine Majesty grant me such spirit and grace that I may govern to Thy glory and service, to the advantage of this realm.'

Her fate was sealed.

JULY 11   1982
PRINCE CHARLES WELCOMES TROOPS HOME FROM THE FALKLANDS CONFLICT

On this day in 1982 Prince Charles welcomed back the liner *Canberra*, which was bringing troops back home to Portsmouth after the military conflict in the Falklands. His brother, Prince Andrew, had experienced active service during the conflict, serving as the pilot of a Sea King helicopter. Andrew's most dangerous moments came when he had used his helicopter as a decoy for the vicious Exocet missiles fired at the British Task Force ships. 'It was horrific and terrible,' he is reported to have said, 'and something I will never forget.' While Prince Andrew was still in the air the *Atlantic Conveyor* supply ship was hit by missiles and Andrew himself helped to rescue sailors from the sea.

Prince Charles was no longer on active service, but he wrote at the time that he felt frustrated at his inability to take part. He spent much time meeting returning units and was an active patron of the South Atlantic Fund, which gave support to those who were bereaved or wounded in the Falklands campaign.

JULY 12   1174
HENRY II DOES PENANCE FOR THE MURDER OF THOMAS BECKET

Henry had already done penance for the murder of Becket at Avranches Cathedral in Normandy. Today, only a stone slab remains of that building, with a notice to tell visitors that Henry knelt here to ask God's pardon. It was inevitable that he should also visit the actual spot in Canterbury Cathedral where Archbishop Becket was hacked down, and on this day in

1174, three-and-a-half years after Thomas's death, Henry came to make a dramatic gesture of repentance for the terrible deed done in his name.

He walked barefoot through the streets of Canterbury dressed in just a woollen shirt and a rough cloak. Then, entering the cathedral, he kissed the sacred stone where Becket had fallen and knelt with groans and tears at the tomb in the crypt, praying.

In penitence he took off his cloak and allowed himself to be beaten with a monastic rod, the *balai*: five strokes from each bishop and abbot, and three more from each of the eighty monks. Finally, he passed the whole night in the crypt, still unwashed and with his feet still bleeding and muddied from his walk through the streets.

Early next morning he heard mass, drank from the Martyr's Well, accepted a phial of water mixed with the saint's blood, and left Canterbury. On returning to London, Henry learned that his great enemy William the Lion, King of Scotland, had been taken prisoner at exactly the time he had been making peace with the martyr. Clearly, the Saint had responded!

Also on this day:

1472   Marriage of King Richard III, aged twenty, and Anne Neville,
         daughter of the Earl of Warwick ('the Kingmaker'), at Westminster Abbey.
1543   Marriage of King Henry VIII, aged fifty-two, and Catherine Parr, his
         sixth wife, daughter of Sir Thomas Parr, at Hampton Court Palace.

JULY 13   1818
WILLIAM AND ADELAIDE – A VERY LOW-KEY
ROYAL WEDDING

George III was still nominally on the throne and Prinny was Regent, but as time went on it became more and more obvious that Prinny's brother William would be the next monarch after Prinny himself. It was therefore a matter of urgency for William to find a proper wife for himself.

It was not a situation he relished. After all, he was living quietly and happily with his partner, an actress called Dorothy Jordan, and their ten children. However, duty called and he sent out proposal after proposal to prospective brides, and with monotonous regularity refusal after refusal came back. Meanwhile he had fallen desperately in love with an English heiress, Miss Wykeham.

Both his brother George and Parliament refused permission for William to marry Miss Wykeham, so the search for a bride had to continue. At last his patience was rewarded: it was to be the 26-year-old Princess Adelaide of the small German Duchy of Saxe-Meiningen. William was fifty-two; unmarried with ten illegitimate children; hopelessly in love with Miss Wykeham; desperately in debt; and on the brink of marriage to an unknown princess exactly half his age. He was miserable. Writing to his eldest son, he poured out his heart:

> The Princess of Saxe-Meiningen is doomed, poor, dear, innocent young creature, to be my wife. I cannot, I will not, I must not ill use her . . .
> What time may produce in my heart, I can not tell, but at present I think and exist only for Miss Wykeham. But enough of your father's misery.

Such was the background when Adelaide arrived in London one July evening in 1818, accompanied by her mother, and settled without any fuss into Grillon's Hotel in Albemarle Street. Prinny and William were summoned to meet them, arriving at about midnight. They all enjoyed a happy supper together – and it was clear that despite everyone's fears, Adelaide would fit in and make an acceptable wife.

William hated ceremony. They were married very quietly on this day in 1818 in old Queen Charlotte's private room at Kew Palace, where an old toilet-table was draped over and turned into an altar with a couple of candles and a prayer book. After this, there was an outdoor family picnic near the Chinese pagoda in Kew gardens. It was a genuinely happy occasion.

1837

THE YOUNG QUEEN VICTORIA TAKES UP RESIDENCE IN BUCKINGHAM PALACE

Victoria's uncle, the extravagant George IV, spent vast sums on enlarging 'Buckingham House' and converting it into a palace for himself. However, he never lived to enjoy it, and when he died in 1830, his brother William IV ridiculed the place and said he would never occupy it.

When the Houses of Parliament were burned down in 1834, William IV came up with the bright idea that the palace might be converted into a new building for the Lords and Commons. It is an intriguing thought that this might actually have happened, but Parliament showed no relish for transferring itself to another site. Reluctantly, therefore, William decided that he would, after all, take it over.

In fact he died just a month after it was completed, and he was succeeded by his niece, the eighteen-year-old Princess Victoria. She had no inhibitions whatsoever, and moved from Kensington into the new palace within three weeks of becoming queen. On July 13 1837 she drove there in state, wildly cheered by her new subjects. And it was Victoria herself who decided that it should be called 'Buckingham Palace'.

Quickly Victoria established a court orchestra, held parties, invited friends and foreign royalty, and a totally new royal scene began to emerge, vastly different from that of the previous occupants of the throne. But by 1845 she was beginning to feel that there was a 'total want of accommodation for our little family'.

Also on this day:

1911   Investiture of the future King Edward VIII as Prince of Wales, at Caernarvon Castle (see FEBRUARY 7).

JULY 14   1746
LUCKY PRINCE CHARLES FINDS A CAVE TO HIDE IN

It was now two months since his disastrous defeat at Culloden, and Bonnie Prince Charlie was still on the run, with the English troops scouring the Scottish landscape for him. Already he had made his famous crossing to the Isle of Skye with Flora Macdonald, dressed as 'Betty Burke', her maidservant, but clearly he could not live there for ever, and so in early July he disguised himself again, this time as 'Lewie Caw', a manservant with a sore face bandaged up with a scarf, and crossed back to the mainland, hoping to find a way back to France.

The next three weeks were the worst of his life as he made his escape. He lived rough, sheltering in barns or ditches, guided by various loyal companions who risked their lives trying to help him. Luckily, on July 14 he met up with a group of men who were also on the run after Culloden, and who were living in a cave near Glenmoriston. They were delighted to accept the prince among them, and shared what little food they could forage with him. In Jacobite lore this group came to be known as the 'eight men of

Glenmoriston' and they solemnly swore an oath of fidelity to their prince. One of them, Patrick Grant, spoke of this time many years later, describing how they would be 'all sitting round in a circle when eating or drinking, every one having his own morsel on his knee, and the Prince would never allow us to keep off our bonnets when in his company'.

Rather ruefully, the prince himself spoke of how they used to bring him his drinking-water in those 'bonnets'!

In all, after the battle of Culloden (see APRIL 16), Bonnie Prince Charlie spent five months as a fugitive from the English troops. It was not until September 19 that he managed to board a French frigate, *L'Heureux*, at Loch nan Uamh, where he had landed fourteen months earlier.

That was the last he saw of Britain.

Also on this day:

1077   Bishop Odo orders a 240ft-long tapestry to be made for the dedication of the cathedral at Bayeux, Normandy, showing the entire story of the Norman Conquest of England.

1789   Fall of the Bastille, signalling the beginning of the French Revolution.

JULY 15   1685
EXECUTION OF THE DUKE OF MONMOUTH

The finale of the great Dorset and Somerset rebellion came on this day, with the execution of the Duke of Monmouth on Tower Hill. He had been desperate for some sort of pardon or reconciliation with his uncle James II, but rumour had it that a final letter which he had written to the king was never delivered.

Early on the morning of his execution Monmouth signed a declaration, witnessed by several bishops: 'I declare that the title of King was forced upon me, and that it was very much contrary to my opinion when I was proclaimed. For the satisfaction of the world, I do declare that the King [i.e. Charles II] told me he was never married to my mother. Having declared this, I hope that the King, who is now, will not let my children suffer on this account.'

On the scaffold he was urged to make a speech of confession, but this he refused to do. 'I will make no speeches. I came to die,' he said, and asked to feel the axe. He complained, 'I fear it is not sharp enough.' He was right. After three unsuccessful strokes, Jack Ketch, the executioner swore: 'God damn me! I can do no more. My heart fails me,' and threw down the axe, leaving the poor victim still alive. The horrified onlookers roared their disapproval and Ketch was forced to carry on with his work: he was notorious for his clumsy bungling.

Two more attempts with the axe still failed to sever his head, so Ketch had to finish the wretched business with his knife.

Monmouth's friend, Lord Bruce, wrote: 'Thus died ignominiously the finest nobleman eyes ever saw as to his exterior, and that was all, save that he was of the most courteous and polite behaviour.'

JULY 16   1377
CORONATION OF THE TEN-YEAR-OLD RICHARD II

On the death of the Black Prince (see JULY 8) the crown had to skip a generation; thus, when Edward III died, his ten-year-old grandson Richard came to the throne. He was very much a puppet-king, ruled by his uncles. His coronation on this day in 1377, just a year after the death of his father and three weeks after the death of his grandfather, was an elaborate and stagy affair. Clearly his uncles were quite ready to give him all the pomp and ceremony so long as they kept the power for themselves.

On the previous day, as he rode through the streets in the traditional procession from the Tower of London, his entourage was dressed in white to symbolise his youth and innocence; little girls, the same age as himself, showered his long golden hair with gold leaf and threw imitation gold florins beneath the hooves of his white charger. And when he reached Westminster he was given a ceremonial bath, as if to wash away any remaining sins or blemishes.

Then, at the lengthy coronation ceremony, Richard wore a special shirt with slits in it to enable him to be anointed, for the holy oil was rubbed on his hands, breast, shoulders, back, elbows and head. He swore to keep the laws of the country, defend the Church, uphold the laws which the people would choose, defend the privileges of bishops and abbots; and he listened to the Bishop of Rochester preaching to him about the dangers of excessive taxation.

Then, having been consecrated, he was loaded with the royal insignia: the alb, the tunicle, buskins, spurs, sword, armilla, imperial mantle, the crown, the ring, the sword, the rod and the sceptre. Understandably, by the end of all this Richard was so exhausted that he had to be carried back to his palace in the arms of his tutor, Simon Burley.

JULY 17 1917
THE HOUSE OF SAXE-COBURG-GOTHA BECOMES THE HOUSE OF WINDSOR

In 1917 the mood against Germany and all things German was so intense that even the royal family, with its German connections, was in grave danger of becoming the focal point of public anger. A letter to *The Times* declared that 'the risk to their people's welfare of monarchs whose spiritual home is Berlin is too great to be borne'. H.G. Wells added fuel to the flames by castigating Britain's 'imported dynasty'. The 'ancient trappings of throne and sceptre are at most a mere historical inheritance,' he argued, and poured scorn on George V and his 'alien and uninspiring court'. King George fulminated. 'I may be uninspiring, but I'll be damned if I'm an alien,' he roared.

Nevertheless, Wells returned to the attack, and a sentence in his next letter may well have been the final goad to spur King George to change his name. Wells wrote: 'The choice of British royalty between its people and its cousins cannot be . . . delayed. Were it made now, publicly and boldly, there can be no doubt the decision would mean a renascence [sic] of monarchy and a tremendous outbreak of royalist enthusiasm in the empire.'

To H.G. Wells, then, we may be indebted to the dramatic declaration which George made on this day in 1917, changing his name to Windsor. Other royals with foreign names and titles were also required to make changes: Battenbergs, for example, became Mountbattens. Many names were suggested: York, Lancaster, Plantagenet, Tudor-Stewart and Fitzroy – but George's private secretary, Lord Stamfordham, finally came up with Windsor. It was an inspired suggestion, which probably saved the monarchy.

Also on this day:
924 Death of Edward the Elder, son of King Alfred the Great, aged fifty-four, at Farndon-on-Dee, Cheshire. He was buried in Winchester Cathedral. King Athelstan succeeded to the throne, aged about twenty-nine, on the death of his father.

1557 Death of Anne of Cleves, aged forty-two, fourth wife of King Henry VIII.
      She was buried in Westminster Abbey.
1717 King George I is entertained on the River Thames and hears Handel's
      Water Music for the first time.

JULY 18   1465
EDWARD IV CELEBRATES A YORKIST TRIUMPH

Edward IV and his Queen Elizabeth Woodville were visiting Canterbury on
this day when news arrived that Henry VI, his rival in the Wars of the
Roses, had been captured near Waddington Hall.

Edward was exultant. A special *Te Deum* was sung in the cathedral, and he
made offerings at the glorious shrine of Thomas Becket, still attracting
thousands of pilgrims every year, though it was destined to last only another
seventy-three years before being destroyed by his grandson, Henry VIII.

For the time being, however, this military success proved, surely, that God
was a Yorkist!

JULY 19   1545
HENRY VIII WATCHES HIS FLAGSHIP
MARY ROSE SINK IN THE CHANNEL

Henry was nearly at the end of his reign when this tragedy occurred. He
was now married to Catherine Parr, his sixth wife, and he had only eighteen
months more to live.

He was in Portsmouth, inspecting his troops and his ships, when news
came that a French invasion fleet was on its way up the channel. Quickly
the *Mary Rose* made ready for action. It had only recently been given a
refit, and it was the pride of Henry's fleet, with two cannon, two demi-
cannon, two culverins, six demi-culverins, two 'sakers' and a 'falcon' (two
other types of small cannon). There were about a hundred crewmen and the
ship was carrying about six hundred soldiers.

Watching from Spithead, the king saw his beautiful refurbished ship
moving out to sea, when suddenly it listed to one side, the guns broke loose,
and within a minute it had sunk to the bottom of the Solent with the loss of
hundreds of lives. It may be that the portholes had been left open, letting
water in.

Henry must have been appalled. But perhaps his anguish would have been assuaged had he known that over four hundred years later a very distant cousin of his, Prince Charles, after fifteen generations, would be present to see the *Mary Rose* raised from the sea-bed. Prince Charles took great personal interest in this enterprise and eagerly watched as the *Mary Rose* came slowly to the surface on October 11 1982.

1821

QUEEN CAROLINE IS REFUSED ENTRY TO WESTMINSTER ABBEY FOR HER OWN CORONATION

On this day in 1821 Prinny was crowned king at last. The ceremony was lengthy and elaborate and the specially designed robes for those who attended him were gorgeous and bordering on the preposterous. The big worry for everyone was the position of the new king's wife, Caroline of Brunswick, who was obviously the legal queen, as there had been no divorce. However, Prinny and Caroline hated each other and had lived apart from the early days of their marriage.

Caroline had pursued an embarrassing lifestyle, living openly with her partner Bartolomeo Pergami. She had toured the continent with her lover, and they had even gone as rather incongruous pilgrims to Jerusalem. She had recently scandalised Italian society by appearing topless at a ball. On hearing of the death of George III, Caroline decided to return to England. After all, she was now queen, despite anything Prinny could say. And despite an attempt in Parliament to dissolve the royal marriage and deny Caroline her right to be queen, the popular support for her was so intense that the Bill was withdrawn at the last moment.

At last the day of the coronation arrived. Caroline had written to the Prime Minister to ask what arrangements had been made for her at Westminster Abbey, but had received no reply. She knew that Prinny, now king, was adamant that she should not be there at all: nevertheless she made herself ready and drove to the abbey where the crowds were agog to see what would happen.

One of the most astonishing scenes ever witnessed by the abbey then took place. Caroline went from door to door, vainly trying to gain admittance. Mostly, the doors were locked against her, but when she found one that was open she found herself barred from entry by a doorkeeper who refused to let her pass without an entrance-ticket! Her companion, Lord Hood, tried to bluster his way in. 'Did you ever hear of a queen being asked for a ticket before?' he cried. 'This is your queen!' But the doorkeeper was resolute. Lord Hood offered to give Caroline his ticket, but this would have meant her going in alone. Suddenly her courage failed her and she turned away.

The crowds watching all these attempts to get into the abbey now turned against her and started hissing and booing. 'Go back to Italy!' they shouted. Deeply humiliated, Caroline drove back to her house in South Audley Street. What would have happened if she *had* managed to get into Westminster Abbey defies imagination.

(For the sequel to this episode, see AUGUST 7.)

Also on this day:
1553 Mary Tudor, aged thirty-seven, daughter of Henry VIII and Catherine of Aragon, was proclaimed queen after the collapse of the Duke of Northumberland's plot to put Lady Jane Grey on the throne. Lady Jane herself was arrested and taken as a prisoner to the Tower of London.
1999 Prince Edward, the youngest son of Elizabeth II and Prince Philip, Duke of Edinburgh, aged thirty-five, married Sophie Rhys-Jones, aged thirty-four, in St George's Chapel, Windsor. The queen created them Earl and Countess of Wessex. The Earldom of Wessex had been in abeyance since the death of Earl Godwin, father of King Harold, in 1053.

JULY 20   1213
KING JOHN IS ABSOLVED FROM THE BAN OF THE CHURCH

In 1212 King John had suffered the humiliation of being excommunicated by the Church, and deposed, at least in theory, from his kingdom; all his subjects were absolved from their allegiance to him. It was a sorry state of affairs.

Now, over a year later, the excommunication was lifted at a ceremony in the Old Chapter House in Winchester Cathedral. Archbishop Stephen Langton came to officiate at this unique service in which John renewed his coronation oath and promised to maintain the ancient laws of the kingdom. Thus twice within the space of less than twenty years two brothers, Richard and John, had each been restored to their kingly authority in Winchester (see APRIL 17).

Visitors to Winchester can see the site of the Old Chapter House just south of the south transept, now in the open air since the dissolution of the monasteries. It is such a tranquil part of the cathedral close that it is difficult to imagine the high drama which was enacted there on this day.

Also on this day:

1588 The Spanish Armada was first sighted off the Cornish coast. Between July 21 and July 29 there were four major engagements: off Eddystone, off Portland, off the Isle of Wight and off Gravelines.

JULY 21   1403
'HOTSPUR' IS KILLED AND PRINCE HAL WOUNDED AT THE BATTLE OF SHREWSBURY

Four years after he had usurped the throne Henry IV was still struggling to maintain his authority. One of the most serious challenges to his position came on this day in 1403 at the Battle of Shrewsbury. Henry Percy ('Hotspur') and his uncle the Earl of Worcester met Henry IV and his son, the fifteen-year-old Prince of Wales ('Prince Hal' – the future Henry V), at a hard-fought battle in Shropshire, about three miles north of Shrewsbury.

The king's army numbered about twelve thousand men and the rebel army about ten thousand. The fighting was ferocious, and Prince Henry was soon wounded in the face. Despite this, however, he refused to leave the battlefield and led his men to victory, attacking Hotspur in the rear. Hotspur himself was slain by an arrow.

Today a beautiful church stands in the middle of the battlefield. It was founded by Henry IV himself in memory of the fallen. Visitors can see the crests of the victors, and it is said that the gargoyles carved there are representations of the rebels.

JULY 22   1939
PRINCESS ELIZABETH MEETS PHILIP, A NAVAL CADET AT DARTMOUTH

The royal yacht *Victoria and Albert* entered the River Dart on this day with the royal family on board. Among the cadets to greet them at Dartmouth

Naval College was Philip, a prince of Greece, whose mother was Princess Alice, great-granddaughter of Queen Victoria. He was eighteen years old.

Royal watchers could note, therefore, that the two youngsters, Princess Elizabeth, then aged thirteen, and Prince Philip, were third cousins through their descent from Queen Victoria. They were also second cousins once removed (from Christian IX of Denmark), and fourth cousins once removed through collateral descendants of George III. Thus they were allowed to meet one another.

For a few days Elizabeth and Philip met quite frequently. 'Crawfie' (Marion Crawford, governess to the Princesses Elizabeth and Margaret) described Philip in much-quoted words: 'a fair-haired boy, rather like a Viking, with a sharp face and piercing blue eyes.' And she noted that 'Elizabeth never took her eyes off him.'

As the royal party left the Naval College, their yacht was followed down river to the sea by a number of boats manned by loyal cadets. One, in particular, rowed by the fair-haired Viking, gained the rapt attention of the teenage princess. Crawfie observed that Elizabeth 'watched him fondly through an enormous pair of binoculars'.

Later, Basil Boothroyd was to remark: 'There's a fair consensus that this was the day that romance first struck.'

JULY 23   1745
BONNIE PRINCE CHARLIE LANDS IN THE OUTER HEBRIDES

Bonnie Prince Charlie, grandson of James II and great-great-grandson of James I, had lived all his days in exile, and now, aged twenty-five, he set foot on Scottish soil for the first time, determined to wrest the throne of Britain from the Hanoverian George II.

His impractical aspirations were awe-inspiring. He landed this day on the minute island of Eriskay in the Outer Hebrides with just seven companions, mostly twice his age. His plan was simple: to raise an army, march against England and seize the throne.

Eriskay lies between Barra and South Uist. The landing place still has the name of the 'Prince's Strand' and, rather romantically, it is said that here grows a little pink convolvulus which is found nowhere else in Scotland, and that the prince himself brought the seeds to the island. If he did bring those seeds, it was just about all that he did bring. And to his dismay the prince, dressed somewhat oddly as an abbé, received a number of Scottish lairds who told him bluntly to his face to go home. They realised the futility of his hare-brained scheme.

Eventually, the Bonnie Prince turned to Ranald Macdonald and said, 'Will not *you* help me?' and was rewarded by the impulsive response, 'I will, though not another man in Scotland draw the sword!'

Ranald's support swayed some of the others. At last the Stuart cause had begun!

JULY 24   1567
MARY, QUEEN OF SCOTS, ABDICATES IN FAVOUR OF HER SON

Mary had never known a time when she was not a queen. She had succeeded her father when she was only one week old and had been crowned at nine months. Now, aged twenty-four, after a life unbelievably crammed with adventure, she was imprisoned in Lochleven Castle, having just miscarried of a pair of twins fathered by Bothwell.

This was probably the lowest point of her fortunes so far. She was still lying in bed after the miscarriage, physically exhausted, having lost a great deal of blood. In this state of weakness she was visited by Lord Lindsay and other Scottish lords, bringing her documents of abdication to sign.

She was outraged, but terrified, for they told her that she might well have her throat cut if she did not comply. These were the cirumstances then, in which Mary, alone, with no protection, desperately ill, on a remote island, was forced to yield her throne.

Five days later, on July 29, her thirteen-month-old son James was crowned King of Scotland at the Church of the Holy Rood, just outside Stirling Castle.

JULY 25   1554
MARRIAGE OF QUEEN MARY AND PHILIP OF SPAIN

This was probably the happiest day in Mary's life. She was being married at last to the husband of her choice, Philip of Spain, the Catholic son and heir of the great Emperor Charles V. The venue for this wedding – Winchester

Cathedral – had been chosen carefully. London might well have been dangerous, because the people were wary of Catholic Spain. Moveover, the Archbishop of Canterbury was not available: he was in prison. And in any case Winchester was nearer to Spain.

At the ceremony Philip was dressed exquisitely in white satin worked with silver, a gold collar studded with diamonds, and round his knee the Garter, for he had been invested in the Order as soon as he had arrived in England. In fact he was still only a prince when he entered the cathedral, but just before the ceremony started a herald announced to the assembled congregation that the Emperor Charles had just created Philip King of Naples. Thus a king would be marrying a queen, and there would be no discrepancy in rank.

As for Mary, she wore red silk stockings beneath her starkly black velvet gown. Philip's wedding gift, a large flat diamond mounted like a rose with a huge pendant pearl, hung round her neck. The bride and groom must have made a sharply contrasting pair.

The nave of the cathedral was hung with a collection of rich tapestries, and visitors to the cathedral today may still see the large hooks specially fitted into the pillars for that royal wedding. They are still used for hanging modern tapestries. The cathedral also keeps other mementoes of the occasion: an impressive portrait of Queen Mary, and the chair on which she sat, a present given to her by the Pope.

Also on this day:

1446 King Henry VI laid the foundation stone of King's College Chapel, Cambridge.

1603 Coronation of King James VI of Scotland, aged thirty-seven, as King James I of England, in Westminster Abbey.

JULY 26   1784
PRINNY COMMUTES FROM BRIGHTON
TO LONDON ON MARIA FITZHERBERT'S BIRTHDAY

Maria Fitzherbert was Prinny's 'secret' wife (see DECEMBER 15). Born Mary Anne Smythe, of an old Roman Catholic family, Mary had already been widowed twice before she met the prince. She had first married a

44-year-old widower named Edward Weld, who was the warden of Lulworth Castle in Dorset, and secondly Thomas Fitzherbert, of Norbury in Derbyshire, a man about ten years her senior.

Both these men had died suddenly and unexpectedly, so in 1784 Maria (she preferred this name to plain Mary) found herself free again, and possessed of a comfortable income of about £2,000 a year. When she decided to end her mourning and enter society again, the *Morning Herald* announced the event in ecstatic terms:

> A new *Constellation* has lately made an appearance in the *fashionable hemisphere* that engages the attention of those whose hearts are susceptible to the power of beauty. The Widow of the late Mr F – h – t has in her train half our young Nobility: as the Lady has not, as yet, discovered a partiality for any of her admirers, they are all animated with hopes of success.

This day in 1784 was her twenty-eighth birthday.

Prinny, that summer, then aged twenty-two, spent ten weeks at Brighton. On this same day, July 26, he travelled up to London and back on horseback – a journey of ten hours in the saddle. One wonders what business he had which demanded such an arduous journey.

Also on this day:

1643 The city of Bristol was stormed and taken by Prince Rupert, nephew of King Charles. Charles soon moved into Bristol, which became the main base for royalist warships.

JULY 27 1850
QUEEN VICTORIA GETS A BLACK EYE IN PICCADILLY

It comes as a surprise to find that Queen Victoria survived no fewer than seven assassination attempts. Her assailants were mentally unstable, and their attempts did not reflect the general public opinion. However, she knew what it was to live in danger.

When she had been thirteen years on the throne she suffered an attack in Piccadilly, just as she was driving along, without an escort, in an open carriage with some of her children. This was not really an assassination attempt, but it must have been an unpleasant moment for the queen.

Her attacker on this occasion was Robert Pate, a retired lieutenant of the 10th Hussars, who hit the queen on the head with his stick. Crowds pulled him away.

Victoria was bruised and came away with a black eye, but was not seriously harmed. (See FEBRUARY 29.)

JULY 28   1540
HENRY VIII MARRIES KATHERINE HOWARD AT OATLANDS, SURREY – AND THOMAS CROMWELL IS BEHEADED ON TOWER HILL

These events took place on the selfsame day, giving satisfaction of different kinds, no doubt, to Henry VIII.

Oatlands Palace in Weybridge, lying less than ten miles west of Hampton Court, had been bought and renovated by Henry VIII for Jane Seymour, but of course was never occupied as intended. The palace no longer exists, and a hotel now stands on the site.

In 1540, however, it was new and unused and just the place for a quiet, almost secret wedding. Within days of his divorce from Anne of Cleves, therefore, Henry took his blushing bride to this private palace and married her without any public pomp or ceremony: at least it saved him money. However, in honour of the event he ordered special gold coins to be struck, bearing the royal arms of England on one side and on the reverse a rose, crowned, in allusion to Katherine, flanked by the initials K R (Katherine Regina) and the motto HENRICUS VIII, RUTILANS ROSA SINE SPINA ('Henry VIII, (his) blushing rose without a thorn'.)

Meanwhile, in London, a very different event was taking place: the execution of Henry's former trusty adviser, Thomas Cromwell. Cromwell had been the organiser of the dissolution of the monasteries, responsible for the destruction of some six hundred beautiful abbeys during the years 1536–9. He had earned for himself the nickname *malleus monachorum*, 'hammer of the monks'.

Now, however, he was in disgrace, having negotiated the unwanted marriage with Anne of Cleves. His downfall was swift, and as Henry was being married to his thornless rose at Oatlands, Thomas found himself in front of the executioner's block on Tower Hill. He made a most pious end by declaring himself a staunch Catholic. The axe-man himself was described as 'a ragged and butcherly miser, which very ungoodly performed the office'.

But Henry was not concerned with these details. He was relishing the words of his young bride promising to be 'bonair and buxom in bed'.

Also on this day:

1683 The future Queen Anne, aged eighteen, daughter of the Duke of York (later King James II), married Prince George of Denmark, second son of King Frederick of Denmark, in the Chapel Royal, St James's Palace, London.

JULY 29   1565
MARY, QUEEN OF SCOTS, MARRIES HER COUSIN LORD DARNLEY

Mary's second marriage was one which she must have regretted almost immediately. At the time, however, she was so passionately besotted with Darnley that people were actually wondering whether he was using witchcraft to gain her affections.

As cousins, they needed a special dispensation from the Pope before they could marry, but such was Mary's impetuosity that she refused to wait for the dispensation to arrive. She bestowed the title Duke of Albany on her future husband and on this day, her wedding-day, it was proclaimed that he was now 'King Henry'.

Only seven months later 'King Henry' was strangled. And four months later still, their son, the future James VI of Scotland and I of England was born.

1567
JAMES VI OF SCOTLAND IS CROWNED, AGED ELEVEN MONTHS

Exactly two years after the marriage of Mary and Lord Darnley, their infant son James was crowned in the Church of the Holy Rood outside Stirling Castle. His father had been murdered and his mother was under house arrest, having been forced to abdicate. It was hardly a recipe for a normal upbringing.

1981
MARRIAGE OF PRINCE CHARLES AND LADY DIANA SPENCER

In the light of subsequent events, the marriage of Charles, Prince of Wales, and Lady Diana Spencer evokes a poignant mixture of emotions. Who could have foretold the disastrous failure of this marriage, or the tragedy of Diana's death?

For those who can remember this brilliant July day it will remain as the most popular and romantic wedding of all time, magnified beyond imagination by the media. No fewer than 750 million viewers watched the service on television – the largest audience ever known up to that time.

The details are all on record, in cuttings and videos all over the world: Diana's 25ft-long train; the spectacular pictures from the television cameras placed high in the dome of St Paul's; the aria from Handel's *Samson* sung by the New Zealander Kiri Te Kanawa; the beauty of the bride as she waved shyly to the crowds from the open horse-drawn carriage as she and the prince were driven back to Buckingham Palace; and then, as the newly-weds appeared on the balcony, perhaps the most memorable shot of all – 'that kiss'.

JULY 30 1418
HENRY V AND THE ENGLISH GODDONS LAY SIEGE TO ROUEN

This day saw the beginning of the ruthless six-month siege of Rouen, which lasted until January 19 1419. Henry had already won his outstanding victory at Agincourt in October 1415, but this had not brought the overall subjugation of France which he so desperately wanted. His campaigns to make his dominance a reality were to continue to the end of his short life.

The siege of Rouen was to be a terrible period for its citizens (see JANUARY 19) and it needed a Joan of Arc to instil new hope and pride in the hearts of the Normans. However, Joan was not to arrive on the scene for another ten years or so. Meanwhile, a new word entered French slang: 'goddons' – a contemptuous term for English soldiers. It derived from their constant swearing: 'God damn'.

JULY 31   1737
POOR FRED'S WIFE GIVES BIRTH BETWEEN A PAIR OF TABLE-CLOTHS

It is a truism that throughout the centuries most Princes of Wales have been on terrible terms with their fathers. Prince Frederick, son of George II, was a conspicuous example of this virtually traditional family feuding.

'Poor Fred' (see MARCH 20) and his pregnant wife Princess Augusta were staying at Hampton Court during this period in 1737 because the king and queen insisted that they should be present to witness the forthcoming birth. They did not want any changeling to be foisted on them, or run the risk of suffering rumours of another 'warming-pan' baby.

On this July evening Augusta suddenly went into premature labour. Fred was desperate that his wife should *not* give birth under his parents' roof, so he secretly hustled his wife out of the palace while the rest of the royal party were enjoying a game of cards. Despite her discomfort he made her take the twelve-mile coach journey to London, to their own home at St James's Palace. Of course, nothing was prepared when they arrived there so Augusta, by now desperate, had to make do with lying between two table-cloths.

Queen Caroline was furious when she woke up the next morning to find that her son and his wife had left them, especially when she learned that Augusta had already given birth to a daughter. On inspecting the rather small infant later that day she admitted that she had no further suspicions about the possibility of a changeling, remarking that 'if, instead of this poor, little ugly she-mouse, there had been a brave, large fat, jolly boy, I should not have been cured of my suspicions'.

Lord Hervey described the royal child as being 'a little rat of a girl, about the bigness of a good large toothpick case'. But this 'little rat of a girl' grew up to become the mother of George IV's controversial wife, Caroline of Brunswick.

Also on this day:
1587 Mary, Queen of Scots, was buried in Peterborough Cathedral. Her body was received by the bishop at 2.00 a.m. for fear of unpleasant demonstrations by Protestants. In 1612 Mary's remains were transferred to Westminster Abbey by her son, King James I (see OCTOBER 3).

AUGUST 1   1086
WILLIAM THE CONQUEROR'S GREAT OATH-SWEARING CEREMONY

Oaths were important to William. He had made Harold swear allegiance to him long before the battle at Hastings, and of course everyone knew what had happened to Harold when he broke that promise. By 1086 William had been settled on his throne for twenty years. The kingdom was his by right and his by conquest. Nevertheless, he did not want any of his nobles to take advantage of him now that they too were settling into their lands and castles. Accordingly he summoned all landholders to the bleak hill-top fortress of Old Sarum, the old city of Salisbury, to swear personal allegiance to him.

Almost nine hundred years later Hitler was to use the same technique. It takes moral courage to turn against a leader after you have looked him in the eyes and sworn to be faithful to him.

After this oath-giving ceremony the large assembly would have worshipped in Salisbury's first cathedral, then in the process of being built by Bishop (later Saint) Osmund.

1714
QUEEN ANNE DIES AT LAST

Queen Anne finally died on this day, aged forty-nine. Rumours of her death had circulated for days beforehand, thus prompting the proverbial saying, 'Queen Anne is dead'. But now, at last, she was.

For years she had suffered from a multitude of illnesses. Nowadays, we can understand her pathetic condition much better than her own ignorant physicians, who merely diagnosed 'dropsy and gout in the bowels.' In fact, Anne probably suffered from a condition known as lupus erythematosus. The symptoms of this include miscarriages, arthritis in many joints, facial skin eruptions and blotching. Kidney damage would lead to water retention, dropsy and obesity. As her wretched life dragged on, she became quite desperately overweight.

Poor Anne had to suffer her physicians' gruesome remedies, being bled and blistered, forced to swallow emetics, and having her head shaved. One of her doctors, Dr Arbuthnot, remarked to Jonathan Swift: 'I believe sleep was never more welcome to a weary traveller than death was to her.'

Her last words were, 'My brother, my poor brother,' referring to James the Old Pretender, who she hoped would be her successor. However, her ministers had already decided to invite Prince George Louis of Brunswick-Lüneburg, Elector of Hanover, to become the next king.

Anne is buried in Westminster Abbey. She had become so fat that her coffin had to be almost twice as wide as it was long.

AUGUST 2   1100
THE RED KING IS FOUND DEAD IN THE NEW FOREST

The circumstances surrounding the death of Rufus (William II, son of the Conqueror) will always remain a mystery. Rufus, the 'Red King', gained his nickname because of his ruddy face and flaming ginger hair. He was viciously cruel, scoffed at the Christian faith and shocked Church leaders by being openly gay. He tolerated no critics. Once, at Old Sarum, he personally ordered an opponent's eyes to be pulled out in his presence and his testicles cut off.

Only the day before Rufus's death, the Abbot of Shrewsbury had preached a vehement sermon against the King's sins and prophesied divine vengeance. He couldn't have been nearer the mark.

It is said that on the day of his death, Rufus actually gave a couple of special arrows to Sir Walter Tyrrel, one of his courtiers, saying, 'Be sure to aim at the mark,' and 'Walter, take good care to carry out the orders I gave you.' Whatever the mysterious significance of these words, the upshot was that when they were hunting in the New Forest together later that day Tyrrel shot at a stag, but his arrow glanced off the beast and somehow hit the king instead. Tyrrel immediately fled the country – he went on a pilgrimage and died in the Holy Land, professing his innocence to the end.

Meanwhile the king's body was found by a charcoal-burner called Purkiss, who trundled the corpse to Winchester Cathedral on his cart. According to William of Malmesbury the king's body was 'dripping with blood all the way'. The monks of Winchester were horrified to receive the wicked king's body and buried it hastily without any ceremony. When a tower of the Cathedral fell down a few years later, the superstitious monks blamed the disaster on the evil influence of the wicked king's corpse.

Some writers have suggested that this death was a planned ritual sacrifice, and that Rufus might have been a member of the old religion connected with a witch cult (after all, the date was just after the old pagan festival of Lammas). Others think it was intentional murder. But was it an accident? Or the fulfilment of some occult prophecy? And, if this were the case, did Rufus know in advance that he was doomed?

Also on this day:

1101   King Henry I and his older brother Robert ('Curthose') signed a
        treaty at Alton, Hants, in which Robert gave up his claim to the throne
        in exchange for Henry's undertaking to surrender his rights in the
        Cotentin pensinsula in Normandy and to give Robert an annual
        allowance of money. It was exactly one year since Henry had seized
        the throne, in Robert's absence, after the death of Rufus.
        (See FEBRUARY 3.)

AUGUST 3   1394
RICHARD II HITS THE EARL OF ARUNDEL FOR BEING LATE AT THE QUEEN'S FUNERAL

Anne of Bohemia, queen of Richard II, had died aged only twenty-eight, and childless. Her husband Richard II was distraught, for they had been deeply attached to each other during the twelve years of their marriage. Her death was sudden, probably the result of the plague.

Elaborate arrangements were made for Anne's funeral. A vast quantity of wax candles and torches had been ordered from Flanders and these were lit to provide a flaming line along the entire route taken by Anne's funeral procession from St Paul's Cathedral to Westminster Abbey. All the peers of the realm and their ladies were required to attend, and to wear long-trained black velvet or cloth cloaks and hoods. It was one of the most memorable funeral processions seen in London.

At Westminster Abbey the Earl of Arundel arrived late, and then asked if he could leave early. Richard was so incensed by this that he struck him to the ground, and the earl's head was cut open by the altar steps. Blood poured out of the wound and the funeral service was lengthily interrupted until the king and the noble earl were reconciled.

Anne had died at the royal palace at Sheen, which was later rebuilt as Richmond Palace. Richard was so deeply grieved at his wife's death that he ordered the palace to be destroyed.

Also on this day:
1557 Funeral of Anne of Cleves, fourth wife of Henry VIII, in Westminster Abbey.

AUGUST 4   1265
SIMON DE MONTFORT IS HACKED TO PIECES AT THE BATTLE OF EVESHAM

Sheer military skill and determination led to the 26-year-old future King Edward I's victory at the Battle of Evesham. He turned the tables on the barons, rescued his father, King Henry III, and killed the man who had virtually taken over the kingdom for the preceding three months – Simon de Montfort.

Henry III was restored to the throne after his period of captivity, and as for Simon de Montfort, he was savagely dismembered and his head was sent as a present to the widow of his arch-enemy, Roger Mortimer.

Simon de Montfort had been guilty of the heinous crime of inventing parliament.

2000
QUEEN ELIZABETH THE QUEEN MOTHER CELEBRATES HER 100TH BIRTHDAY

On this day Queen Elizabeth the Queen Mother became the first centenarian in royal history. The Queen Mum's birthday was marked by a huge surge of love and loyalty.

Newspapers and magazines were filled with congratulations. Special picture supplements galore pointed out that her life had exactly spanned the most eventful century in the history of mankind. They pointed out, too, what a crucial role she had played, particularly in wartime Britain, to boost Londoners' morale by her courage and sympathy.

Already, in the preceding month, there had been a special service of thanksgiving in St Paul's Cathedral, and a joyful procession on Horse Guards Parade. Now, on the birthday itself, there was a relatively simple ceremony, watched by thousands outside her home at Clarence House, and by millions more on TV. This consisted of a parade past her former residence by the King's Troop Royal Artillery. Then, bringing up the rear, came the Queen's Postman in an electric van. He was bringing the expected congratulations card from the Queen to her mother, who was standing at the gate of Clarence House to receive it.

A moment of dilemma came as it was realised that the Queen Mum couldn't easily open the envelope as she was supporting herself on two walking sticks. Smiling cheerfully, she asked her equerry, 'Can you use your sword?' Gallantly, he did so, to the laughter and cheers of the onlookers. It was a unique moment during a unique royal occasion. The card summed up everyone's feelings: '. . . our loving best wishes for this special day.' It was signed 'Lilibet'.

Shortly afterwards, the Queen Mother rode in an Ascot landau, adorned with blue and yellow flowers – her racing colours – to a lunch at Buckingham Palace. She appeared on the palace balcony at first with twenty-seven members of her family; and then, finally, she stood with just her two daughters, the Queen and Princess Margaret, at each side of her. It was a memorable replica of their VE Day balcony appearance in 1945 – over fifty-five years before. Sadly, however, this was destined to be the last time that either the Queen Mother or Princess Margaret would be seen on that balcony. (See FEBRUARY 9 and MARCH 30.)

AUGUST 5 1100
HENRY I BECOMES THE FIRST
POST-CONQUEST USURPER

The death of Rufus (see AUGUST 2) paved the way for his younger brother Henry to seize the throne, which he did with spectacular efficiency. It is quite likely that Henry was a member of the royal hunting-party when Rufus was killed in the New Forest: indeed he may have witnessed his brother's death. One could even speculate that he engineered the whole affair.

The fact is, the moment Henry learned of his brother's death he galloped as fast as he could to Winchester to demand the keys of the treasury. Then he made the 60-mile dash to London and within four days, on August 5, he was crowned King of England by Maurice, Bishop of London, in Westminster Abbey. Henry was not quite thirty-two, and still unmarried.

His speed and determination were a prelude to a very successful reign, but it has to be admitted that Henry was a usurper. The crown should have gone to Rufus's older brother Robert Curthose (the name means 'short trousers' – apparently he had stocky little legs) but Robert was away on a crusade at the time, so missed the opportunity to become Rufus's successor.

Of course, Robert was not likely to take the situation lying down, and returned to England breathing fire and eager for revenge. (For his ultimate fate see SEPTEMBER 28.)

AUGUST 6   1307
THE KING'S GAY PARTNER IS CREATED EARL OF CORNWALL

Edward II had succeeded to the throne on July 7 on the death of his father Edward I, but he still had not been crowned. However, he was assuredly king, and determined to do whatever he pleased.

Less than a month after his accession he shocked and angered his nobles by creating his homosexual lover, Piers Gaveston, Earl of Cornwall. Great wealth and lands went with this title, but what shocked the barons most was that traditionally it was given to members of the royal family.

Clearly this move was in defiance of his dead father's wishes, for Edward I had banished Gaveston from England earlier in this year. He had been enraged when his son had actually asked permission to give a gift of land to Gaveston.

'You baseborn whoreson,' the old king is reputed to have shouted. 'Do you want to give away lands now, you who never gained any? As the Lord lives, if it were not for fear of breaking up the kingdom you should never enjoy your inheritance.'

The king's fury was such that he grabbed his son's hair with both his hands and yanked tufts of it out until he was so exhausted that he simply threw him out.

AUGUST 7   1821
AN 'OFFENSIVE' INSCRIPTION ON A QUEEN'S COFFIN

Just three weeks after the dramatic snub given to Queen Caroline at George IV's coronation (see JULY 19), she was dead. One might suppose that she died of sheer mortification, but the fact was she suddenly suffered a bowel obstruction. On July 30 she was enjoying a performance at Drury Lane Theatre when she was taken ill with abdominal pains. These became worse, and it became increasingly clear, as the days went by, that she was dying. She died during the evening of August 7.

The king, her husband, was in Anglesey at the time, on his way to Ireland to celebrate his coming to the throne. However, he was careful to observe five days of mourning and to avoid any public show or celebration which might have betrayed just how relieved he was at her disappearance from his life.

Before she died Caroline expressed two wishes: first, to be buried back in Germany; and second, to have a special inscription put on her coffin: CAROLINE OF BRUNSWICK, THE INJURED QUEEN OF ENGLAND.

A mob of demonstrators ran riot in London as her funeral procession passed through the streets, and one man was killed in the disturbances.

King George IV had objected to the proposed wording on Caroline's coffin, which he found to be 'offensive': nevertheless, her supporters managed to fix this inscription on the coffin as she had wished. (See AUGUST 18.)

Also on this day:

1385   Death of Joan of Kent, the first Princess of Wales, widow of the Black Prince and mother of King Richard II. She was buried in Canterbury Cathedral.

AUGUST 8   1588
ELIZABETH I REVIEWS HER TROOPS AT TILBURY

The Armada had just been defeated, but fears of a Spanish invasion were still uppermost in many people's minds. Elizabeth arrived at Tilbury on this day, in her state barge, to review her army, encamped there to counter this possible threat.

She rode a milk-white steed, and was dressed in white velvet with a shining silver breastplate. A young page went before, bearing her silver helmet on a white cushion, and the Earl of Ormonde ceremonially bore her sword of state. It was a moment of dazzling pageantry as she inspected rank upon rank of foot soldiers and well-turned-out cavalry all wearing plumes. 'God bless you all!' she cried; and they responded with 'Lord preserve our Queen!'

The next day she came again to the camp, and received a tumultuous burst of welcoming cheers. It was then that she delivered her most famous speech – probably the finest ever made by any English king or queen. Here is just a part:

My loving people, we have been persuaded by some that are careful of our safety to take heed how we commit ourselves to armed multitudes, for fear of treachery; but I do assure you, I do not desire to live to distrust my faithful and loving people.

Let tyrants fear. I have always so behaved myself that, under God, I have placed my chiefest strength and safeguard in the loyal hearts and goodwill of my subjects, and therefore I am come amongst you, as you see, at this time, not for my recreation and disport, but being resolved in the midst and heat of the battle to live or die amongst you all, to lay down for my God and for my kingdom, and for my people, my honour and my blood, even in the dust.

I know I have the body of a weak and feeble woman, but I have the heart and stomach of a king, and of a king of England too, and think it foul scorn that Parma or Spain, or any prince of Europe, should dare invade the borders of my realm; to which, rather than any dishonour shall grow by me, I myself will take up arms, I myself will be your general, judge, and rewarder of every one of your virtues.

This famous speech is known to us because one of the queen's chaplains took it down in writing, and it was read to the troops again the next day, in case anyone had missed it. Indeed copies of the speech were circulated far and wide for years afterwards.

AUGUST 9   1902
EDWARD VII IS CROWNED ON THE DATE
RECOMMENDED BY HIS FORTUNE-TELLER

Count Louis Hamon, or 'Cheiro' as he often called himself, was a fortune-teller of international reputation. He had already been awarded the Order of the Lion and the Sun by the Shah of Persia because he had successfully predicted an assassination attempt on the Shah, which had been foiled because of Cheiro's warning.

King Leopold II of Belgium and King Humbert I of Italy were also clients of Cheiro, so advising royalty was not new to him when Edward VII asked him to suggest a propitious date for his coronation. Unfortunately, the date first chosen for Edward's coronation had had to be abandoned, literally at the last moment, because the king had been taken seriously ill with appendicitis.

Cheiro reassured Edward that his illness would not be fatal despite the fears of many of his subjects. He actually indicated when the king was likely to die (he told him he would live to be sixty-nine) and finally he came up with August 9 as the perfect coronation date!

Some years later, in June 1911, Cheiro told another client, William Stead, not to travel by water during April 1912. Stead ignored Cheiro's warning, bought a ticket for the maiden voyage of the *Titanic* – and was duly drowned on April 14 of that year. (See MAY 6.)

Also on this day:

1192 Richard I ('Lionheart') made the treaty with Saladin by which Christians were allowed to make pilgrimages to Jerusalem. This was the end of the Third Crusade.

AUGUST 10   1675
CHARLES II ECONOMISES IN BUILDING THE ROYAL OBSERVATORY AT GREENWICH

Various sites were suggested for the proposed Royal Observatory, among them Hyde Park and Chelsea. However, Sir Christopher Wren's suggestion of the highest spot on Greenwich Hill met with the King's favour.

Charles allowed stone to be taken from the old castle there, and gave bricks, iron and lead from a demolished part of Tilbury Fort. Some spoilt gunpowder was sold off to provide £500 to pay the workmen. As a final economy, he required John Flamsteed, his first Astronomer Royal, to pay his assistants and buy his own instruments out of the non-too-generous salary of £100 per annum. It is sad to record that Charles had promised to buy the necessary instruments, but never honoured this commitment.

Flamsteed laid the foundation stone of the new observatory on this day in 1675, thus literally putting Greenwich on the world map.

Also on this day:

1414 King Henry V, aged twenty-seven, made a formal claim to the throne of France.

AUGUST 11 1403
THE EARL OF NORTHUMBERLAND SUBMITS TO HENRY IV

On this day, at York, King Henry IV grimly forced the proud Earl of Northumberland to make a formal submission to him, and to acknowledge his royal authority.

It was just three weeks after the battle of Shrewsbury, in which the king and his son Prince Hal (the future King Henry V) had inflicted a crushing defeat on the rebel forces led by 'Hotspur', the Earl of Northumberland's son. It had been the worst crisis of King Henry's reign, but he had survived. Hotspur had been slain and in a gruesome gesture Henry sent his severed head back to his widow.

As for the earl, he was to rebel yet again a few years later, and after another unsuccessful battle at Bramham Moor in Yorkshire, he was executed on February 19 1408.

As Shakespeare wrote, it was 'a scrambling and unquiet time'.

AUGUST 12 1484
RICHARD III MOVES HENRY VI'S BONES

Henry VI had always wished to be buried in Westminster Abbey. Even as a young man he had marked out the exact spot on the floor next to the tomb of Edward the Confessor. However, this would have been far too public a place, and would have attracted unwelcome publicity, embarrassing to Edward IV, who had deposed him. Accordingly, after his murder in 1471, Henry was buried in the Lady Chapel at Chertsey Abbey – a relatively obscure place, well away from the London crowds.

Thirteen years later Richard III ordered the monks of Chertsey to give up Henry's body for reinterment in St George's Chapel, Windsor. It was to lie near his lifetime rival, Edward IV. The reburial took place on this day in 1484.

Immediately Henry's resting-place became a focal point for pilgrims. Scores of miracles were recorded there, and pilgrims would put their offerings in a curious iron money-box with twenty slots in it. It is still to be seen next to his tomb.

Thomas Fuller, in his *History of the Worthies of England* (published in 1662), wryly observed about Henry VI:

He was both over-subjected and over-wived . . . This Henry was twice crowned, twice deposed and twice buried (first at Chertsey, then at Windsor), and once half sainted . . . This Henry was a saint . . . with the people repairing to this monument from the farthest part of the land, and fancying that they received much benefit thereby.

Also on this day:

1762 The future King George IV, son of George III and Queen Charlotte, was born at St James's Palace, London.

AUGUST 13 1704
QUEEN ANNE REJOICES OVER THE VICTORY AT BLENHEIM

The Anglo-Austrian army under the command of John Churchill, Duke of Marlborough, defeated the French army at Blenheim on this day. The Duke calculated that he had spent seventeen hours in the saddle, and after he had routed the enemy he looked around for a scrap of paper. The only bit he could find was an old bill for expenses in a French tavern, saying '16 May. For six loaves and one candle . . .' Still on horseback, he wrote a note on the back of the bill to his wife Sarah, 'with a leaden pencil':

> I have not time to say more than to beg of you to present my humble duty to the queen, and to let her majesty know that her army has had a glorious victory. M. Tallard, and two other generals, are in my coach, and I am following the rest. The bearer, my aide-de-camp, Colonel Parkes, will give her majesty an account of what has passed. I shall do it, in a day or two, by another more at large.
>
> MARLBOROUGH

The news of the victory was received in England with ecstasy. After all, this was the first foreign battle-victory since Agincourt, and the English were still hankering after rescuing their lands in France, and the French were still regarded as the traditional 'enemy'.

Queen Anne received the good news at Windsor Castle while playing dominoes with Prince George. She offered Colonel Parkes, the messenger, 500 guineas. And when he begged for a miniature of the Queen instead, she impetuously gave him both miniature *and* 1000 guineas.

St Paul's Cathedral was still incomplete, but Queen Anne attended a great service of thanksgiving in the unfinished building, with guns from the Tower booming out over London at the singing of the *Te Deum*.

AUGUST 14   1369
NOSEY PARKER SPREADS GOSSIP ABOUT QUEEN PHILIPPA

Queen Philippa, wife of King Edward III, died on this day. She had been a good queen and had borne her husband no fewer than twelve children, including the Black Prince and John of Gaunt, father of Henry IV.

A curious bit of gossip, however, relates how she made a most extraordinary confession on her deathbed to William of Wykeham, Bishop of Winchester and the famous founder of Winchester College. According to this rumour, Philippa confessed that she had given birth to a daughter while she was in Ghent and had accidentally killed the little princess. She was so upset, and dreaded the anger of her husband King Edward if he heard about his infant daughter's death. To avoid the king's wrath, therefore, she arranged to smuggle a baby boy into her apartments, a porter's son who had been born at the same time. The king was delighted with his new 'son' and the boy grew up knowing nothing about his real background – and everyone knew him simply as John of Gaunt, Duke of Lancaster.

Probably there was no truth in this, but gossipy rumours have a habit of hanging around for centuries, and Matthew Parker, Archbishop of Canterbury under Elizabeth I, recounted the story in his *Ecclesiastical History*, printed in 1575. The good archbishop enjoyed prying into other people's affairs, and is widely credited with being the original 'Nosey Parker'.

Visitors to Westminster Abbey can enjoy Queen Philippa's beautiful effigy there. She was only fifty-five when she died, and she did not live to see the squabbles of her grandsons as Henry IV seized the throne from Richard II.

AUGUST 15   1947
GEORGE VI CEASES TO BE EMPEROR OF INDIA

On the stroke of midnight, August 15 1947, the Indian sub-continent which had been for many years a part of Britain's Empire became two independent nations, India and Pakistan. George VI at the same time ceased to be

Emperor. His great-grandmother Queen Victoria had been given the title Empress by Disraeli in 1877 (see JANUARY 1) so in effect the Indian Empire had lasted only seventy years.

Lord Mountbatten, the last Viceroy of India, immediately became Governor-General of the new dominion of India. The days of the Raj were over.

Also on this day:

1057 Death of Macbeth, killed by Malcolm, at Lumphanan, about 20 miles west of Aberdeen.

1945 Surrender of Japan and the formal end of the Second World War.

1950 Birth of Princess Anne, daughter of Queen Elizabeth and Philip, Duke of Edinburgh, at Clarence House, London.

AUGUST 16   946
THE FOURTH CORONATION AT KINGSTON UPON THAMES

Just outside the town hall at Kingston upon Thames, Surrrey, is a large stone, roughly cube-shaped and about four foot in height and width, where traditionally many of the Saxon kings were crowned. Whether they were crowned on it or beside it we do not know, and the history of this ancient stone is obscure.

Nowadays it rests on a modern stone plinth and it is surrounded by low railings. There is nothing special to draw attention to it, and visitors to the town may easily miss it, despite its size. Nevertheless it clearly had great importance for the Saxons, for no fewer than seven kings were invested with their authority next to this 'Coronation Stone'.

For the record, these are the kings who were crowned there, with the traditional dates, all in the tenth century:

Edward the Elder	(son of Alfred the Great)	June 8 900
Athelstan	(son of Edward the Elder)	September 4 925
Edmund I	(Athelstan's half-brother)	940
Edred	(brother of Edmund I)	August 16 946
Edwy	(nephew of Edred)	January 956
Edward the Martyr	(nephew of Edwy)	975
Ethelred II	(half-brother of Edward	April 14 979
(the Unready)	the Martyr)	

Ethelred's son, Edmund II ('Ironside'), was not crowned here, and reigned only briefly in 1016. Then the Danish kings forced themselves on the throne (Sweyn Forkbeard, Canute, Harold Harefoot and Hardecanute). The last two Saxon kings were Edward the Confessor, who was crowned in Winchester, and Harold II who was the first monarch to be crowned in Westminster Abbey.

Since 1066 every English monarch has been crowned at Westminster, except Edward V, who disappeared, probably murdered in the Tower of London, and Edward VIII, who abdicated and married Mrs Simpson.

AUGUST 17   1579

'A FROG HE WOULD A-WOOING GO'

On this day in 1579 there arrived at Greenwich the foreign prince who most nearly succeeded in marrying Queen Elizabeth I – the Duke of Alençon, the youngest son of Catherine de' Medici. The duke was then aged only twenty-three and Elizabeth was twice his age at forty-six; nevertheless, despite the difference in their ages, Elizabeth had found his love-letters intriguing and arguably she was still, perhaps, young enough to conceive an heir to the throne.

It was obvious that Elizabeth found the duke attractive, despite the fact that he was much shorter than she was. He was witty, self-assured, a prince of France, and – unlike many of her other suitors – he had actually come in person to press his claim. Elizabeth herself teasingly called him 'her frog'.

For some months the wooing seemed to be going well, and she told her Council that they should recommend her to marry him. Unanimously they agreed. After all, a union with France would be a safeguard against Spain. Fickle as ever, however, Elizabeth changed her mind at the last moment, and told the duke that she felt she must put her people's welfare before her own happiness.

The duke took her refusal in good part, but stayed so long in England that he had to be bribed with £10,000 to go home, with a promise of £50,000 more when he was actually on board ship for France.

As for Elizabeth, as always it was difficult to penetrate her real feelings, but it does seem that for a while she was emotionally torn. She wrote a moving little poem entitled 'On Monsieur's Departure':

> I grieve, yet dare not show my discontent;
> I love, and yet am forced to seem to hate;
> I dote, but dare not what I meant;
> I seem stark mute, yet inwardly do prate.
> I am, and am not – freeze, and yet I burn,
> Since from myself my other self I turn.

And she wrote to her young lover, saying that she would give a million pounds to see her frog swimming again in the Thames.

AUGUST 18   1821
FIGHTING BREAKS OUT IN COLCHESTER OVER QUEEN CAROLINE'S COFFIN

After riots and deaths in London as the crowds swarmed round Caroline's funeral procession on its way back to Germany, there were yet more scenes of violence as her coffin arrived at Colchester on this day in 1821.

Caroline's body rested in St Runwald's Church, and fighting broke out between her supporters, who wished to fix the 'offensive' inscription to her coffin: 'CAROLINE OF BRUNSWICK, THE INJURED QUEEN OF ENGLAND' (see AUGUST 7), and the King's supporters, who wished to remove the inscription. In the event, the king's party won, and the funeral carriage went on to Harwich without offence.

Poor Caroline! Eventually she arrived back in her native Brunswick and was buried in the vaults of St Blaize Cathedral between her father and her brother, both killed in the Napoleonic wars. Her mother (see JULY 31) had died alone and in exile. Her sister, Charlotte of Württemberg, was imprisoned and never heard of again. It was demonstrably not a happy family.

AUGUST 19   1274
GRAND JUNKETINGS AT THE CORONATION OF EDWARD I AND ELEANOR

The records which have come down to us about Edward I's coronation feast are almost unbelievable. It went on for days, and required 380 cattle, 430 sheep, 450 pigs, 18 wild boars, 20,000 chickens and 278 flitches of bacon, and wine literally flowed through the water-conduits. There was a frantic free-for-all as hundreds of horses were let loose in the streets and anyone who could catch one could keep it. London itself was rich with decorations: tapestries hung from the houses, banners hanging out of windows, and all the nobility of England were accoutred in splendid attire.

It was the first occasion when a king and queen were crowned together in Westminster Abbey, and both Edward and Eleanor were young and popular.

It was also the last coronation to be held without the famous Stone of Scone, for it was Edward himself who stole it from Scone Abbey in 1296 and brought it back to London. He was pleased to pay a Master Adam 100 shillings for a wooden seat to enclose this stone and 13 shillings 4 pence for carving and painting two leopards as decoration. Since then, all other coronations have used Edward's chair.

Also on this day:
1561 The widowed Mary, Queen of Scots, aged eighteen, returned to Scotland after the death of her first husband, Francis II, King of France.

AUGUST 20   1589
JAMES VI IS MARRIED BY PROXY, AND THEN BRAVES THE WITCHES TO MARRY HIS WIFE IN OSLO

King James VI of Scotland (and the future King James I of England) was twenty-four when he decided for political reasons to marry the sixteen-year-old Princess Anne of Denmark. Accordingly, on this day in 1589 they were married by proxy at the Danish court.

Anne then set sail for Scotland but twice the fleet carrying her was driven by violent winds back to the coast of Norway. When a third storm blew her adrift to Oslo it was clear to everyone that witchcraft was at work. After all, the admiral in charge of bringing Anne to Scotland had recently slapped the face of a Danish magistrate who happened to be married to a witch.

The witch was duly burnt, whereupon King James decided to brave the storms himself and sail to Oslo to marry his wife in person. This wedding took place in November, after which the newly-weds went to Kronenburg in Denmark for a third wedding, this time according to Lutheran rites. James is unique in having been married three times to the same wife!

When James eventually sailed back to Scotland his ship was again bewitched, seeming to have a special wind blowing against it, different from the winds affecting the other ships.

Later, James personally examined the Scottish witch Agnes Sampson, who claimed to have put the spell on his ship. She explained to him that she had christened a cat, tied bits of a dead man to it, and then thrown it into the sea, thus causing a tempest and sinking a vessel carrying wedding gifts for Queen Anne.

James was unnerved at the witch's words, especially at what she told him privately:

> And therupon taking his Maiestie a little aside, she declared vnto him the verye woordes which passed betweene the Kings Maiestie and his Queene at Vpslo [Oslo] in Norway the first night of their mariage, with their answere eache to other: whereat the Kinges Maiestie wondered greatlye, and swore by the liuing God, that he beleeued that all the Diuels in hell could not haue discouered the same: acknowledging her woordes to be most true, and therefore gaue the more credit to the rest which is before declared.

AUGUST 21   1765
A FUTURE KING IS BORN IN BUCKINGHAM HOUSE

This day saw the birth of the future King William IV in 'Buckingham House' – recently bought by his father, King George III, for £28,000. Buckingham House was known as 'The Queen's House' from 1775 to 1820, but when Prinny became king it became known as 'The King's House, Pimlico' or 'The New Palace in St James's Park'. It wasn't until Queen Victoria moved into the building in 1837 that it acquired its present name, Buckingham Palace.

Prinny had been born at St James's Palace in 1762, but over the following years his fourteen siblings were all born in Buckingham House. His younger brother Frederick (the original 'Noble Duke of York who had ten thousand men') was born there in 1763 and the future William IV was born there on this day in 1765.

But despite having been born in Buckingham House, William hated the place and as king he never lived there.

Also on this day:
1930 Birth of Princess Margaret, younger sister of Queen Elizabeth II, at Glamis Castle, Scotland.

AUGUST 22   1485
A CROWN IS LOST – AND FOUND UNDER A HAWTHORN BUSH

The battle of Bosworth Field was fought on this day, ending the long line of fourteen Plantagenet kings which had lasted 330 years. It was a turning-point in English history: the Wars of the Roses finally came to an end; Richard III was killed; Henry Richmond won the day; and the age of the Tudors began.

Nowadays, next to the site of the battle there is an excellent visitors' centre and museum to explain exactly what happened on this day. It was a cliff-hanger of a battle, which might easily have gone the other way if Lord Stanley and his brother William Stanley had not decided at the very last moment to support Henry Tudor rather than King Richard. In fact, neither Henry nor Richard knew what the Stanleys would do. It was one of those crucial decisions which alter the course of history for ever.

It's easy to dismiss the legendary details as mere romanticism. No one will ever know whether Richard's crown really was found under a hawthorn bush, or whether Lord Stanley actually crowned Henry on the spot, but the tradition is strong. Why else would Henry adopt the crown and hawthorn as his personal badge and have it appear on his tomb in Westminster Abbey?

As for Richard, his naked body was ignominiously strapped on to his horse and he was taken back to Leicester for the public to gape at.

1642
A KING MAKES WAR ON HIS PEOPLE

In a dramatic gesture Charles I raised his royal standard at 6.00 p.m. in a field a little to the north of the main gate of Nottingham Castle. It was a declaration of war against his enemies. The day was wet and windy and only a handful of supporters shouted 'God save the King and hang all roundheads'. The townsfolk of Nottingham were distinctly cool towards the diminutive king.

A herald tried to make himself heard as he read out the text of Charles's proclamation, but as Charles had rewritten a part of it, the poor herald found it extremely difficult to decipher.

In fact it was a silly place to try to rally support: Charles's own advisers had told him that he should go elsewhere, to a part of the country where he had real support. In Nottingham popular opinion was against him, especially as some years before, when he and Henrietta Maria had stayed five days in the town, the town council had been ruined financially because of the costs involved in entertaining them. They even had to mortgage some public land to pay off their debts.

During the night the royal standard was blown down in the gales, and in the ensuing civil war Nottingham quickly supported the Parliamentarians. The next time Charles saw Nottingham Castle was when he was taken there as prisoner in 1647.

Also this day:

1358   Death of Isabella of France, aged sixty-six, widow of King Edward II. She was buried at Grey Friars Church, London.

1553   John Dudley, Duke of Northumberland, was beheaded for his treasonable act in attempting to place Lady Jane Grey on the throne.

1705   Marriage of the future King George II, aged twenty-one, to Caroline of Ansbach, daughter of John Frederick, Margrave of Brandenburg-Ansbach, at Hanover.

AUGUST 23   1305
THE END OF SIR WILLIAM WALLACE ('BRAVEHEART')

The impressive Wallace monument near Stirling Castle is a rugged tribute to 'Braveheart', the great Scottish soldier and patriot. After Wallace's notable victory against the English at the battle of Stirling Bridge (September 11 1297) Edward I had beaten him at Falkirk (July 22 1298). Eventually, after waging guerrilla war against the English for the next few years, Wallace was betrayed into their hands in 1304 and taken to London in chains in August 1305.

On this day Wallace suffered a dreadful death. His hands tied behind him, he was taken on horseback to Westminster Hall where he was crowned in mockery with a wreath of silvered laurel leaves. Condemned to die the death of a traitor, he was taken to West Smithfield, where he was hanged, drawn and quartered.

His head was cut off and stuck on a pole, as the crowds danced and cheered. It was taken to the Tower and set up over the principal gate. The riotous mob celebrated around it for hours until soldiery had to be called out to restore order.

Edward I, the 'Hammer of the Scots', must have been grimly satisfied by the day's events.

AUGUST 24   1200
KING JOHN MARRIES A TEENAGE BRIDE

John had already been married to his second cousin, Isabella of Gloucester, but the Pope had never given his approval and had in fact forbidden them to live together. It was easy enough, therefore, to annul this marriage in favour of a political union with Isabella of Angoulême.

No one quite knows exactly how old Isabella was when they were married in Bordeaux Cathedral on this day in 1200, but she was probably about thirteen or fourteen. John himself was thirty-two.

Mediaeval chroniclers made much of the fact that John was voluptuously in love with his child-bride, and recounted how, in the early months of their marriage, he kept in bed with her till midday. A prudish nineteenth-century writer adds that 'his young queen shared some of this blame, as the enchantress who kept him chained in her bowers of luxury'. Oh dear!

Also this day:
1804   King George III and his family arrived in Weymouth once again for their annual holiday.

AUGUST 25   1482
MARGARET OF ANJOU, WIDOW OF HENRY VI, DIES IN FRANCE

So many consort queens in previous centuries have had appallingly miserable lives! Margaret, queen of Henry VI, perhaps suffered more than most the occupational hazards of being royal. She had to cope with her husband's uniquely unsuccessful reign, desperately trying to cover up for his weaknesses. She gave birth to their son when her husband was in an eighteen-month coma and had to introduce the baby to him as a stranger when eventually his long period of unconsciousness ended. She had to fight his wars; she had to put up with his being deposed twice; she saw her son killed at the Battle of Tewkesbury; and finally she was thrust into prison when her husband's rival, Edward IV, ultimately took over the kingdom.

Eventually she returned to France and lived the last years of her life in obscurity, accepting a pension from her cousin, Louis XI of France, in return for agreeing to give up all her royal rights.

Margaret died on this day in 1482 and a French writer who saw her at the end of her life tells us that 'the once peerless Margaret had become a horror to look upon. Grief had turned the whole volume of her blood to water; her once superb eyes were swollen and red with weeping, and her skin covered with blotches like leprosy.'

She died aged fifty-one and was buried in the tomb of her father and mother in Angers Cathedral. She was given no epitaph or inscription.

AUGUST 26   1346
THE PRINCE OF WALES WINS A BATTLE
AND HIS SPURS

Edward, Prince of Wales and son of King Edward III, was only sixteen when he commanded the English army at the Battle of Crécy and won an astonishing victory.

The battle took place in the late afternoon, just after a tremendous thunderstorm had broken. Tradition has it that the crossbows of the enemy were ruined by the rain, but that the English archers, using long bows which they had had the foresight to keep dry, produced a blizzard of arrows, shooting into the French forces who were blinded by having to look into the gleam of the setting sun.

Tradition also tells how Edward III watched the course of the battle from the top of a windmill, and deliberately let his teenage son gain the full honour of victory. 'Let the child win his spurs,' he said, 'and let the day be his.'

It was the age of chivalry, knightly honour and rhetoric, and after the battle the king publicly embraced the young prince in front of the troops. 'Sweet son,' he said, 'God give you good perseverance; you are my true son

– right loyally have you acquitted yourself this day and worthy are you of a crown.' And the next day, walking with his son through the battlefield still littered with blood and corpses, he is alleged to have asked: 'What think you of a battle, is it an agreeable game?'

It was at this battle that the young Prince of Wales first wore the 'armure noire' which was to give him his nickname – the 'Black Prince'.

Also on this day:
1819   Birth of Prince Albert of Saxe-Coburg-Gotha, future Prince Consort and husband of Queen Victoria, at Rosenau in Bavaria.

AUGUST 27   1979
EARL MOUNTBATTEN, THE QUEEN'S COUSIN, IS KILLED BY TERRORISTS

Earl Mountbatten of Burma, aged seventy-nine, great-grandson of Queen Victoria, cousin of Queen Elizabeth and uncle of Prince Philip, was killed instantly by an IRA bomb which blasted his 29ft fishing boat to bits off the coast of Mullaghmore, County Sligo, Ireland. He was enjoying a peaceful holiday at the time. Also killed were his fourteen-year-old grandson Nicholas and a young local boatman. The earl's daughter and son-in-law and a friend of the family were badly injured.

The earl had been Supreme Allied Commander in Asia during the Second World War and had played a major part in the recapture of Burma from the Japanese. After the war he became the last Viceroy of India and prepared the partition of India and Pakistan and the transfer of power to these countries in 1947.

Fifteen British soldiers were also killed on this day in a huge bomb-blast at Warrenpoint, County Down.

AUGUST 28   1883
VICTORIA ASKS LORD TENNYSON TO WRITE AN EPITAPH FOR JOHN BROWN

John Brown, the 'Queen's Highland Servant', had died on March 29 1883, and Victoria grieved deeply: she was used to grief. At the time of Brown's death, Tennyson had written her letters of condolence: he too, as author of

In Memoriam, was almost professionally committed to grief. It was an emotion which bound them together.

The result of his letter was an invitation to Tennyson to come to Osborne. An audience was held which Victoria described:

'After luncheon saw the great Poet Tennyson in dearest Albert's room for nearly an hour; – and most interesting it was. He is *shaky on his legs*. But he was very kind. Asked him to sit down. He talked of the many friends he had lost and what it would be if he did not feel and know that there was another World, where there would be no partings.

. . . I told him what a comfort *In Memoriam* had again been to me which pleased him. . . . When I look leave of him, I thanked him for his kindness and said I needed it, for I had gone through so much – and he said you are so alone on that 'terrible height, it is Terrible. I've only a year or two to live but I'll be happy to do anything for you I can. Send for me whenever you like.' I thanked him warmly.

Following this meeting, an extraordinary friendship developed between monarch and poet. They wrote to each other at a personal level, with Victoria describing her innermost feelings for Brown ('The comfort of my daily life is gone – the void is terrible – the loss is irreparable!') and signing herself 'Yours affectionately' – a unique tribute to her feelings for her Poet Laureate.

On this day in 1883 Victoria wrote to Tennyson, asking him to produce a fitting epitaph for John Brown, to put on the pedestal of a statue. Tennyson sent the following:

> Friend more than servant, loyal, truthful, brave!
> Self less than duty, even to the grave!

Victoria thought this 'so very fine'.

AUGUST 29   1483
KING RICHARD AND QUEEN ANNE ENJOY
A GREAT RECEPTION AT YORK

The 'hunchback' Richard III ('Now is the winter of our discontent') has had such a bad press, partly owing to Shakespeare and other Tudor writers, that it comes as quite a surprise to learn that he and his wife Anne were received with wild enthusiasm by the citizens of York when they came to the city in progress on this day in 1483. Richard had been a popular Lieutenant in the North during the reign of his brother, Edward IV, and retained his popularity there to the end.

On this day the city of York was hung with rich tapestries, and the royal visitors were entertained by three pageants as they processed through the cheering crowds. The welcome was so impressive that Richard decided he would invest his nine-year-old son Edward as Prince of Wales while staying in the city.

This investiture took place on September 8 in York Minster, with all pomp and ceremony. Forty trumpeters produced a fanfare for the occasion and after the investiture King Richard, Queen Anne and Prince Edward, all wearing crowns, once more paraded through the streets, 'to the honour, joy and congratulations of the inhabitants, as in show of rejoicing they extolled King Richard above the skies'.

Richard had less than two years more as king before being killed at the Battle of Bosworth Field (see AUGUST 22); Prince Edward died 'an unhappy death' on March 31 1484, only seven months after this investiture; and Queen Anne, aged thirty-one, died on March 16 1485. Perhaps luckily for her, she did not live to see her husband killed.

AUGUST 30   1548
CATHERINE PARR, HENRY VIII'S LAST QUEEN, GIVES BIRTH TO A DAUGHTER

Catherine Parr, sixth wife of Henry VIII, gave birth this day to a daughter at her home at Sudeley Castle in Gloucestershire. Her husband, whom she had married secretly in 1547, after Henry's death, was Thomas Seymour, brother of Jane Seymour, Henry's third wife, who had died after giving birth to Henry VIII's son and heir, Edward VI.

Alas, Catherine Parr was to suffer and die in exactly the same way as Jane Seymour. She fell mortally ill with puerperal fever and died a week later, on September 5. Lady Jane Grey, a few days short of her eleventh birthday, was staying at Sudeley Castle at the time and acted as godmother for the baby girl, who was christened Mary, after the future Mary I. Lady Jane also acted as chief mourner for the dead former queen, who had always shown her much kindness.

As for the baby, little Mary Seymour, she lived on for a couple of years, but then disappears from the records – although odd rumours suggest that she survived into the next century.

AUGUST 31   1997
DEATH OF DIANA, PRINCESS OF WALES

Chased by the paparazzi along the streets of Paris, Princess Diana and her friend Dodi Fayed were killed in a spectacular car-crash shortly after midnight on this day in 1997. Dodi Fayed died at the scene of the accident in a road tunnel close by the River Seine, and Princess Diana died soon afterwards, at 4.00 a.m. at the Pitié-Salpetrière Hospital.

World grief at the death of the princess can hardly be described. Those who experienced the almost surreal events in Britain during the days which followed and who saw her funeral either in person or on television will never be able to convey the emotional impact to later generations, nor will they be able to explain just how increasingly mesmeric the princess had become in the sixteen years she had been in the public eye, since her engagement to Prince Charles. Her dazzling beauty, her refreshing informality, her deep sympathy with the sick and underprivileged, her sense of fun: all these combined to produce a heady mixture which was given unequalled media coverage during her life.

The unbelievable quantity of flowers left at the gates of Kensington Palace and at public places throughout the country bore some testimony to the outpouring of public grief. The royal family itself came virtually under siege as a vague feeling of accusation was whipped up by some sections of the media. The absence of a Union Jack flying at half-mast over Buckingham Palace was seen to be somehow cruel and unfeeling, and the protocol which disallowed it was felt to be meaningless and irrelevant. After a few days the flag was allowed to fly there, to everyone's relief. Trivialities like these became hugely important to those gripped by the almost tangible sense of loss.

The day of the funeral was filled with unforgettable moments: the brilliant sunshine heightened the splendour of the royal coffin, draped with the royal standard edged with white linen; the wreath of white roses with the hand-written card inscribed 'Mummy'; the courage of the two princes, William, aged 15, and Harry, 12, as they accompanied their father on foot behind the gun-carriage; the painfully beautiful performance of a specially written version of *Candle in the Wind* by Elton John; the defiantly proud oration by the princess's brother, Earl Spencer; the haunting music by John Tavener as the procession wound its way out of the abbey; and finally the end of the princess's journey as her cortège disappeared behind the gates of her family home at Althorp in Northamptonshire.

Our photographs, colour supplements and videos remain to remind us of that day. Surely no public funeral has ever engendered such deep and complex emotions of grief, love, sympathy and painful shock. The princess had literally touched so many in her concern for ordinary people, especially the sick and the dying, and it was only after her own death that we realised just how full her life had been.

Future generations will never be able to share the overwhelming sense of loss that filled the nation on this day.

Also on this day:

1422   Death of King Henry V, aged thirty-five, of dysentery, at the castle of Vincennes, near Paris.

1669   Death of Henrietta Maria, aged sixty, widow of Charles I and mother of King Charles II, at the Château de Colombes, near Paris. She was buried at St Denis, France.

SEPTEMBER 1 1422
A NINE-MONTH-OLD BABY BECOMES
KING OF ENGLAND

Like Mary, Queen of Scots, and James I of England, King Henry VI never knew what it was like *not* to be a monarch: he became king at the age of nine months, on the death of his father, Henry V.

His mother was Catherine of Valois, the princess who appears so coyly in Shakespeare's *Henry V*. Although she and her husband seem to have been happily married, she certainly did not take kindly to his insistence that in no circumstances should she give birth to her baby at Windsor Castle while he was away fighting in France. He seemed to think there would be a kind of bad-luck spell on the newly-born child if Windsor was the birthplace. However, while Henry was away, Katherine made no attempt to leave Windsor as her labour-pains came on.

Henry V was strongly displeased to learn that his son was born at Windsor, and tradition has it that he foretold great disaster. In the years ahead he was proved right. He was a strong believer in omens and spells, and had even put his stepmother, Queen Joanna, in prison for being a witch (see JULY 9).

Little Henry VI himself was the intended victim of witchcraft, too, for his aunt, the Duchess of Gloucester, employed various people including 'a woman . . . surnamed the Witch of Eye [to] devise an image of wax like unto the King . . . [and] by their devilish incantations . . . make the King's life dwindle away . . . as they little and little consumed that image'.

Luckily, however, he lived to be almost fifty before he was murdered.

SEPTEMBER 2 1666
CHARLES II AND THE FUTURE JAMES II HELP TO
PUT OUT THE FLAMES

In the early hours of Sunday, September 2, a fire started in Master Farryner's bakery in Pudding Lane. No one realised it at the time, but this fire was to spread across London to destroy Old St Paul's Cathedral, eighty-seven other churches and over thirteen thousand dwelling-houses. In just five days the Great Fire of London was to devastate almost 400 acres. Strong winds helped to spread the blaze, and after a hot summer the houses simply burned like paper.

King Charles II himself went into the thick of the smoke and flames and insisted on blowing up houses near the Temple Church, while the Duke of York (the future James II) was personally responsible for saving Westminster Abbey, by blowing up old wooden houses nearby, and organising a chain of buckets. We must be grateful to these two brothers for saving two of London's most important buildings.

Both Charles and James gained much popularity from their prompt and purposeful actions. Afterwards, the Monument, 202ft high and designed by Sir Christopher Wren, was put up exactly 202ft from the spot where the fire began. It was to have had a statue of Charles II on the top, but Charles declined this honour, saying it might look as if he had been responsible for starting the fire!

SEPTEMBER 3   1658
OLIVER CROMWELL DIES ON HIS 'FORTUNATE DAY'

Cromwell always regarded September 3 as his 'fortunate day' as this was the date on which he had won two of his important battles: at Dunbar against the Scottish army in 1650, and at Worcester against the royalists in 1651. The Scots explained their defeat at Dunbar by saying that the Lord had not wished to support an army who fought for an unconverted king. At Worcester, the Scottish general David Leslie, who had fought and lost at Dunbar, was too wary of the Roundheads to act decisively, and pulled back at a crucial moment.

Now, in 1658, Cromwell was sick and still heavily depressed by the death of his daughter, who had died just a month before. George Fox, the founder of the Quakers, met him in Hampton Court Park in these final weeks of his life and wrote in his journal: 'I saw a waft of death go forth against him, and when I came to him he looked like a dead man.'

Cromwell died aged fifty-nine, in the early hours of his 'fortunate day', at times slipping into a delirium during which he spoke incoherently about his sins. Finally, as he passed away, London was devastated by a terrific thunderstorm. The Thames overflowed its banks, church steeples were blown down, and hundreds of houses lost their roofs. It was one of the most dramatic gales ever seen. It was an awesome end.

Also on this day:

1189 Coronation of King Richard I, aged thirty-one, in Westminster Abbey.

1651 The second battle of Worcester (see SEPTEMBER 23), where the troops of Charles II were defeated. Charles managed to escape.

1660 Marriage of James, Duke of York, future King James II, aged twenty-six, to his first wife, Anne Hyde, eldest daughter of Edward Hyde, Lord Chancellor and 1st Earl of Clarendon, at Worcester House, The Strand, London.

1752 The dates from September 3 to September 13 1752 inclusive do not exist. This was because England adopted the Gregorian Calendar, following an Act of Parliament passed in 1751. This brought England into line with the continental countries. Eleven days were 'lost', prompting disgruntled crowds to protest, shouting 'Give us back our eleven days !'

1939 Beginning of the Second World War.

SEPTEMBER 4   924
A KING GAINS ALL: THE CORONATION OF KING ATHELSTAN

This day is the anniversary of the coronation of Athelstan, son of Edward the Elder and grandson of Alfred the Great, at Kingston upon Thames.

Athelstan became the first Saxon king to exercise full control over the entire country, proudly minting coins bearing the inscription 'King of All Britain'.

1651
A KING LOSES ALL: CHARLES GOES INTO HIDING AFTER THE BATTLE OF WORCESTER

Just before dawn, at 3.00 a.m., the 21-year-old King Charles II arrived at White Ladies Priory on the Giffards' Boscobel estate, just over 30 miles north of Worcester. He had been travelling since the previous evening, leaving Worcester after he knew he had lost the battle against Cromwell.

He had already been in exile for over two years since the execution of his father Charles I, but it would be nearly nine more years before he could reclaim his kingdom. (See SEPTEMBER 6.)

SEPTEMBER 5   1186
A SCOTTISH KING MARRIES IN AN ENGLISH PALACE

William the Lion, King of Scotland, married Ermengarde of Beaumont, cousin of King Henry II, on this day at Woodstock Palace. The circumstances were perhaps a little strained, as Henry had captured William at Alnwick some years before, in 1174, and he was released only on condition that he accepted Henry as overlord of Scotland. William bided his time, and after Henry's death he bought back the sovereignty of Scotland from Richard I, paying £6,600 towards the Third Crusade.

This day in 1186, however, was a relatively happy occasion as the two kings, William and Henry, came to Woodstock for this marriage to take place. Woodstock, alas, is no more, but it was a famous royal residence for seven hundred years. Ethelred the Unready held a council here; Henry I built a zoo here; Henry II kept his mistress Rosamund Clifford here; the Black Prince was born here; and Elizabeth I was held here under house arrest by her half-sister Mary Tudor.

Visitors to Blenheim Palace should remember this historic spot, which was sited near the present huge edifice, built to reward the Duke of Marlborough for his victory over Louis XIV in 1704. Woodstock was pulled down to make room for it.

Also on this day:

1548   Death of Catherine Parr, aged thirty-six, sixth wife of Henry VIII. She died from puerperal fever following the birth of her daughter (see AUGUST 30) and was buried in the chapel of Sudeley Castle, Gloucestershire.

SEPTEMBER 6   1651
CHARLES II HIDES IN AN OAK TREE

Royal Oak pubs all over the country are named to commemorate the famous incident which took place this day, when King Charles II hid with Colonel Carlos up an oak tree at Boscobel. They peeped out of the branches and watched the Roundhead troops searching the woods below them. The King's own account describes the events:

Major Carlos had . . . told me that it would be very dangerous for me either to stay in that house, or to go into the wood, there being a great wood hard by Boscobel; that he knew but one way how to pass the next day, and that was, to get up into a great oak, in a pretty plain place, where we might see round about us; for the enemy would certainly search at the wood for people that had made their escape.

Of which proposition of his I approving, we (that is to say, Careless [sic] and I) went, and carried up with us some victuals for the whole day – viz., bread, cheese, small beer, and nothing else, and got up into a great oak, that had been lopped some three or four years before, and being grown out again, very bushy and thick, could not be seen through, and here we stayed all the day.

Memorandum – That while we were in this tree we see soldiers going up and down, in the thicket of the wood, searching for persons escaped, we seeing them, now and then, peeping out of the wood.

Also on this day:

1701 Death of the former James II, aged sixty-seven, in exile at St Germain-en-Laye, France. He was buried in the Church of the English Bénédictines, Paris, and his remains were later transferred (in 1813) to the parish church at St Germain-en-Laye.

SEPTEMBER 7 1533
BIRTH OF ELIZABETH I,
AT GREENWICH PALACE

Much to Henry VIII's displeasure and disappointment, Anne Boleyn gave birth to a daughter on this day, a Sunday, at about 3.00 p.m. Doctors and fortune-tellers had been telling the king for weeks that the child would be a boy. To be presented with a girl was a most unpleasant turn of events for him.

The infant princess was christened Elizabeth after her grandmother, Elizabeth of York, Henry VII's queen. Archbishop Cranmer stood as godfather to the child, but Henry was too upset even to attend the christening service, and he cancelled the joust which he had been planning to celebrate the birth of a son.

1573
ELIZABETH I SPENDS HER 40TH BIRTHDAY WITH NOSEY PARKER

By the time she was forty, Elizabeth was an experienced monarch who had coped with extraordinary stresses and difficulties in her youth. Now, aged forty, she was able to enjoy a fortnight's stay with her archbishop, Matthew Parker, in Canterbury, who entertained her with a masque put on by the Kentish Mariners (see AUGUST 14).

One of Elizabeth's great gifts was the ability to choose her advisers wisely, and she had appointed Matthew Parker to be her archbishop as early in her reign as 1559. At one time he had been the personal chaplain to her mother, Anne Boleyn. He resisted being made archbishop for many months but, once having accepted, he filled the post with distinction at a difficult and crucial time in Church history.

He was noted for his keen inquiries into Church affairs and the conduct of the clergy, and it is believed that his conscientiousness led to his memorable nickname 'Nosey Parker'.

SEPTEMBER 8   1761
GEORGE III BLUSHES TO HEAR THE NAME OF HIS SWEETHEART

George III was twenty-three when he married Princess Charlotte of Mecklenburg-Strelitz and was desperately in love with a lovely court beauty, Lady Sarah Lennox. She had already rejected him, and in any case it wasn't done in those days to marry a mere commoner. Nevertheless, he was still love-smitten.

Charlotte had only just arrived in England to marry George, but within twenty-four hours of meeting each other they were married in St James's Palace. During the service, when a Bible reading mentioned Abraham and Sarah, it was noted that George blushed scarlet.

Charlotte was no beauty. In the streets people shouted out 'Pug! Pug! Pug!' when they first saw her upturned nose. Poor Charlotte couldn't make out what they were saying. 'Vat means *poog*?' she asked.

'It means "God bless Your Royal Highness",' was the tactful reply.

1831
WILLIAM IV WANTS TO ABANDON HIS CORONATION

William IV hated fuss and ceremony of any kind. No doubt he had been somewhat embarrassed by the spectacularly elaborate coronation which his brother George IV had given himself ten years before, so when it came to his turn he tried hard not to have any coronation at all.

Tradition dies hard, however, and William was obliged to have a ceremony. He contented himself with a very muted affair on this day in 1831, spending as little as possible on it. The number of musicians was cut to a minimum; he omitted many of the customs; and his queen, Adelaide, even refused to spend money on a crown, but had a special item made up for herself with her own jewels.

When it came to the church offering, William had nothing to put into the gold basin when it was put before him. 'I have not got anything,' he whispered to the archbishop. 'I will send it to you tomorrow!'

Also on this day:
1157 Birth of the future King Richard I, son of Henry II and Eleanor of Aquitaine, in Beaumont Palace, Oxford.

SEPTEMBER 9 1087
WILLIAM THE CONQUEROR IS STRIPPED NAKED ON HIS DEATHBED

The death of William the Conqueror came after six weeks of agony. He had been riding through the little town of Mantes, which his forces had just devastated, when his horse trod on hot cinders and reared up. The king was thrown forward on to the iron horn of his saddle, suffering serious internal injuries.

On this day in 1087, aged about sixty, William died in Rouen. Astonishingly, after the nobles had left the room the household servants plundered the whole apartment, even stripping the dead king of his clothes. It was left to just one loyal supporter to convey William to Caen for burial. He was buried in the abbey he himself had founded as a penance for having disobeyed the Pope in marrying his cousin Matilda.

William's bones were thrown into the River Orne at the time of the French Revolution and lost. One thigh-bone seems to have been rescued, however, and this was solemnly reburied as recently as 1987 under a new memorial stone which can be seen today in front of the altar at the Abbaye aux Hommes at Caen.

SEPTEMBER 10   1658
RICHARD CROMWELL BECOMES LORD PROTECTOR II

Just two days before his death Oliver Cromwell told his ministers that he had decided to nominate his son Richard to be his successor as Lord Protector. This was in accordance with the biblical tradition that the eldest son should inherit the responsibilities of the father. It was a disastrous decision. It was said at the time: 'The vulture died, and out of his ashes rose a tit-mouse.'

Richard opened Parliament for the first time in January 1659, but through sheer lack of experience he found himself quite unable to bear the burdens of office and resigned the office of Protector three months later, on April 21.

Parliament gave Richard £60,000 to pay for his father's funeral, but he spent more than he should have done and got himself heavily into debt as a result. He had to flee the country and it was not until 1680 that he dared to return, and even then he went under the assumed name of 'John Clark'. (See MAY 16.)

Also on this day:
1087 William II ('Rufus'), aged about thirty-one, succeeded to the throne on the death of his father, William the Conqueror.
1169 Death of the Empress Matilda, aged sixty-five, daughter of King Henry I and mother of King Henry II, near Rouen, France. She was buried at the Abbey of Bec.
1299 King Edward I, aged sixty, married his second wife, sixteen-year-old Margaret of France, daughter of King Philip III of France, at Canterbury.

SEPTEMBER 11   1939
THE DUKE OF WINDSOR IS BROUGHT BACK TO AN ENGLAND AT WAR

Eight days after the outbreak of the Second World War the Duke of Windsor was picked up from France and brought back to Portsmouth in the destroyer *Kelly*, commanded by Louis Mountbatten. It was the first time the duke had set foot in Britain since his abdication in 1937; on that occasion he had sailed out of Portsmouth, from the same quay, in the destroyer *Fury* (see DECEMBER 12).

There was a very real problem deciding what the ex-king should do. Two jobs were offered: he could be Deputy Regional Commissioner for Wales or a liaison officer with the British Military Mission in France. He picked Wales, but ended up in France, being given the rank of major-general.

When France fell in 1940 the Windsors were in Biarritz and from there they moved first to Spain and then to Portugal. Winston Churchill offered to bring them back in a flying-boat, but the duke refused to return unless the duchess was accorded the dignity of being a Royal Highness.

Eventually, for the duration of the war, he was made Governor of the Bahamas. 'Naturally, we loathe the job,' wrote the duchess to her Aunt Bessie.

SEPTEMBER 12   1940
BUCKINGHAM PALACE IS HIT BY
FIVE GERMAN BOMBS

King George VI and his wife Queen Elizabeth were just 80 yards from two of the five bombs which landed in the quadrangle of Buckingham Palace in the middle of the morning. The other three bombs landed in the forecourt, gardens, and on the palace chapel, which was completely destroyed.

The king and queen saw the German bomber as it flew straight down the line of the Mall towards the palace, and they could actually see the bombs dropping. George pulled Elizabeth to the floor, where they lay as debris fell around them. Water splashed everywhere as the mains burst and underground sewers were smashed. As a result of this damage, the palace grounds were plagued with rats during the following days.

By now, London was experiencing the horrors of the blitz, and the king and queen toured the blitzed areas day after day, picking their way among the wreckage. Famously, the queen (i.e. the future Queen Mother) remarked, 'I'm glad we have been bombed. It makes me feel I can look the East End of London in the face.'

All told, the palace was hit by bombs, flying bombs and rockets nine times during the war.

1945
LOUIS MOUNTBATTEN RECEIVES
JAPAN'S FINAL SURRENDER

Exactly five years later, the Japanese forces in south-east Asia surrendered to the Allied Supreme Commander, Louis Mountbatten. Shortly afterwards, King George created Mountbatten a viscount, and a little later an earl, with the unique privilege that, as he had no son, the title could descend through the female line. (See AUGUST 27)

SEPTEMBER 13   1598
DEATH OF PHILIP OF SPAIN,
FORMER KING OF ENGLAND

Although it was an empty title, without any powers attached, Philip enjoyed the title King of England during the lifetime of his sadly neglected wife, Mary Tudor.

He went back to Spain and married two more wives, sent his vast unsuccessful Armada against England, and built his huge palace, El Escorial, in honour of his favourite saint, St Lawrence. He had won his famous battle of Saint-Quentin on St Lawrence's Day, 1557.

To the end of his days he was filled with animosity against Protestant England, and even on his deathbed in 1598, forty years after the death of Mary Tudor, he found strength to write an encouraging letter to the Catholic Irish rebel, Hugh O'Neill, Earl of Tyrone, who was creating trouble for Elizabeth I.

Philip had married Mary Tudor with great pomp in Winchester Cathedral (see JULY 25), but it is notable that in the church of the Escorial he is depicted kneeling with his three other wives, Anne of Austria (whom he had married before Mary Tudor), Isabelle of Valois and Maria of Portugal. Significantly, there is no reference at all to his marriage to Mary Tudor, daughter of Henry VIII. For him, she had never existed.

Philip died on this day in his modest apartment in the Escorial, exactly fourteen years to the day after the palace had been completed.

Also on this day:

1409 Death of Isabelle of France, aged twenty, second wife of King Richard II, and daughter of King Charles VI of France. She died in childbirth, having married the Duke of Orleans as her second husband. She was buried first in the Abbey of St Laumer, Blois, but was later transferred to the Church of the Celestines, Paris.

SEPTEMBER 14   1141
THE EMPRESS MATILDA IS ROUTED AND WINCHESTER GOES UP IN FLAMES

The civil war between the Empress Matilda and King Stephen reached a climax in Winchester when Stephen's brother, the powerful Bishop of Winchester, Henry of Blois, suddenly switched sides and turned against Stephen's cousin Matilda, who was fighting for her right to the throne.

The events at this time were confused and dramatic. The bishop had cunningly invited Matilda's supporters to a banquet in his new castle at Wolvesey, just to the south of the city centre. No sooner had they arrived than he locked the gates, thus in effect capturing them. But fortune turned in Matilda's favour as one of these supporters, the chief magistrate of Winchester, managed to escape and fled to the royal castle on other side of the city (near today's modern magistrates' court) and alerted Matilda's forces.

But then fortune turned against her, as reinforcements arrived from London to help the bishop. In the ensuing conflict the bishop set fire to the entire city of Winchester, trying to force Matilda out of any possible hiding-place. Tragically, Winchester's Saxon past was completely destroyed: the royal palace, twenty churches, the monastery of St Grimbald, the Abbey of St Mary's, Hyde Abbey, Wherwell Priory and hundreds of dwellings were all lost. The city burned for weeks.

Although at this time Matilda was still 'Domina' or 'Lady of the English', her days as uncrowned queen were numbered, and just seven weeks later, on November 1, Stephen regained the throne.

SEPTEMBER 15   1984
BIRTH OF PRINCE HARRY

On this day Diana, Princess of Wales gave birth to her second son, Prince Henry Charles Albert David, to be known simply as Prince Harry. The baby, weighing 6lb 14oz (3kg), was born at St Mary's Hospital in Paddington at 4.20 p.m. At present, Prince Harry is third in line to the throne (see JUNE 21).

After well over a thousand years of royal records, it is possible to trace Harry's descent back to King Alfred and beyond. His ancestors include some startlingly varied figures: through his grandfather Earl Spencer he is descended from Charles II and Lady Castlemaine (see OCTOBER 9), and from his grandfather Prince Philip he is descended from Sweyn Forkbeard, father of King Canute (see NOVEMBER 12).

SEPTEMBER 16   1387
MARY DE BOHUN GIVES BIRTH TO A SON AT MONMOUTH

Mary de Bohun, aged eighteen, was the first wife of Henry Bolingbroke, Earl of Hereford. On this day, in Monmouth Castle, she gave birth to a son who would have much influence on the history of England – the future Henry V, or 'Henry of Monmouth' as he called himself.

Mary little knew, in 1387, that in a few years' time her husband would seize the throne and become Henry IV and that her baby son would grow up to be his successor, Henry V. Sadly, she died five years before these events took place. She bore Henry seven children in all, and was only twenty-five when she died in childbirth at Leicester.

She was originally buried in St Mary de Castro in that city, but her remains were later removed to Trinity Hospital, Leicester.

SEPTEMBER 17   1588
ELIZABETH I IN TRIUMPH AND GRIEF

After the defeat of the Spanish Armada in the summer of 1588, Queen Elizabeth had every reason to be triumphant. She wished to reward her 'Sweet Robin', the Earl of Leicester, who had been in command of her troops at Tilbury, by appointing him Lieutenant Governor of England and Ireland. He had been the one constant love of her life, if ever she had allowed herself the luxury of loving.

But Robin was a sick man. Quite unexpectedly, only a few weeks later, on September 4, aged only 55, he died. Rumours circulated that he had been poisoned by his jealous wife Lettice, but it is more likely that he was suffering from stomach cancer. On his way to Buxton in Derbyshire, hoping to find comfort there from the healing waters, he wrote his last letter to the queen:

> I most humbly beseech Your Majesty to pardon your old servant to be thus bold in sending to know how my gracious lady doth, and what ease of her late pain she finds, being the chiefest thing in the world I do pray for, for her to have good health and long life. For my own poor case, I continue to still your medicine, and it amends much better than any other thing that hath been given me. Thus hoping to find a perfect cure at the bath, with the continuance of my wonted prayer for Your Majesty's most happy preservation, I humbly kiss your foot.
>
> From your old lodgings at Rycote this Thursday morning, by Your Majesty's most faithful and obedient servant, R. Leicester.
>
> P.S. Even as I had written this much, I received Your Majesty's token by young Tracy.

Elizabeth was plunged into intense grief when she learned of his death. It was reported to the Spanish Ambassador, Bernardino de Mendoza, on September 17, that 'The Queen is sorry for his death . . . She was so grieved that for some days she shut herself in her chamber alone and refused to speak to anyone until the Treasurer and other councillors had the door broken open and entered to see her.'

Steeling herself, Elizabeth hid her sorrow. But she inscribed the letter she had received from her sweet Robin 'His last letter', and kept it in a little box by her bedside.

SEPTEMBER 18 1714
GEORGE I ARRIVES WITH THE MAYPOLE AND THE ELEPHANT

On this day in 1714 the 54-year-old Elector of Hanover arrived in England to become the country's new monarch. He was accompanied by his son, the future George II. It was a foggy night when they landed at Greenwich so torches and candles were necessary to help the new king see his new kingdom.

As the king could speak no English, he was dependent on his secretaries, attendants and some negro servants. He left his divorced wife behind him, still locked up in the castle of Ahlden in Germany where she was imprisoned for having taken a secret lover and planning to elope.

But George was not bereft of female company, for he also brought his two mistresses with him: one who was tall and thin, Ermengarda Melusina von Schulenburg, who quickly became known as 'The Maypole'; and another who was large and fat, Sophia von Kilmansegg, who was promptly nicknamed 'The Elephant'.

SEPTEMBER 19   1356
THE BLACK PRINCE CAPTURES THE KING OF FRANCE AT POITIERS

The Black Prince's triumph at the Battle of Poitiers, fought this day in 1356, was even greater than his victory at Crécy ten years before. He brilliantly outmanoeuvred the French forces with his army of 8,000 men against an estimated French army of 60,000. Thousands of Frenchmen were taken prisoner, including the French King John II.

In a magnanimous chivalrous gesture the Black Prince invited King John and his son, together with a large number of the captured French nobility, to a great celebration supper that night, and humbly waited on them at table. According to the French historian Froissart, who was about twenty at the time of this battle, the Black Prince would not sit down with the king, saying that 'he was not sufficient to sit at the table with so great a prince as the king was,' and complimented his royal guest on the 'valiantness' he had shown during the day. 'I say not this to mock you,' said the prince, 'for all that be of our party, that saw every man's deeds, are plainly accorded by true sentence to give you the prize and chaplet.'

Despite this rhetorical compliment, however, the English struck a hard bargain with the French, demanding three million gold pieces for the king's release, and King John was kept a prisoner at Windsor for four years until the ransom was paid.

Poitiers has been described as the most brilliant of English victories over the French. It gave the English sovereignty over Gascony, Poitou, Calais and other territory in northern France.

Edward, the Black Prince, was still only twenty-six at the time of this battle, although it was ten years since his previous great triumph at Crécy. He was still one year younger than Napoleon had been at the beginning of his campaigns.

SEPTEMBER 20   1258
HENRY III AND QUEEN ELEANOR ATTEND THE CONSECRATION OF SALISBURY CATHEDRAL

Henry III, the greatest patron of church architecture that England has ever known, came to Salisbury to attend the consecration of the beautiful new cathedral which had been begun earlier in his own reign, in 1220.

He had been only twelve when his half-uncle William Longespée, (one of Henry II's dozen or so bastards), had laid one of the five foundation stones, but as the building continued Henry had frequently visited the site to follow its progress, riding over from one of his favourite hunting palaces at nearby Clarendon.

Henry's practical gift to the cathedral was to provide the massive timbers needed for the tower and roof. He is often remembered for his work in enlarging Westminster Abbey, but seldom gets full credit for his widespread generosity to other great works of art which were being constructed during his reign. Salisbury is just one example.

1486
PRINCE ARTHUR IS BORN IN 'CAMELOT'

Henry VII was insistent that his son should be born in Winchester, the ancient capital of England. Henry wanted to link his son with the romantic past of Arthurian legend and of course it was in Winchester Castle that Arthur's legendary Round Table was to be found. Some even believed that Winchester *was* Camelot.

Accordingly, he brought Elizabeth of York, his queen, to Winchester on September 1, and now, three weeks later, the royal parents rejoiced in the birth of a son who, they hoped, would successfully continue the new Tudor dynasty. Significantly, the infant prince, born on this day, was christened Arthur.

Arthur's baptism in Winchester Cathedral was one of the most splendid royal occasions ever to take place there. Costly hangings decorated the nave and a staging with seven steps led up to a special silver gilt font, over which hung a rich canopy. After the baptism Arthur was solemnly placed on the High Altar to the accompaniment of choral music.

It was just over a year since Henry's victory at Bosworth. He must have been a proud and happy father. (See APRIL 2.)

Also on this day:

1643 The first battle of Newbury: King Charles I took charge of the royalist forces himself, and the outcome was confused and bloody. Charles and his army withdrew to Oxford.

1714 King George I made his state entry into London.

SEPTEMBER 21   1327
THE MURDER OF EDWARD II

One of the most horrific events in English history took place today in Berkeley Castle, Gloucestershire. Edward II was murdered by having a red-hot poker thrust up his anus.

Visitors to Gloucester Cathedral, where a magnificent tomb was erected in Edward II's memory by his son Edward III, can enjoy the beautiful architecture which was largely paid for by the constant stream of medieval sight-seers visiting the king's last resting-place. Indeed, the new style known as 'perpendicular' gothic was introduced here.

There is a lingering tiny doubt, however, about Edward's tomb. Who lies in it?

According to the papal notary Manuele de Fieschi, Edward II was not murdered. At the last minute, he exchanged clothes with his gaoler, who volunteered to take his place while the king crept down to the door of the castle. Here, Edward killed the sleeping porter to gain the keys, and then fled into the night. When the knights came to the castle to murder Edward and found that he had escaped, they were afraid to go back to his queen and confess that they had been unsuccessful. Accordingly, as they had a corpse to hand, they cut the heart out of the dead porter, and took it back to Isabella, saying that it was the king's.

Later, apparently, it was the porter whose body was buried in Gloucester Cathedral.

As for Edward, Manuele de Fieschi recounts how he spent his final years doing penance for his sins in a hermitage somewhere on the continent.

Also on this day:

1745 Bonnie Prince Charlie and his Jacobite supporters won a victory over the English at the battle of Prestonpans, about 10 miles east of Edinburgh.

SEPTEMBER 22 1761
A POPULAR CORONATION –
BUT WHO CAME TO SEE IT?

George III was twenty-two and had been married to Charlotte of Mecklenburg-Strelitz for just a fortnight when the royal newly-weds were both crowned in Westminster Abbey on this September day. The popularity of the young couple was astonishing. Horace Walpole was amazed at how much people were paying for seats and stands. Westminster Abbey itself was fitted up with wooden viewing compartments, each holding about a dozen occupants, perched high up on scaffolding near the tops of the stone columns: fifty guineas was the going rate for one of these. London was packed with visitors with crowds sleeping all night in the open streets. Those in the abbey were treated to a magnificent ceremony, hearing Handel's stirring anthem *Zadok the Priest*, which had been sung for the first time at the coronation of George III's grandfather, George II, in 1727.

George was in a quandary as he took Holy Communion. Should he remove his crown? No one was willing to advise him, so he made the decision and took it off. The congregation was delighted at such a modest display of humility. But poor Charlotte found that her crown had got stuck in her hair, and she couldn't manage to take it off.

At the banquet afterwards everyone was amused at the Lord Steward's horse, which had been so well trained to walk backwards that it insisted on walking towards their majesties rump-first! It was a jolly, happy coronation, despite the shambles, auguring well for the future of the Hanoverians.

But afterwards a curious rumour went around that among the guests had been the Young Pretender, Bonnie Prince Charlie himself, who had come secretly to London to watch the proceedings. The prince is supposed to have declared: 'the person who is the object of all this pomp and magnificence is the person I envy the least.' Was it true? Who can say? But the very existence of such a rumour indicates the way people's minds were working in those days.

SEPTEMBER 23 1642
WORCESTER, THE 'FAITHFUL CITY'

The Battle of Edgehill, in Warwickshire, is often described as the first battle of the civil war, (see OCTOBER 23) but in fact exactly a month before this, on September 23, a company of royalist supporters defeated a parliamentary army at Powick Bridge. This victory must have given Charles I some much-needed encouragement.

Worcester's support for the king was constant throughout the civil war; in fact, as it was the only town of importance to remain loyal to the king, Charles II rewarded the citizens by granting them the motto *Civitas fidelis* – the 'Faithful City'.

Visitors to the city today can see statues of Charles I and Charles II standing in niches on each side of the entrance to the Guildhall. Charles I is holding a model of a church in his left hand and the sceptre in his right; Charles II holds the orb and sceptre, to symbolise regal government.

Also, above the doorway of the Guildhall there is a stone head 'nailed up' by its ears, representing the arch-enemy of royalists, Oliver Cromwell.

SEPTEMBER 24   1645
CHARLES I SEES HIS ARMY DEFEATED AT ROWTON HEATH NEAR CHESTER

Just three years after the first Battle of Worcester Charles knew that he was on the brink of final defeat. On this day in 1645 Charles mounted a tower in the northern city wall of Chester and watched as the remnants of his cavalry were utterly routed beneath him, just outside the city walls. Visitors to Chester can walk along these walls and go into the tower where Charles watched this battle. (It now houses a museum explaining the details of this royal disaster.)

In despair, knowing that he had no further hope of success, Charles made his way south, to Denbigh. His cause was lost.

SEPTEMBER 25   1066
KING HAROLD WINS THE BATTLE OF STAMFORD BRIDGE

In the autumn of 1066 Harold knew that he was doubly in danger: from his brother Tostig and the invading King Hardrada of Norway in the north; and from certain invasion by the Norman army led by Duke William in the south.

In the event, it was Hardrada who claimed his attention first. Harold quickly collected his army together and force-marched them 200 miles north at speed, arriving at York after just a few days. Tostig and Hardrada were waiting for him at Stamford Bridge, about 8 miles to the east.

Before joining battle, Harold briefly met his brother for the last time, offering him a third of his kingdom if he would desert Hardrada. But it was a forlorn hope. Tostig was in no mood for bargaining. 'And what will you give to Hardrada?' he asked. Harold's reply is memorable: 'I will give him six feet of English earth, or since he is taller than other men, seven feet of earth for a grave.' Then the brothers parted, and on this day in 1066, less than three weeks before that other great battle at Hastings, Harold fought the bloody Battle of Stamford Bridge. Both Tostig and Hardrada were killed.

True to his word, Harold did give Hardrada seven feet of English earth. As for Tostig, his features were so badly mangled that the only way Harold could identify him was by a wart he remembered his brother had between his shoulders. As a gesture of forgiveness, he gave him a Christian burial at York.

SEPTEMBER 26   1087
CORONATION OF WILLIAM RUFUS

Rufus was crowned on this day, a Sunday, in Westminster Abbey by Lanfranc, the Archbishop of Canterbury. It was the third coronation to take place there, and so Westminster was already becoming the traditional place for English coronations.

Rufus had been abroad when his father died, so his first thought was to reach England as soon as possible, make sure of the royal treasure at Winchester, and then to find Lanfranc and persuade him that his claim to the throne was valid. He showed him a letter which the Conqueror had dictated on his deathbed, bequeathing him the kingdom. The point was that Rufus's elder brother Robert arguably had a stronger claim, being the senior heir. However, he had already been disinherited for rebellion. Probably to Rufus's relief, Lanfranc accepted the letter and crowned him as William II.

History was to repeat itself almost thirteen years later, when Rufus's younger brother Henry also outmanoeuvred Robert to have himself crowned. One has to sympathise with Robert, the king who never was (see FEBRUARY 3).

Also on this day:

1943 King George VI visited St Paul's Cathedral to attend a thanksgiving service for victory in the Battle of Britain.

SEPTEMBER 27   1938
QUEEN ELIZABETH LAUNCHES
THE *QUEEN ELIZABETH*

Crisis was in the air on this day in 1938. Neville Chamberlain was urgently talking to Herr Hitler, as the newspapers politely called him; trenches were being dug in the London parks; gas-masks were being distributed; evacuation of children from the major cities was being organised; and King George VI was crucially occupied in discussing plans for the outbreak of war, likely at any time.

As the king felt that he should remain in London, Queen Elizabeth (later the Queen Mother) took his place in going to Clydebank to launch what was then the world's largest liner. She named the ship after herself, the *Queen Elizabeth*; it was a sister ship to the *Queen Mary*, which had been launched four years before. Both ships were to be used as troop ships during the Second World War – in fact the *Queen Elizabeth* was refitted as a troop ship even before making her maiden voyage.

Queen Elizabeth returned to London in time to hear of the agreement between Chamberlain and Hitler that Britain and Germany would 'never go to war with one another again'.

SEPTEMBER 28   1599
THE EARL OF ESSEX INVADES THE
QUEEN'S BEDROOM

This was the day when Robert Devereux, Earl of Essex, sealed his fate by striding unannounced into Elizabeth I's bedroom in the early morning, before she had had time to dress, put on her make-up, or even decide which of her eighty wigs she would wear.

The occasion was his return from a disastrous campaign in Ireland, in which, time after time, he had abused the power she had vested in him and had deliberately ignored her express commands. He had suffered defeats; he had dissipated his resources on unnecessary skirmishes; his army was deserting him. Above all, he was plainly afraid to confront the rebel Earl of Tyrone in battle, which was the specific reason he had been sent to Ireland. 'We absolutely command you to continue and perform that resolution,' Elizabeth wrote to him. But before he could receive her letter, he had decided to leave his army and speak to the queen himself.

At dawn on this day Essex arrived back in London, but when he learned that Elizabeth was at her favourite palace of Nonsuch, about 6 miles from Hampton Court, he leapt on his horse and galloped off alone through the rain. Arriving at the palace bespattered with mud, he marched straight into the queen's presence.

He grovelled before her and smothered her hands with kisses. But the damage was done. Elizabeth knew that he was a failure and an impetuous fool; knew, too, that he might well be planning rebellion against her. Nevertheless, with her thin grey hair straggling about her face, she received him with courtesy and promised to speak further when she was dressed.

Essex had offended the elderly queen more deeply than he realised – and by the end of the day he was under arrest.

Also on this day:
1853 Queen Victoria laid the foundation stone of Balmoral Castle.

SEPTEMBER 29　1399
ABDICATION OF RICHARD II

Imprisoned in the Tower of London, King Richard abdicated on this day. At least, Henry Bolingbroke summoned a Parliament in Westminster Hall on September 30 and announced that this abdication had taken place and therefore he, Henry, was claiming the throne which was there before them, symbolically empty.

The details of Richard's end are understandably obscure. He was probably starved to death in Pontefract Castle (Shakesperare's account is pure fiction). By mid-February 1400 Richard was dead.

Also on this day:
1200 Isabella of Angoulême, wife of King John, aged about fourteen, was crowned queen in Westminster Abbey.

SEPTEMBER 30　1673
MARY OF MODENA MARRIES A MAN SHE HAS NEVER HEARD OF

Mary Beatrice of Modena was only fifteen when she was told that she was to marry the English Duke of York. She had never heard of him. Perhaps she was happier when she was told that he was the brother of the King of England. But then, she had hardly heard of England either. However, she burst into tears when she learned that he was forty, and protested that she would rather be a nun.

Nevertheless, on this day in her home town of Modena in northern Italy she was married by proxy to the future King James II of England. After the ceremony was over she packed her bags, made the journey through France to Calais, crossed the Channel and went to London to meet the man she had just married.

Also on this day:

1399 Henry Bolingbroke, aged thirty-three, succeeded to the throne as King Henry IV, having forced King Richard II to abdicate.

OCTOBER 1   1553
MARY TUDOR IS CROWNED

Mary Tudor – or 'Bloody Mary' as she came to be called – has had such a bad reputation because of the cruelties done in her name in the latter part of her reign that it comes as something of a surprise to read of the great jubilations and festivities which marked her coronation. After the huge religious upheavals during the reign of her father Henry VIII, and the fanatical Protestantism of her half-brother Edward VI, most people looked forward eagerly to a return to the times their parents had known.

The day before the coronation the streets of London were lined with cheering crowds, and all kinds of entertainments were laid on for the new queen, who was thirty-seven at the time, and of course still unmarried. Orations were given from four giants; there was a trumpet solo and a huge angel in green with a moving arm; and the conduits at Cornhill and Cheapside ran with wine. Perhaps the most dramatic event put on to please Mary was an exhibition of gymnastics performed by an acrobat called Peter the Dutchman, who dazzled everybody by his daring antics on the weathercock of Old St Paul's.

For the coronation Westminster Abbey was richly decorated with elaborate hangings and the choir was well strewn with rushes. All the details of the traditional coronation services were observed, and Bishop Gardiner of Winchester, who officiated, declared to all present:

Here present is Mary, rightful and undoubted inheritrix, by the laws of God and man, to the crown and royal dignity of this realm of England, France, and Ireland; and you shall understand, that this day is appointed by all the peers of this land for the consecration, unction, and coronation of the said most excellent princess Mary. Will you serve at this time, and give your wills and assent to the same consecration, unction, and coronation?

With one voice everyone present answered: 'Yea, yea, yea, God save Queen Mary.'

Religious rumblings were in evidence, however. Bishop Gardiner had been invited to take the service as Thomas Cranmer, Archbishop of

Canterbury, was in prison charged with treason – he had supported the Protestant Lane Jane Grey.

As for the Archbishop of York, Robert Holgate, he too had been deprived of office and put in prison for the heinous crime of being married! He later got himself released by declaring that he repented of his marriage and that he had only married for fear of being thought a papist. He offered to disown his wife, obey the queen, and pay £1,000. His offer was accepted.

Also on this day:

957   Death of King Edwy, aged about nineteen. He was succeeded to the throne by his younger brother King Edgar ('The Peaceful'), aged about fifteen.

1207   Birth of the future King Henry III, son of King John and Isabella of Angoulême, in Winchester.

OCTOBER 2   1501
'SEÑORA PRINCESS CATALINA' IS GIVEN
A GRAND RECEPTION AT PLYMOUTH

On this day Catherine of Aragon, accompanied by attendants, prelates, princes, clerics, governess, duenna and many other donnas, landed at Plymouth, 'where the señora princess Catalina was grandly received, with much feasting and rejoicing'. Aged sixteen at the time, she was on her way to marry Arthur, Prince of Wales.

She must have been excited and probably a little nervous, but she never lost sight of her religious obligations or her royal dignity. On the way to the coast she had prayed for a whole night at the shrine of St James of Compostella, and she boarded the very best royal ship of Spain, of 300 tons, no less.

Arriving at Plymouth she was given a lavish welcome with West Country sports and entertainments before she began a slow and stately journey towards London. One of the stopping-places was Amesbury Abbey, founded in 980 by Queen Elfrida as a penance for having murdered her stepson, King Edward the Martyr, at Corfe Castle. It had become an abbey of royal connections: indeed it had close links with Fontevrault Abbey in France. Among other high-born ladies who had lived in Amesbury had been Queen Eleanor of Provence,who retired there as a nun after the death of her husband Henry III.

Amesbury also had even older legendary links with the story of Arthur, who had bidden farewell to his Guinevere in this abbey, before his last 'great battle in the West'. Clearly, the young Spanish princess was becoming acquainted with British royal traditions as she went on her way to meet her own future King Arthur. (See OCTOBER 7.)

Also on this day:

1452 Birth of the future King Richard III, fourth son of Richard, 3rd Duke
      of York, and Lady Cecily Neville, at Fotheringhay Castle,
      Northants.

OCTOBER 3 1612
MARY, QUEEN OF SCOTS, REACHES
HER FINAL RESTING-PLACE

James I had been ten years on the throne when he decided that he would bring the remains of the mother he had hardly known to be reinterred in Westminster Abbey. Accordingly, he wrote to the Dean of Peterborough Cathedral, where she had lain for the preceding twenty-five years, commanding him to have 'the corp of his dearest moder, lifted in as decent and respectfull a manner as is fitting,' and conveyed to Westminster, so that it might 'rest in a place where the Kings and Queens of these Realms are commonly interred, that the like honour might be done to the body of his dearest mother, and the like monument be extant to her, that had been done to his *dear sister*, the late Queen Elizabeth.'

The bodies of Queen Elizabeth and Mary, Queen of Scots, lie in the vaults of Westminster Abbey within feet of each other – an ironic juxtaposition in death. The reinterment took place on this day in 1612, when Mary's vast leaden coffin (she was six foot tall) was ceremonially brought to the abbey, drawn by six black horses.

For a while, Roman Catholic pilgrims began to visit her tomb, and hers was the last royal tomb in England at which miracles were said to have been wrought.

Also on this day:

1470 Henry VI, having been deposed on March 4 1461, was restored to the
      throne.

OCTOBER 4 1066
HAROLD MARCHES SOUTH FROM VICTORY AT STAMFORD BRIDGE

After his astonishing 200-mile march to Yorkshire to fight Hardrada and Tostig in Battle at Stamford Bridge (see SEPTEMBER 25), King Harold learned on October 1 that Duke William had already landed at Pevensey Bay, and was waiting with his Norman army to meet him.

The very next day, on October 2, Harold began his *second* 200-mile march back to London. He did it with his Saxon army in just five days – averaging about 40 miles per day. They arrived in London on October 6. On this day, then, October 4, he was about half-way back to London, probably near Peterborough or Leicester.

Orders were sent out, en route, for reinforcements to come and join them as they journeyed south: various meeting points were arranged between York and London. Men came from Lincolnshire, Nottingham, Bedford, Norfolk and Suffolk. Further south, contingents from Buckingham, Berkshire and the Thames Valley joined Harold's growing army. The Sheriff of London led troops from Middlesex. Many others came from further afield: Wiltshire, Gloucester, Worcester, Dorset and Somerset.

The Saxon army showed colossal stamina and endurance. But beyond the physical effort, Harold also faced the enormous problems of reorganising and reinforcing his troops. It was the greatest military feat achieved by any English king. The astonishing thing is how narrowly he missed victory at Hastings, just ten days later.

Also on this day:

1626 Birth of Richard Cromwell, future Lord Protector II, son of Oliver and Elizabeth Cromwell.

OCTOBER 5 1376
THE BLACK PRINCE IS BURIED NEAR THOMAS BECKET'S SHRINE

During his lifetime the Black Prince held a special veneration for Thomas Becket. He endowed not one but *two* chantries in Canterbury Cathedral in Becket's memory, and in his will he gave precise instructions that he should be buried close to the saint's shrine. Clearly it was a decision of great importance to him. Indeed this holy spot was believed to be the most sacred place in England.

On this day in 1376, seventeen weeks after his premature death at the age of forty-six, the great prince was laid to rest according to his own wishes. He was one of the greatest kings we never had. As he had died in Westminster Palace his body had to be conveyed to Canterbury, taking the very route that Chaucer's pilgrims would have taken. In fact Chaucer, who worked for the royal family and knew them well (Edward III granted him a pitcher of wine daily), was just beginning to write *The Canterbury Tales* at this time.

OCTOBER 6   1651
CHARLES II HIDES AMONG THE STONES AT STONEHENGE

It was now more than a month after his army had been defeated at Worcester, and Charles was still on the run, hiding, moving on, trying to make plans. For a while in October he was staying at Heale House, about 4 miles north of Salisbury, and on this day he spent his hours hiding among the stones at Stonehenge. Here he could easily see anyone approaching and would be able to conceal himself. At any rate, it was a lonely, unvisited spot, unlike the tourist-infested place it is today.

After the Battle of Worcester on September 3 Charles spent six weeks on the run, before he finally managed to escape to France on October 16. Here is his full itinerary during that time:

September
3 (Wed.) 6.00 p.m. leaves Worcester with Lords Wilmot and Derby, and Charles Giffard.
4 (Thurs.) 3.00 a.m. arrives at White Ladies Priory near Boscobel, about 30 miles north of Worcester. After dark goes on to Madeley, about 10 miles west of White Ladies Priory, and sleeps in the straw in a barn.
5 (Fri.) Tries to cross the Severn, but as this is closely guarded he returns to Boscobel.
6 (Sat.) Arrives at Boscobel at 5 a.m. Hides in an oak tree (see September 6)
7 (Sun.) Goes south to Moseley Hall, about 4 miles north of Wolverhampton. Spends the day talking with Father John Huddleston and hides in a priest-hole when a troop of militia come to the hall. He remains at the hall.

9 (Tues.) Leaves Moseley Hall at midnight, disguised as 'William Jackson', accompanying Jane Lane as her servant. They travel south.

10 (Wed.) Arrives at Long Marston, about 5 miles south of Stratford upon Avon, with Jane Lane, and stays at Bentley Hall.

11 (Thurs.) Continues south, through Chipping Campden to Cirencester, where the royal party spends the night at the Crown Inn, overlooking the market-place.

12 (Fri.) Continues through Chipping Sodbury and Bristol, arriving at Abbotsleigh, a little west of Bristol, where the party stay with friends for three days.

16 (Tues.) Travelling south, they spend the night at the Manor House, Castle Cary.

17 (Wed.) Continuing south, they arrive at Trent House, near Yeovil, the home of Colonel Francis Wyndham. Here Charles sees villagers celebrating his 'death', believing him to have been killed at Worcester. Jane Lane leaves him and returns home. Charles stays at Trent House until September 22.

22 (Mon.) Again disguised as a servant and accompanied by Juliana Coningsby, niece of Lady Wyndham, Charles travels to Charmouth on the south coast, and spends the night at the Queen's Armes Inn. (This pub is still there!) He hopes to find a boat at Lyme Regis to take him to France, but when this project fails he moves on to Bridport.

23 (Tues.) At the George Inn at Bridport Charles is recognised, and has to escape, travelling north, spending the night at a house at Broadwindsor.

24 (Wed.) Goes back to Trent House, near Yeovil. Stays with the Wyndhams until October 6, while his supporters try to find a suitable ship.

October

6 (Mon.) Leaves Trent House and travels to Heale House, about 4 miles north of Salisbury. He stays here for a week, and spends his days hiding among the stones at Stonehenge, returning to Heale House each day after dark.

13 (Mon.) Travels east to the house of Thomas Symonds at Hambledon in Hampshire.

14 (Tues.) Continues on to the Old George Inn at Brighton. Lord Wilmot rejoins him.

15 (Wed.) Exactly six weeks after the Battle of Worcester, Charles leaves Brighton early and travels 6 miles west, to Shoreham-by-Sea, where he boards the brig *Surprise*. The royal party sets sail at 8.00 a.m. towards the Isle of Wight but at dusk they cut across to Fécamp on the French coast.

16 (Thurs.) Lands at Fécamp at 10.00 a.m. The following day Charles and
Wilmot continue to Rouen and from there to Paris, where they are
welcomed by Henrietta Maria, Charles's mother.

OCTOBER 7   1922
THE PRINCE OF WALES MAKES THE FIRST ROYAL BROADCAST

Edward, Prince of Wales and future Edward VIII (later Duke of Windsor),
made history on this day by becoming the first member of the royal family
to make a radio broadcast.

The occasion was a National Scout Rally at Alexandra Palace. As patron
of the Scout Movement Prince Edward was making the broadcast in order
to reach those scouts who were unable to be present at the rally. His
broadcast to the boy scouts of Britain was made from York House via the
Marconi Co. Station 2LO.

OCTOBER 8   1191
JOHN TAKES CONTROL

King Richard I spent only a few months in England during his ten-year reign,
so obviously he needed a good deputy to look after the kingdom in his absence.
He chose William Longchamp, Bishop of Ely, Chancellor and papal legate.

Richard's younger brother John was naturally somewhat put out not to
be given the authority to rule in England as Richard's deputy. Taking
advantage of the fact that William Longchamp was making himself
thoroughly unpopular, John managed to persuade the barons and bishops
to impeach him for misconduct. Longchamp, who was virtually 'king' for a
while, was deposed on this day in 1191 and had to flee to the continent.

Probably much to his relief and pleasure, John now took over.

OCTOBER 9   1662
SAMUEL PEPYS HEARS THE QUEEN IS PREGNANT

Pepys records in his diary for this day that he was staying at an inn at Ware,
where he met a Mr Brian, 'with whom I supped, and was very good
company, and a scholar. He tells me, that it is believed the Queene is with
child, for that the coaches are ordered to ride very easily through the streets.'

It was a likely piece of news: Catherine of Braganza was twenty-four and had been married to Charles for just five months. Clearly, the country was in need of an heir to the throne, and the young queen provided hope and expectation. Sadly, Catherine was destined never to produce a child. How different the course of English history would have been, if only she had. For Charles, however, it was quite a different story: the *Dictionary of National Biography* reports that 'The task would be too arduous to endeavour to give an accurate list of his mistresses.'

CHARLES II's MISTRESSES AND BASTARDS

Here are the most notorious of Charles II's mistresses and their bastard children – but no list can ever pretend to be complete:

Lucy Walter	His favourite partner when in exile, and by whom he had James, Duke of Monmouth and Buccleuch, born in 1649. Lucy may also have had a daughter, Mary, by Charles.
Barbara Palmer (née Villiers)	Rather confusingly, Barbara Palmer was successively known as the Countess of Castlemaine and then as the Duchess of Cleveland. She gave Charles no fewer than six illegitimate children: Charles FitzRoy, Duke of Southampton and Cleveland, b. 1662; Henry FitzRoy, Duke of Grafton, b. 1663; George FitzRoy, Duke of Northumberland, b. 1665; Anne, Countess of Sussex; Charlotte, Countess of Lichfield; and Barbara FitzRoy, who became a nun in France.
Louise de Kéroualle	Nicknamed 'Fubbs', Louise was ennobled with the title of Duchess of Portsmouth. She gave Charles a son, Charles Lennox, Duke of Richmond, born 1678.
Hortense Mancini	She became the Duchess of Mazarin.
Nell Gwynne	Charles's favourite during his later years. Her son by him was Charles Beauclerk, Duke of St Albans, b. 1670. Nell herself was to be given the title Countess of Greenwich, but Charles died suddenly before he could confer this upon her.
Margaret Davis	An actress, who gave him a daughter, Mary Tudor, Countess of Derwentwater.
Katharine Pegge	She gave Charles a son named Charles FitzCharles, Earl of Plymouth, born 1657, and a daughter, Katherine, who became a nun in France.
Elizabeth Killigrew	Also known as Lady Shannon, she gave him a daughter named Charlotte FitzRoy, Countess of Yarmouth.
Frances Stuart	'La Belle Stewart', who was the original model for 'Britannia' on British coins.

Lesser-known names include Margaret de Carteret of Jersey, by whom he had one son, named James; Eleanor Needham (Lady Byron); Margaret Hughes, an actress; Winifred Wells; Mary Knight; and Jane Roberts, a clergyman's daughter.

OCTOBER 10   1839
QUEEN VICTORIA FALLS IN LOVE

Victoria noted the exact time in her private journal: '*10 October*: At ½p. 7 I went to the top of the staircase and received my 2 dear cousins Ernest and Albert – whom I found grown and changed, and embellished. It was with some emotion that I beheld Albert – who is *beautiful*.'

She had met Albert briefly a few years before, but now, as a blushing twenty-year-old, Victoria instantly and instinctively knew she had met her future husband. The following day she described Albert's beauty in detail: 'Albert really is quite charming, and so excessively handsome, such beautiful blue eyes, an exquisite nose, and such a pretty mouth with delicate moustachios and slight but very slight whiskers; a beautiful figure, broad in the shoulders and a fine waist.'

The attraction was mutual. In rapture, the queen noted how Albert 'was *so* kind, *so* dear, we kissed each other again and again and he called me 'Liebe Kleine. Ich habe dich so lieb, ich kann nicht sage wie.' ('Dear little one. I love you so much. I can't say how much.'). . . . Oh! what *too* sweet delightful moments are these!! . . . We sit so nicely side by side on that little blue sofa; no two Lovers could ever be happier than we are!'

Within days she had proposed to him.

1844
VICTORIA AND ALBERT FIND OSBORNE

Coincidentally, exactly five years later to the day, Victoria and Albert came across Old Osborne House on the Isle of Wight. In her diary (where she expressed all her innermost thoughts) Victoria wrote, 'It is impossible to imagine a prettier spot – we have a charming beach quite to ourselves, we can walk anywhere without being followed or mobbed.'

Albert immediately set to work to redesign and rebuild the house according to his own fastidious tastes. It was complete within a few years and here their growing family grew up. It was at Osborne that Victoria spent the idyllic years of her married life, and when in 1861 Albert suddenly died, here she spent the remaining forty years of her widowhood, expecting the whole world to come to her in her prolonged grief.

And it was at Osborne that she died, cradled by the Kaiser (her favourite grandchild), and surrounded by her family.

Also on this day:
1361 Marriage of Edward, Prince of Wales (the 'Black Prince'), aged thirty-one, to the Countess Joan of Kent.

OCTOBER 11   1521
HENRY VIII BECOMES THE 'DEFENDER OF THE FAITH'

It was just four years since Luther had nailed his famous ninety-five theses on the door of the church at Wittenberg arguing against the beliefs and practices of the Church of Rome. Whatever else he was, Henry VIII was no supporter of the views of this great German reformer – indeed only five months before this date, on May 12, Luther's works had been publicly burned in Old St Paul's churchyard in front of Cardinal Wolsey and a crowd of thirty thousand staunch Catholics.

Henry enjoyed a fight, and he loved theological disputation: so he had written his counterblast to Luther in a book he called *Assertio Septem Sacramentorum* – 'The Assertion of Seven Sacraments'. In it, among other things, Henry argued the case for the authority of the Pope and the indissolubility of marriage! Of course, he had the help of biblical scholars in writing this book; nevertheless, he was enjoying the fame of authorship at this time, only weeks after the publication of his work.

On this day in 1521 Pope Leo X rewarded Henry for his efforts by bestowing upon him the proud title *Fidei Defensor* ('Defender of the Faith'). Most British coins since that day – even the present decimal coinage – have carried the initials 'F.D.' in token of the fact that our monarchs are 'Defenders of the Faith'. Ironically, subsequent monarchs since Mary Tudor have defended a very different version of the Christian faith.

Also on this day:
1727 Coronation of King George II, aged forty-three, in Westminster Abbey.

OCTOBER 12   1537
AT LAST, A LEGITIMATE SON FOR HENRY VIII

Jane Seymour went into labour at Hampton Court Palace. It was a lengthy labour, which began on the afternoon of October 9, and the baby was finally born in the early hours of October 12. Henry VIII had a son at last! It is said that the king wept as he held the new-born prince in his arms.

It was the eve of the feast-day of Edward the Confessor, so what name could be more suitable than this for the future King of England? Edward VI had arrived.

OCTOBER 13   1399
HENRY IV IS CROWNED AND ANOINTED WITH SPECIAL OIL

Today saw the formal coronation of Henry Bolingbroke as King Henry IV. Although he was usurping the throne, he felt he had every legal and moral right to do so, and so his coronation observed every tradition and custom. Indeed, he was keen to use some very special oil for his anointment.

Legend had it that centuries before, St Thomas Becket had seen a vision of the Virgin Mary at Sens in France, and that she had given him a phial containing some special holy oil. Apparently, St Thomas had hidden this precious treasure, and it was lost until Richard II discovered it in the Tower of London. Naturally, Henry felt that it was his to use by right.

It must have been powerful stuff, for the Welsh historian Adam of Usk noted that when it was poured over Henry's head, all the lice rushed out.

1470
HENRY VI IS CROWNED AGAIN, IN ST PAUL'S CATHEDRAL

Henry IV's grandson, Henry VI, began his second period of kingship on this day. The Earl of Warwick (the 'Kingmaker') had landed from France the previous month and had gathered forces around him. Entering London, he found the capital in chaos, with King Edward no longer there. They went immediately to the Tower of London, where Henry had been kept prisoner, and released him from his captivity.

Poor Henry! He was 'not so worshipfully arrayed, nor so cleanly kept' as he should have been, and was described as 'a man amazyd and utterly dullyd with trubbles and adversitie'. He hardly knew what was happening to him.

Nevertheless, he was a useful figurehead, so on this day in 1470 he was taken to Old St Paul's and given a second coronation. Perhaps it would be truer to say a *third* coronation, for he had been crowned King of France in St Denis in Paris on 16 December 1431, as well as being crowned King of England in Westminster Abbey on 6 November 1429.

Sadly this second period of kingship was to last just six months. His wits were not quite with him, but he did find time to send a greeting at Christmas to his college at Eton.

OCTOBER 14   1066
THE BATTLE OF HASTINGS

In just a few hours the fate of England was changed for ever. For a long time the Saxon army had held its own against the Norman attack, but then William sent back to his base-camp at Pevensey for a new supply of arrows. When these were fired high into the sky Harold received his famous mortal wound in his eye. The Saxon defences crumbled and William's horsemen and foot soldiers closed in for the kill.

The final moments of Harold, the last Saxon king, were terrible. Not only was he hit in the eye by that fatal arrow, but he was also run through by two lances and struck on the head by a sword. A group of Norman knights surrounded him, and one of them, Ivo of Ponthieu, tried his best to hack off Harold's leg.

Harold's mother Gytha and his lifetime mistress Edith of the Swan Neck had been watching the battle, standing under a massive oak tree, later called the Watch Oak. They must have been sickened at what they saw. On that day the old lady Gytha lost three sons and a nephew, and the corpses on the battlefield were so mangled and jumbled together that she simply couldn't recognise them. It was left to Edith of the Swan Neck to unfasten the chainmail on one of the victims. Only then could she identify the tattoo marks on Harold's body.

After the battle, Gytha pleaded with the Conqueror to give Harold a proper burial, but William was adamant. Harold had been merely a usurper in his eyes, and did not deserve that honour. He was left on the beach, covered by a pile of stones. Only much later were his mutilated remains transferred to Waltham Abbey.

Gytha kept up her opposition to William the Conqueror to the very end. She spent her final years at Brompton Regis, a village about 12 miles south of Minehead in Somerset. And when William came there in 1068, she positively refused to yield her manor up to him. William knew when he was beaten. He let her stay there in peace until she died. It is still Brompton's proud boast that it was the last piece of free Saxon territory.

Also on this day:

1633 Birth of the future King James II, second son of King Charles I and Henrietta Maria, in St James's Palace, London.

OCTOBER 15   1399
HAL BECOMES
PRINCE OF WALES

Two days after his coronation (see OCTOBER 13) the newly self-appointed King Henry IV invested his eldest son Henry as Prince of Wales. Henry, or 'Hal' as he appears in Shakespeare's plays, was of course destined to become the heroic victor at Agincourt.

Shakespeare has given us a memorable image of young Hal as a high-spirited ne'er-do-well while he was Prince of Wales, living a riotous life-style with the notorious old rogue Falstaff. He evidently had something of a squeamish nature at this time, however. He went to watch the burning of John Bradbury at Smithfield, accused of heresy.

John Bradbury was rolled to the place where he was to be burned in an empty beer-barrel. Prince Hal could not bear to witness the man being burnt, so he offered him a free pardon if he would recant his Wycliffite beliefs. Bradbury rejected the offer, and the bonfire was kindled. In his agony he cried out to God, praying for strength to bear the flames. Prince Hal was so unnerved by this that he ordered the poor man to be dragged out of the fires, and then he promised to pay him a pension of threepence a day in compensation if only he would recant.

Bradbury, half-roasted, still refused, much to the prince's grief. He was cast back into the flames and perished.

Also on this day:

1839 Queen Victoria proposed to Prince Albert. He accepted.

OCTOBER 16   1834
THE PALACE OF WESTMINSTER GOES UP IN FLAMES

The original Palace of Westminster had been built for Edward the Confessor, but after 1066 it was used by William the Conqueror and his court.

Rufus, the Conqueror's son, intended to extend it with an immense building project: his legacy, which remains to this day, is Westminster Hall, almost 240ft long and 68ft wide, built in 1097–9. In a famous boast Rufus said that this huge hall was 'a mere bed-chamber' compared with the palace he intended to build beside it. But fate intervened and he was dead before he could even start it.

The palace remained the main residence of the kings of England until Henry VIII abandoned it for Whitehall Palace in 1512, but still it remained the administrative centre of the kingdom.

On this day in 1834 a gigantic fire burned the entire complex: the palace, the crypt of St Stephen's Chapel and the cloisters were totally destroyed. Luckily, Westminster Hall, Rufus's 'bed-chamber' remained intact. The cause of this fire was the burning of a vast quantity of 'tally sticks' – a curious and out-dated system of keeping accounts which involved notched elm-wood sticks split in halves: one half being kept by the Exchequer at Westminster and the other being kept as a receipt by those who had paid.

Charles Dickens amused an audience at Drury Lane by explaining 'it would naturally occur to any intelligent person that nothing could be easier than to allow them to be carried away for firewood by the miserable people who live in that neighbourhood. However, they never had been useful, and official routine required that they never should be, and so the order went forth that they should be privately and confidentially burned.'

The decision was made to burn these tally sticks in a big furnace beneath the House of Lords. The blaze got out of control and by six o'clock that evening the whole higgledy-piggledy sprawl of buildings was alight.

Charles Barry, who was to design the new Houses of Parliament, happened to see the burning glow in the sky over London as he was approaching the city that night on the stage-coach from Brighton. He little realised how significant that glow would be for his future career.

Also on this day:

1555   Hugh Latimer and Nicholas Ridley were burned at the stake in Oxford for upholding their Protestant faith (see NOVEMBER 10).

1651   Charles II finally landed on French soil, at Fécamp, after forty-three days on the run after his defeat at Worcester (see OCTOBER 6).

1653   Oliver Cromwell was installed as Lord Protector in Westminster Hall. It was tantamount to a coronation and the Coronation Chair was taken to Westminster Hall for the occasion.

1793   Marie Antoinette, Queen of France and wife of Louis XVI, was guillotined in the Place de la Révolution (now called the Place de la Concorde), Paris.

OCTOBER 17   1980
QUEEN ELIZABETH II VISITS THE VATICAN AND MEETS THE POPE

After several centuries during which a meeting between an English sovereign and the 'Bishop of Rome' would have been unthinkable, on this day Queen Elizabeth, wearing black, paid a state visit to the Vatican and met Pope John Paul II.

An equally significant and historic moment came on May 28 1982, when the Pope returned the visit and spent thirty-five minutes alone with the queen at Buckingham Palace.

'I will pray for your son in the Falklands,' the Pope is reported to have said. But naturally the private conversation between priest and monarch is a matter which cannot be known. The break from Rome had lasted four-and-a-half centuries.

OCTOBER 18   1216
PEACHES AND NEW CIDER, OR WAS IT POISON?

King John died in the castle at Newark-on-Trent, Nottinghamshire. He was just forty-eight. Only one week before, his convoy of horse-drawn luggage-carts had been swallowed up in the boggy marshes of the Wellstream estuary in East Anglia, where the old River Ouse flowed out to the Wash. Dangerous tidal waters had rushed in from the sea, engulfing wagon-load after wagon-load of John's priceless valuables.

He had been in the habit of carrying these treasures about with him, afraid to leave them behind. Thus in this disaster he lost his own personal belongings, most of them inherited from his mother, Eleanor of Aquitaine, who had been the richest woman in the world. Beautiful jewels, necklaces, bracelets, precious ornaments, hundreds of gold and silver cups, crosses, chalices, holy relics: all these were lost for ever. Worse still, the royal regalia also disappeared: including a crown which had belonged to his grandmother, the Empress Matilda.

One has to feel sorry for John, who was now suffering from dysentery, an illness that had developed after a session of over-eating and drinking at a banquet laid on for him by the citizens of King's Lynn. Sick, angry and miserable, he moved on to Swineshead Abbey, Lincolnshire, on his way to Lincoln. Here he indulged himself too freely on peaches and new cider – not the best diet for someone with dysentery! Later chroniclers, always ready to spread malicious gossip about the unpopular monarch, told the tale that a monk at Swineshead had poisoned the peaches.

John's condition worsened, but he dragged himself on, first to Sleaford, and then to the Bishop of Lincoln's castle at Newark in Nottinghamshire. By now he was so ill that he could go no further. The Abbot of Croxton, a monastic physician, was called in to help, but he could do nothing for the sick king. John managed to dictate his will, asking to be buried in Worcester Cathedral, so as to lie near his favourite saint, St Wulfstan. Then he died. Legends tell how savage gales shook the roof-tops as he received the last rites.

Also on this day:

1016 Battle of Ashingdon, Essex, after which King Edmund II ('Ironside') was forced to partition the country with the Danish King Canute.

1216 King Henry III, aged nine, succeeded to the throne on the death of his father, King John.

OCTOBER 19   1483
RICHARD III SIGNS A DEATH WARRANT

Richard was in Grantham on this day and had been disturbed to hear that his former friend, the Duke of Buckingham, was stirring rebellion against him. Staying in 'the king's chamber of the hospice of the Angel at Grantham', he signed a death warrant for the duke, having previously sent for the Great Seal of the kingdom.

Exactly a fortnight later the Duke of Buckingham was duly beheaded in Salisbury market-place. Today, there is a plaque on the wall of Debenham's store in that city, to commemorate the Duke's execution.

OCTOBER 20   1604
KING JAMES I OFFICIALLY DECLARES THE NAME 'GREAT BRITAIN'

Despite some parliamentary opposition, King James proclaimed himself 'King of Great Britain, France and Ireland' on this day in 1604.

Being king of both Scotland and England posed something of a constitutional problem. Were the two countries united as a single entity? Or were they still separate? In fact, it was not until 1707 that a formal Act of Union joined England and Scotland under one parliament. The old Scottish Parliament last met on April 28 1707, when it was formally dissolved. A few days later, on May 1 1707, the new parliament of Great Britain met for the first time.

To bring the story up to date, it was on Thursday May 6 1999 that the people of Scotland were again given the opportunity to vote for candidates in a new, independent Scottish Parliament. Tony Blair, the 'British' Prime Minister, had managed to reverse history.

In 1604, anticipating the union of the two countries, James had come up with a strange new name – 'Great Britain'. He made his constitutional position quite clear: 'What God has conjoined, let no man separate. I am the husband and my whole isle is my lawful wife.' However, it was pointed out to him that to cross a rose with a thistle might well produce a monster.

Also on this day:
1714   King George I, aged fifty-four, was crowned in Westminster Abbey.

OCTOBER 21   1936
KING EDWARD VIII RECEIVES THE FIRST WARNING ABOUT MRS SIMPSON

It was on this day at Fort Belvedere, about 5 miles from Windsor Castle, that King Edward VIII had a sticky interview with his Prime Minister, Stanley Baldwin.

Fort Belvedere was the king's private retreat. Originally a kind of mock-gothic folly built by 'Butcher' Cumberland, it was used occasionally by George IV. When Edward asked his father George V for permission to turn the 'fort' into a country house for himself the old king replied: 'What could you possibly want that queer old place for? Those damn weekends, I suppose.' But it was at those 'damn weekends' that Edward and Wallis Simpson built up their powerful relationship that ultimately led to the king's abdication.

Stanley Baldwin's visit on this day gave Edward the first intimation that the nation was concerned about his relationship with Wallis, who was just about to divorce her second husband. 'Must the case really go on?' asked Baldwin, 'almost bluntly' according to the king's own memoirs.

Baldwin kept up the pressure. It was just fifty days later that the king, who described himself as being in 'a personal situation of almost indescribable complexity', made his final decision to abdicate.

Also on this day:

1805   Lord Nelson led his fleet to victory at the Battle of Trafalgar but was killed on board his ship, *Victory*.

OCTOBER 22   1695
WILLIAM III STAYS AT ALTHORP AS A GUEST OF ROBERT SPENCER

The attention of the world was centred on Althorp in 1997, when the body of Diana, Princess of Wales, was brought here to be laid to rest in the grounds of her family home.

The Spencers had been friends and supporters of royalty for generations: indeed Sir Robert Spencer (1570–1627), who was created 1st Baron Spencer in 1603, owned no fewer than 19,000 sheep, and was reputed to own more ready money than anyone else in the entire country at the time of James I. The king was pleased to use his services as ambassador.

Henry, 3rd Baron Spencer, was a brave supporter of Charles I, who created him Earl of Sunderland when he was aged only twenty-three, but sad to say only a few months later Henry was killed fighting in the royalist army at the Battle of Newbury, leaving Robert, his two-year-old son, to become the 2nd Earl of Sunderland. Robert grew up to be, in the words of Raine, Countess Spencer, 'one of the most brilliant, devious and enigmatic politicians of his time,' and gave his services in advising three kings: Charles II, James II and William III.

It was on this day in 1695 that the recently bereaved William III arrived at Althorp in Northamptonshire to begin a week's stay with the Spencers. Twelve generations of Spencers later (it was in 1765 that John Spencer (1734–83) was created the 1st Earl Spencer), Lady Diana Spencer was to marry into the Royal House of Windsor.

OCTOBER 23   1642
THE GHOSTLY AFTERMATH OF THE BATTLE OF EDGEHILL

The Battle of Edgehill was fought between the royalist troops led by Prince Rupert and the parliamentarian army led by the 3rd Earl of Essex. The battlefield is in Warwickshire, about 11 miles south-east of Stratford upon Avon. Neither side could claim a victory, though Charles did manage to keep open the road to Oxford and London. Charles was personally present in the thick of the fighting, and was almost captured by Essex's infantry.

As the first major conflict in the civil war, the Battle of Edgehill is well known to everyone. Far less well known is the extraordinary story that three days afterwards the entire scene, lasting several hours, was re-enacted before a group of local shepherds, by *ghosts*! It was a spooky illusion which ranks as one of the most astonishing demonstrations of paranormal phenomena ever witnessed in England.

Even more astonishing to relate is that the same illusion was replayed not once but several times during the following weeks, including a ghostly battle on Christmas Eve!

Hundreds of sightseers turned up to witness these phantom encounters, and an account was eventually printed in London in January 1643. The king was so intrigued that he sent a team of special observers to report on what was happening. And when they returned they told Charles that they had seen the ghostly battle with their own eyes, twice on consecutive days. They had heard clashes of swords and screams of wounded soldiers, and they even claimed, on oath, to have recognised their own comrades who had been killed in the real battle.

These Edgehill soldier-ghosts have been seen even in the twentieth century.

OCTOBER 24   1537
DEATH OF QUEEN JANE SEYMOUR

There is no doubt of the sincerity with which Henry mourned Jane. She died this day, aged twenty-eight, twelve days after giving birth to the future Edward VI.

It had been a difficult labour lasting two days and three nights. A popular ballad recounted, wrongly, that the queen had a Caesarean birth after a labour of 'six weeks or more' and that she was already dead when the baby was 'set free'. It described how the surgeon

> . . . gave her rich caudle [warm drink]
> But the death-sleep slept she
> Then her right side was opened
> And the babe was set free.
>
> The babe it was christened
> And put out to nurse
> While the royal Queen Jane
> She lay cold in the dust.

Henry is reported to have wept with joy as he held the newly born prince in his arms, and of course joyful preparations went ahead for the christening three days later. But the effort of birth and the constant noise and hullabaloo of the celebrations must have exhausted Jane. Lack of proper medical care and poor hygiene led to puerperal fever, and Jane could not escape the fate which befell so many in those times.

In his last will Henry commanded that his own body should lie with the bones of 'our true and loving Wife Queen Jane', and this was duly done.

OCTOBER 25   1415
'ONCE MORE UNTO THE BREACH, DEAR FRIENDS, ONCE MORE!'

Thanks to Shakespeare, Henry V's victory at Agincourt on this day, the feast day of Saints Crispin and Crispian, is still remembered more than any other English military success. Crécy, Poitiers, Blenheim and even Waterloo are merely names, but the name of Agincourt still reverberates with the royal shout of 'God for Harry, England, and Saint George!' This is the victory of 'we few, we happy few,' that still lingers in the minds of Englishmen, and probably will continue to do so 'from this day to the ending of the world'. But Shakespeare's patriotism was justified: it was indeed a remarkable victory, against enormous odds.

Henry's army of about six thousand men, weakened by dysentery and short of rations, utterly defeated a French force of twenty thousand men equipped with greatly superior armour and much heavier weapons. In fact, they were too heavily equipped. Badly organised and lacking manoeuvrability, they simply fell on top of each other in heaps on the boggy ground. The English butchered them where they lay, completely unable to get up. It has been estimated that the French losses amounted to about ten thousand, compared with fewer than five hundred English casualties.

Apart from the bad weather and poorly deployed French forces, the victory was largely won by the unrivalled English longbowmen. Their skill with six-foot bows, shooting arrows tipped with good Sheffield steel and flighted with goose feathers, was unmatched throughout Europe.

No English monarch has been given such a splendid welcome as that given to Henry V on his return to England. Crowds plunged into the sea at Dover and carried him shoulder-high to the shore. London gave him a tumultuous reception and fountains literally flowed with wine.

Also on this day:

1154 Death of King Stephen, aged fifty-seven, at St Martin's Priory, Dover, Kent. He was buried in Faversham Abbey (though his remains are now lost). King Henry II, aged twenty-one, succeeded to the throne as a result of an agreement made between the two men (see JANUARY 13).

1760 Death of King George II, aged seventy-six, in Westminster Palace, London.

1760 King George III, aged twenty-two, succeeded to the throne on the death of his grandfather, King George II.

OCTOBER 26 899
THE GHOST OF KING ALFRED WALKS IN WINCHESTER

Arguably the greatest king ever to rule over England, Alfred died this day in his own capital city of Winchester. He was only fifty when he died, but his achievements in the face of appalling difficulties were incalculable and enduring. His biographer, Bishop Asser of Sherborne, wrote of him that he was the 'unshakeable pillar of the western people, a man replete with justice, vigorous in warfare, learned in speech, above all instructed in divine learning'.

Fighting many battles, he saved England from the Danes, brought learning to the land, initiated the first history of the nation, strengthened the army, built fortified towns, drew up a legal system, personally translated several books, established religious foundations, and even invented candle-clocks. As for Winchester, he had the roads properly cobbled, built monasteries, and made it a centre of culture renowned throughout Europe.

The *Anglo-Saxon Chronicle*, which Alfred himself began, laconically reports in AD 899:

> In this year died Alfred, son of Ethelwulf, six nights before All Hallows' Day. He was king over all England except that part which was under Danish domination, and he ruled the kingdom twenty-eight and a half years.

Sadly his bones are lost. Originally he was buried in Winchester's Old Minster, but when his ghost started walking about there, perhaps unquiet at the place chosen for his resting-place, the monks begged his son, King Edward the Elder, to allow them to transfer his remains to the New Minster, which Alfred himself had built.

This was done. However, two centuries later the royal bones were moved again, this time to Hyde Abbey, just to the north of the city walls. At the time of the Reformation the abbey was sold to Henry VIII's Lord Chancellor, Thomas Wriothesley. Unforgivably, in the eighteenth century, when the buildings were finally turned into a House of Correction, the bones of both Alfred and his queen, Elswitha, disappeared for ever.

Even now, archaeologists are investigating the site, hoping to locate them.

Also on this day:
899   King Edward the Elder, aged twenty-nine, succeeded to the throne on the death of his father, King Alfred the Great.

OCTOBER 27 1553
MARY TUDOR SOLEMNLY SWEARS TO MARRY PHILIP OF SPAIN

Mary had managed to survive the crude plot to put Lady Jane Grey on the throne, and it was now just over three weeks since her coronation (see OCTOBER 1). Clearly it was now time to marry. She knew that Parliament was petitioning her not to 'marry a stranger or a foreigner', but she had already made up her mind: it was to be Philip of Spain.

In the evening of this day, a Sunday, in 1553, she sent for the Spanish ambassador and asked him to follow her into her private chapel. Here she knelt before the altar in the presence of the consecrated Host. She repeated the hymn *Veni Creator*, and then called God to witness that while she lived she would never wed any man other than Philip of Spain.

Also on this day:
939 Death of King Athelstan, aged about forty-four, son of Edward the Elder and grandson of Alfred the Great. He was buried in Malmesbury Abbey, Wilts. His half-brother, King Edmund I, aged eighteen, succeeded him to the throne.

OCTOBER 28 1216
NINE-YEAR-OLD HENRY III IS CROWNED IN GLOUCESTER

When King John died, his queen Isabella of Angoulême and their children, including Henry, his nine-year-old son and heir, were staying in Gloucester.

These were difficult and dangerous days. John had been far from popular, and although the accession of the boy-king Henry was announced in the streets of Gloucester, it was by no means certain that he would be accepted by all the barons as their king. After all, it was only a year since they had forced John to put his seal to Magna Carta: royalty was not having an easy time.

Hastily Isabella sent her second son Richard to Ireland for safety's sake, and then arranged for young Henry to have at least a preliminary coronation, to pre-empt possible rivals seizing the throne. No crown was available, so she gave her own golden throat-collar for the ceremony.

On this day, using Isabella's collar, the Bishop of Winchester, Peter des Roches, crowned the young king in the church of the Benedictine Abbey of St Peter in Gloucester – the church which later became Gloucester Cathedral. During the service, Henry swore that he would show strict justice to the people committed to him, that he would destroy evil laws and unjust customs, if there were any in his realm, and that he would observe the good and make everyone else observe them. It was a tall order for a nine-year-old!

It was not until May 17 1220, almost four years later, that Henry was 'properly' crowned in Westminster Abbey.

Also on this day:
1708 Death of Prince George of Denmark, aged fifty-five, husband of Queen Anne. He was buried in Westminster Abbey.

OCTOBER 29   1618
JAMES I ORDERS THE EXECUTION OF SIR WALTER RALEIGH

Sir Walter Raleigh, one of the greatest of all the Elizabethan adventurers, was beheaded on this day in Old Palace Yard at Whitehall. King James, poverty-stricken as always, had hoped to make use of Raleigh by sending him on an expedition to the Orinoco River in South America to find a gold mine. But alas, Sir Walter lost everything: his fleet, his son, and on this day, in retribution, his head.

The problem was that Raleigh had been too rash in his dealings with the Spaniards, and James had to bow to diplomatic pressure from Spain.

Raleigh inspected the axe just before he put his head on the block. 'This is sharp medicine,' he remarked, 'but it is a sure cure for all diseases.' The executioner was not happy at the job he had to do, and Raleigh had to urge him to get on with it.

It took two blows to sever his head. Afterwards his body was taken to St Margaret's, Westminster, where it is said to have been interred in front of the altar – though possibly it was smuggled out to be buried in West Horsley, Surrey. Lady Raleigh, his wife, managed to retrieve his head, and she kept it with her in a red leather bag for the rest of her life.

OCTOBER 30   1485
HENRY VII INVENTS THE BEEFEATERS

On this day, Sunday October 30 1485, the victor at Bosworth Field had himself properly crowned in Westminster Abbey. He had previously been crowned on the battlefield by one of the Stanleys, according to the oft-told tale, with Richard's gold circlet, retrieved from a hawthorn bush.

The coronation went according to tradition, but for this occasion Henry had created a special personal bodyguard for himself – the Yeomen of the Guard. These Yeomen are now the oldest royal bodyguards in the world.

It is easy to confuse them with the Yeomen Extraordinary of the Guard, who were appointed as Warders of the Tower of London by Henry's grandson, Edward VI. Both the Yeomen of the Guard and the Yeomen Extraordinary of the Guard have scarlet tunics, white ruffs and black Tudor hats, but Henry's original Yeomen can be recognised by their crossbelts, which were originally intended to support their 'arquebuses' – an old-fashioned type of handgun.

The popular nickname 'Beefeater' came to be applied to the Yeomen of the Guard about the middle of the seventeenth century, but nowadays it is more frequently used to refer to the colourful guards of the Tower. Picturesque they may be, but when Henry VII created his Yeomen he knew that as a newcomer to the throne he urgently needed special protection from his enemies. The Yeomen of the Guard were, for him, a vital necessity and not just a tourist attraction.

Also on this day:
1683 Birth of the future King George II, son of Crown Prince George of Hanover and Sophia Dorothea of Celle, at the Herrenhausen Palace, Hanover.

OCTOBER 31   1955
THE QUEEN'S SISTER CHOOSES 'DUTY'
AND REJECTS HER LOVER

Later generations find it difficult to imagine why Princess Margaret, the younger sister of Queen Elizabeth II, decided after weeks of anguish to relinquish the idea of marrying a man whom she clearly loved. Group Captain Peter Townsend had been an equerry to King George VI and had had a distinguished record of service in the RAF during the Battle of Britain.

The one reason that was put forward to make her abandon her natural wishes was simply that Peter Townsend was a divorcee. As such, he was unacceptable to Church and Parliament. It made no difference that he had been the innocent victim of his wife's adultery.

Pictures taken of the princess at this time show her to be deeply unhappy, and even until the last moment she had hoped to brave the storm and marry, but in the end she made this announcement on the last day of October:

> I have been aware that, subject to my renouncing my rights of succession, it might be possible for me to contract a civil marriage. But mindful of the Church's teaching that Christian marriage is indissoluble, and conscious of my duty to the Commonwealth, I have resolved to put these considerations before others. I have reached this decision entirely alone, and in doing so I have been strengthened by the unfailing support and devotion of Group Captain Townsend.

On May 6 1960 the princess married Anthony Armstrong-Jones.

NOVEMBER 1 1141
STEPHEN IS RELEASED FROM CAPTIVITY AND BECOMES KING AGAIN

King Stephen had been held captive by his cousin, the Empress Matilda, since February 2 of this year, and so she had temporarily become England's ruler, with the unique title 'Domina' – or 'Lady of the English'. He had been captured near Lincoln, and was held first in Gloucester before being taken to another dungeon in Bristol. For a while, it looked as if Matilda had won the crown which had been bequeathed to her by her father Henry I.

However, the fortunes of war had turned against her (see SEPTEMBER 14) and when her half-brother Robert was captured at Stockbridge, near Winchester, the two sides in this wretched civil war came to an agreement to exchange prisoners: Stephen for Robert.

Thus on November 1, Stephen was released from Bristol and Robert was released from Rochester. Meanwhile Stephen's queen and son were held hostage at Bristol and Robert's son was held hostage at Winchester until the king and Robert were known to have been given their freedom. It was like some gigantic chess-game.

Stephen, of course, now became king again, and Matilda lost whatever claim she could make to be 'ruling' the country.

NOVEMBER 2 1726
DEATH OF 'QUEEN' SOPHIA DOROTHEA IN EXILE

Sophia Dorothea never was a queen – but arguably she should have been. When George I came to England to be its king, he brought his two mistresses with him: a fat one, Sophia von Kilmansegg, nicknamed 'The Elephant'; and a thin one, Ermengarda Melusina von Schulenburg, nicknamed 'The Maypole'. Later on, he took another mistress, Anne Brent, who had such black hair and dark skin that she became known as 'The Sultana'. His wife Sophia Dorothea, however, he left behind to languish in prison. Poor Sophia Dorothea had married George when she was only sixteen and he was twenty-two. It was, of course, a political marriage and although they had a son and daughter (the son became our George II) they disliked each other from the start.

Sophia was foolish enough to take a secret lover, the handsome Swedish count Philip Konigsmarck, and they planned to elope together. However, Philip was already tangled up in another love-affair with Countess Platen, who was so furious when she heard of Philip's intentions to elope with Sophia that she naturally had him murdered.

As for George, *he* was furious that his wife was double-crossing him. It was all very well for men to have mistresses, but it was quite a different matter for women to have lovers. Promptly he divorced her and had her kept in a castle under house arrest for the rest of her life – another thirty-two years. As a kind gesture, he allowed her out for a walk every afternoon. Sophia never came to England. Indeed she never went anywhere.

A fortune-teller told George that he would not live more than a year after the death of Sophia, so when she died George left her unburied for six months and then left England to make the funeral arrangements, telling his son and daughter-in-law that he would never see them again. On arrival at Osnabrück he predictably died.

Also on this day:

1083 Death of Matilda of Flanders, wife of William the Conqueror, aged about fifty-two, at Caen, Normandy.

1470 Birth of Prince Edward, future King Edward V, in the sanctuary of the abbot's house, Westminster. The son of Edward IV and Elizabeth Woodville, he was one of the 'Princes in the Tower', supposedly murdered on the orders of King Richard III.

NOVEMBER 3 1403
HENRY IV SENDS A GIFT TO HOTSPUR'S WIDOW

Fifteen weeks after the battle of Shrewsbury (see JULY 21), Henry IV ordered that Hotspur's severed head should be returned to his widow. It must have been a gesture with mixed intentions. As well as giving the poor woman the comfort of being able to bury her husband's head it also sent out the message to her part of the country that he, Henry, would brook no opposition.

Rebel heads were usually left to rot for decades, perched on poles above city gates. In the north, Micklegate Bar in York was a favourite place for displaying heads, and the heads of Lord Mowbray and Archbishop Scrope were among scores of heads put on view there. In the south, Westminster Hall, London Bridge and Temple Bar were usually surmounted with these grisly relics. It comes as something of a shock to realise that even in Samuel

Johnson's time London was still receiving its quota of rebel heads. One of the last heads to be left there was blown down on April 1 1772.

NOVEMBER 4   1396
RICHARD II MARRIES HIS SECOND WIFE –
A SEVEN-YEAR-OLD PRINCESS

It was an extraordinary match! Richard's first wife, Anne of Bohemia, had died in 1394, to his intense grief. But now he was proposing to marry Isabella of Valois, daughter of Charles VI ('The Mad') of France. Like so many royal marriages, it was a political affair, and Isabella brought with her an enormous dowry of 800,000 francs in gold. Although still a child, just a few days short of her eighth birthday, she was pretty and intelligent. When the English Earl Marshal introduced himself to her, kneeling and saying 'Madam, if it please God, you shall be our lady and queen,' the little princess had the dignity and maturity to reply: 'Sir, if it please God and my lord and father, that I be queen of England, I shall be well pleased thereat, for I have been told I shall then be a great lady.'

The French historian Froissart was staying at Eltham Palace at the time of this marriage, and he tells us that 'it was pretty to see her, young as she was, practising how to act the queen.'

The marriage took place on this day in 1396. There was such a dense crowd on London Bridge as people tried to catch a glimpse of her that nine people were crushed to death.

Also on this day:
1650 Birth of the future King William III, son of Mary (daughter of King Charles I) and Stadtholder William II, Prince of Orange-Nassau, at the Hague, Holland.
1677 Marriage of the future King William III to his cousin Mary, future joint sovereign, eldest daughter of the Duke of York (future James II), at St James's Palace, London.

NOVEMBER 5   1605
'REMEMBER, REMEMBER, THE FIFTH OF NOVEMBER'

Remember, remember, the fifth of November,
Gunpowder, treason and plot!

Thanks to this old doggerel, the date of the discovery of the Gunpowder Plot is etched permanently into English minds. The year may be forgotten, and perhaps even the motive of the plot, but the date itself is unforgettable.

In the early hours of this day in 1605, the Catholic Guy Fawkes was discovered in the precincts of Parliament with about thirty-six barrels of gunpowder nearby – quite sufficient to blow up the entire House of Lords, where the king and his Parliament were shortly to assemble. Estimates vary, but the amount of gunpowder may have been as much as 10,000lb.

Even now, the exact details of how the plot was discovered remain somewhat vague, but certainly a letter was intercepted and King James was alerted. Guy Fawkes, in this situation, was the 'fall-guy' who had the appalling task of keeping the names of his fellow-conspirators from his torturers. Immediately after his arrest, he gave his name as 'John Johnson' and was dragged before the king in the middle of the night.

James, whose life had been filled with plots and assassinations, was amazed at John Johnson's defiance. Fawkes told him bluntly to his face that his purpose was 'to blow the Scots back to Scotland again!'

Later, poor Guy was tortured so much that he could hardly hold the pen to sign the confession. And over the centuries, sentries in the Tower of London where the torture took place have sworn that his ghostly shrieks of pain can still be heard there.

Also on this day:

1688 Prince William of Orange (the future King William III) landed at Brixham, Devon, with an armada of nearly 300 ships. He was openly challenging his father-in-law, King James II, for the throne.

NOVEMBER 6   1612
DEATH OF THE PRINCE OF WALES

On this day Henry, the eighteen-year-old elder son of James I and Anne of Denmark, died of typhoid fever. He had been a young man of great promise. The Earl of Dorset wrote at the time: 'Our rising sun is set ere scarce he had shone and all our glory lies buried.'

It is a sad fact of English history that so many heirs did not live to succeed to the throne, or were prevented in some way from taking over.

Also on this day:

1429 First coronation of King Henry VI, aged eight, in Westminster Abbey.

1817 Death of Princess Charlotte, aged 21, in childbirth, only daughter of the Prince Regent, the future King George IV and Caroline of Brunswick, at Claremont House, Esher, Surrey. She was buried in St George's Chapel, Windsor. Had she lived she would have been heir to the throne when her father became king.

THE MONARCHS BRITAIN NEVER HAD

King Robert	son of William the Conqueror, instead of Henry I	(outmanoeuvred)
King William	son of Henry I, instead of Matilda or Stephen	(drowned)
Queen Matilda	daughter of Henry I, instead of Stephen	(outmanoeuvred)
King Henry	son of Henry II, instead of Richard I (Lionheart)	(died)
King Edward	son of Henry VI, instead of Edward IV	(killed)
King Edward*	son of Edward IV, instead of Richard III	(disappeared)
King Arthur	son of Henry VII, instead of Henry VIII	(died)
King Henry	son of James I, instead of Charles I	(died)
King James	son of James II, instead of William and Mary	(in exile)
Queen Sophia	mother of George I instead of George I	(see below**)
King Frederick	son of George II, instead of George III	(died)
Queen Charlotte	daughter of George IV, instead of William IV	(died)
King Edward	son of Edward VII, instead of George V	(died)

* Perhaps this name should not appear, for he was legally King Edward V for seventy-seven days, from the death of his father Edward IV on April 9 until June 25 1483, when his uncle Richard III seized the throne. He was one of the murdered 'Princes in the Tower'.
** 'Queen Sophia' was actually nominated as the heir to Queen Anne, but unfortunately she died, aged eighty-three, just six weeks before Anne herself died, and so her son, George I succeeded to the throne instead. Sophia would have been the oldest monarch to ascend the throne. She had remained in good health to the last, and had been expected to outlive Queen Anne, who died aged only forty-nine.

NOVEMBER 7   1501
HENRY VII INSPECTS CATHERINE OF ARAGON

As Catherine of Aragon and her attendant lords and ladies, including a Spanish archbishop, drew nearer to London on their slow progress from Plymouth (see OCTOBER 2), Henry VII and Arthur, Prince of Wales and Catherine's bridegroom, travelled to Dogmersfield in Hampshire to meet and view the princess. They wanted to assure themselves that Catherine was in fact suitably attractive and marriage-worthy.

At this point, however, King Henry was astounded to be met by a company of Spanish nobles whose duty it was to inform him that in no way would Catherine allow herself to be inspected. She would lift her veil and reveal her countenance only at the marriage altar, and then only after the marriage ceremony itself was over.

It was now Henry's turn to be regal. He positively insisted that she reveal herself to him! He pointed out that she was now his subject, and so he would see her 'even were she in her bed'. So, despite her misgivings and pride, Catherine made herself ready and grudgingly received him in a private chamber, where Henry viewed his daughter-in-law for the first time. Luckily, she passed inspection, and Prince Arthur was fetched to meet his future bride. All conversation had to be in Latin.

Catherine had learned her first important lesson in England: that kings must always be obeyed.

NOVEMBER 8   1745
THE JACOBITE ARMY CROSSES INTO ENGLAND

Towards the end of October Bonnie Prince Charlie reviewed his troops and found that his army now consisted of about 5,000 foot-soldiers and 500 horse. He judged that this was now the moment to move into England.

The prince wanted to take the town of Newcastle himself. An English army had only just arrived there, and the prince argued that they would be tired from travelling, and thus easy prey. However, he was persuaded that a more westerly route into England might be advisable, as Lancashire and Cheshire were likely to be stronger supporters of his Jacobite cause.

The prince allowed himself to be over-ruled, and on this day in 1745 he made his crucial decision and with his troops he crossed the River Esk into England.

NOVEMBER 9   1841
BIRTH OF THE FUTURE EDWARD VII

Born in Buckingham Palace, Edward was the second of Victoria's nine children. He was 'a wonderfully strong and large child with very large dark blue eyes, a finely formed but somewhat large nose and a pretty little mouth', according to a letter Victoria wrote to her uncle, King Leopold of Belgium.

Albert, his perfectionist father, was determined from the start that the newly born heir to the throne should be given the finest upbringing possible. Samuel Wilberforce, the Bishop of Oxford, agreed that 'the great object in view is to make him the most perfect man.' Baron Stockmar, Victoria's friend and confidant, went even further, and advised that the baby prince, as the future 'executive Governor of the State', should become 'the repository of all the moral and intellectual qualities by which it [the state] is held together and under the guidance of which it advances in the great path of civilization'. Thus he would become 'a man of calm, profound, comprehensive understanding, with a deep conviction of the indispensable necessity of practical morality to the welfare of the Sovereign and People'.

As he grew up, Edward began to have his own priorities.

Also on this day:

1901   Investiture of the future King George V as Prince of Wales.

1918   George V himself noted in his diary that this had been his father's birthday, and coincidentally the date on which Wilhelm II left Germany and abdicated as Kaiser and King of Prussia. 'Kaiser Bill' was Edward VII's nephew and George V's cousin. (See JANUARY 22 and OCTOBER 10.)

NOVEMBER 10   1558
MARY TUDOR BURNS HER LAST VICTIMS

According to John Foxe's *Book of Martyrs*, the last five Protestant victims of Mary I's persecution went to the flames on this day in Canterbury. They were John Corneford, Christopher Browne, John Herst, Alice Snoth and Catherine Tynley. Mary herself died just one week later, on November 17, thus putting an end to the horrific killings done in her name.

Foxe's list contains 314 names, including some who died in prison. The first name recorded is that of John Rogers, a priest of Smithfield, burnt on February 4 1555. Those who follow include a pathetic tally of butchers, weavers, cooks, barbers, wheelwrights, widows, labourers, ironmongers, and two youngsters who are simply described as 'blind girls'.

The Martyrs' Memorial in Oxford is the best-known memorial in the country to remind us of those days. It was set up in memory of two bishops, Hugh Latimer and Nicholas Ridley, who were both burned in Oxford on October 16 1555, and Archbishop Thomas Cranmer, that useful servant of Henry VIII, comforter of his wives, and author of the Anglican Prayer Book, who was also burned in Oxford, a few months later, on March 21 1556.

NOVEMBER 11 1920
KING GEORGE V ATTENDS THE BURIAL OF THE UNKNOWN WARRIOR

The idea of bringing the body of a nameless, unknown soldier to be buried in Westminster Abbey was not easily accepted. George V was sceptical at first, but with the persuasion of his advisers, including Lloyd George, he soon became enthusiastic, and deeply committed to this unique burial.

To make quite sure of the anonymity of the body, the military authorities were asked to dig up six coffins, each marked 'Unknown', one from each of the main battlefields: Ypres, the Marne, Cambrai, Arras, the Somme and the Aisne. Then these were assembled in an army hut and a blindfolded officer was led inside. He was required to move forward and touch one coffin at random. Thus selected, it was brought to London.

The coffin was never opened. It was enclosed in a bigger, massive oak casket, made from a tree from Hampton Court. Two wrought-iron straps went round it, under which was fastened an ancient sword which George V had chosen from his own collection. This was the background to the unforgettable scene in Westminster Abbey on this day in 1920, two years after the ending of the First World War.

One of the texts on the grave had already been used before in Westminster Abbey – for Richard II had had it inscribed on the tomb of his friend and supporter John Waltham, Bishop of Salisbury, buried in the abbey in 1395. The words were deemed appropriate for the Unknown Warrior:

> 'They buried him among the Kings because he had
> done good toward God and towards His house.'

Also on this day:

1100 Marriage of King Henry I, aged thirty-two, to Matilda, daughter of King Malcolm III of Scotland (he makes the final speech in Shakespeare's play *Macbeth*) in Westminster Abbey.

NOVEMBER 12 1035
DEATH OF KING CANUTE AT SHAFTESBURY

Shaftesbury Abbey was founded by Alfred the Great, and his daughter was its first abbess: thus its links with early royalty were strong. Edmund Ironside's queen was buried here in 971, and here too lay the remains of the young murdered Saxon King Edward, buried in 979. He was later canonised as a saint and his shrine brought countless pilgrims to this Dorset township.

King Canute died here on this day in 1035, but then his remains were taken to the Old Minster in Winchester, to lie with the old Saxon kings. Later in the same century his bones were ceremonially transferred to the new Norman cathedral. He lies there still, in one of the mortuary chests near the high altar. However, sad to relate, in the seventeenth century parliamentarian soldiers tipped his bones out on to the cathedral floor, together with those of many of the other ancient kings and bishops. They even threw them up at the stained-glass windows to break them. Later, all these remains were put back, all jumbled up, so that no one nowadays will ever know whose bones are whose.

Also on this day:

1918 The day after the signing of the Armistice that ended the First World War, King George V and Queen Mary went to St Paul's Cathedral to attend a thanksgiving service for the ending of hostilities.

NOVEMBER 13 1687
DEATH OF NELL GWYNNE

Of all Charles II's mistresses, 'Nelly', the orange-seller turned actress, is the one who is remembered with most affection. There is something rather cold and calculating about some of the others. Indeed, a famous story is told of Nell that once, when London crowds were mobbing her coach, thinking that she was Louise de Kéroualle, the Catholic Frenchwoman who was one of Charles's other mistresses, Nell Gwynne poked her head out of the window and shouted to them: 'Pray, good people, desist! I am the *Protestant* whore!' They roared their approval, and let her go!

Charles was kind to all his mistresses. He once confessed to having about thirty-nine of them – as being the right number for the head of the Church of England with its 'Thirty-Nine Articles'. And indeed he was kind to all his thirteen or so illegitimate children, giving them grand titles. He created one of Nelly's sons the Duke of St Albans. She herself was to have been made Duchess of Greenwich, but Charles died before he could confer the title upon her (see OCTOBER 9).

Nelly called the king 'Charles III' because she had had two previous lovers both named Charles.

Charles's last words are reputed to have been 'Let not poor Nelly starve,' and it is pleasing to know that Charles's brother King James II, honoured this request: he paid off her debts and gave her several generous sums of money. Sadly, however, she died young, aged only thirty-seven, two years after Charles. She is buried in St Martin-in-the-Fields, London, but unfortunately, owing to rebuilding in the 1720s, the exact site has now been lost.

Also on this day:
1312   Birth of the future King Edward III, son of King Edward II and Isabella of France, at Windsor Castle.

NOVEMBER 14   1948
NO OFFICIAL WITNESSES AT THE BIRTH OF PRINCE CHARLES

Prince Charles was born on this day in 1948 in Buckingham Palace. To give him his full title, he is His Royal Highness the Prince of Wales and Earl of Chester, Duke of Cornwall and Duke of Rothesay, Earl of Carrick and Baron Renfrew, Lord of the Isles and Great Steward of Scotland.

All the expertise of twentieth-century medicine was on hand at his birth. Gone were the days when anaesthetics were considered immoral for childbirth: Queen Victoria herself had pioneered this change of opinion. At birth, Prince Charles weighed 7lb 6oz and he was delivered with the help of forceps by the royal gynaecologist Sir William Gilliatt.

Things were definitely different for this birth. For the first time since the seventeenth century this was a royal birth without official witnesses or a government minister to overlook the event. The new baby's grandfather, George VI, had changed the regulations just before Princess Elizabeth was due to give birth.

Almost incredibly, the custom of having official witnesses at royal births dated back to the time when Mary of Modena, wife of James II, had given birth in 1688 to her son James, later known as the 'Old Pretender'. Rumour had spread that Queen Mary had not really been pregnant at all, and that the child had been smuggled into the bedchamber concealed in a warming-pan (see JUNE 10).

One has to trust that Prince Charles was no warming-pan baby.

Also on this day:

1501   Marriage of Prince Arthur, aged fifteen, Prince of Wales and son of King Henry VII and Elizabeth of York, in Old St Paul's Cathedral.

1973   Marriage of Princess Anne, aged twenty-three, daughter of Queen Elizabeth II and Prince Philip, to Captain Mark Phillips, in Westminster Abbey.

NOVEMBER 15   1638
BIRTH OF CATHERINE OF BRAGANZA,
QUEEN OF CHARLES II

Probably Catherine is the least known of all English queens. Her husband's many mistresses are much more vividly remembered (see OCTOBER 9). She had no children to perpetuate her memory, but her importance to England was the very rich dowry she brought with her. Three hundred and fifty thousand pounds was the largest sum any queen had given to an English husband – and poverty-stricken Charles, recently returned from exile, was in dire need of it. And territorial gifts came as well: Tangier in Africa, and Bombay in India.

As a wife, poor Catherine was treated abominably by Charles, but she suffered her humiliations with superhuman patience. As Charles lay dying she came to his bedside to say goodbye to him. She was so overcome with emotion that she had to be carried away fainting. She sent word to Charles to beg his forgiveness. 'Alas poor woman!' replied the king. 'She asks my pardon? I beg hers with all my heart: take her back that answer.'

After his death, Catherine lived for a few years in Somerset House, and then decided she would be much happier back in Portugal. She is buried in Santa Maria de Belém, in Lisbon. Having no memorial in England, even in death she is almost completely forgotten.

NOVEMBER 16   1499
EXECUTION OF 'RICHARD IV'

'Richard IV' – as he called himself – is probably better known to historians as Perkin Warbeck, one of the non-royal imposters who stirred up trouble for Henry VII in the early years of his reign.

Perkin was incredibly audacious. Coming on the scene in 1490, he claimed to be the Duke of York, one of the two Princes in the Tower who had disappeared so mysteriously, probable victims of their wicked uncle, Richard III. He certainly had a regal manner about him which fooled even the nobility, including his 'aunt' the Duchess of Burgundy, and he was given a warm royal welcome by Charles VIII, King of France.

The pinnacle of his impudence came when he stayed with James IV of Scotland in Stirling Castle, and actually married one of the king's own distant cousins, Lady Catherine Gordon, while he was there! He tried to invade England in 1497, aged only twenty-five. He landed near Land's End, but he had no military skill and was quickly captured at Taunton. Probably his most embarrassing moment came when he was compelled to confess publicly to his noble-born wife that his real name was Piers Osbeck, and that he was just a poor lad from Belgium.

Perkin was treated leniently at first, but as he continued to give trouble, Henry had him beheaded on this day in 1499.

Also on this day:

1272 Death of King Henry III, aged sixty-five, in Westminster Palace. He was buried in Westminster Abbey.

1940 King George VI visited Coventry just hours after the city and its cathedral had been devastated by German bombers in the Second World War. (See MAY 25.)

NOVEMBER 17   1558
'QUEEN ELIZABETH'S DAY'

Nowadays no one remembers this day as a public holiday, but it was kept as such for over a century, as it was the day on which Queen 'Bloody' Mary died, and of course as a natural consequence it marked the accession of Queen Elizabeth I. Such was the rejoicing at the accession of Elizabeth in 1558 that the day was kept as a day of celebrations not only throughout her reign, but until well into the eighteenth century, dying away only in the reign of George I.

'Queen Elizabeth's Day' became more and more riotous in the later years of the reign of Charles II, with an increasingly strong anti-Catholic flavour about it. A pamphlet entitled *London's Defiance to Rome* describes 'the magnificent procession and solemn burning of the Pope at Temple Bar, November 17, 1679', and it tells how 'the bells generally about the town began to ring about three o'clock in the morning . . . At the appoach of evening (all things being in readiness), the solemn procession began, setting forth from Moorgate, and so passing first to Aldgate, and thence through Leadenhall Street, by the Royal Exchange through Cheapside, and so to Temple Bar. Never were the balconies, windows, and houses more numerously lined, or the streets closer thronged, with multitudes of people, all expressing their abhorrence of popery with continued shouts and exclamations, so that 'tis modestly computed that, in the whole progress, there could not be fewer than two hundred thousand spectators.'

This observance of 'Queen Elizabeth's Day' seems remarkably like the celebrations held in Lewes on Guy Fawkes' Night, with effigies of unpopular figures of the day being paraded through the streets on their way to being burnt.

In the reign of Queen Anne the annual procession was still going strong with banners proclaiming:

> God bless Queen Anne, the nation's great defender!
> Keep out the French, the Pope, and the Pretender.

Also on this day:
1818 Death of Charlotte of Mecklenburg-Strelitz, wife of King George III, at Kew. She was buried in St George's Chapel, Windsor.

NOVEMBER 18   1518
CATHERINE OF ARAGON HAS A STILLBORN DAUGHTER

At the age of thirty-three, Catherine of Aragon still had time to produce the necessary son. Nevertheless, the birth of a stillborn daughter on this day in 1518 instead of the hoped-for lively boy was a bitter disappointment.

All the same, Henry VIII had something to be pleased about, because he had just managed to make his mistress Bessie Blount pregnant, and he awaited the birth with keen anticipation. Just as he wanted, Bessie gave him a strong and lusty boy at the beginning of June the following year.

It says much about Henry's attitudes to his womenfolk that when Bessie did give birth, he naturally expected his wife Catherine of Aragon to attend the elaborate court festivities arranged to celebrate the event.

NOVEMBER 19   1688
JAMES II HAS AN INCONVENIENT NOSEBLEED IN SALISBURY

William of Orange had landed at Brixham on November 5 and James travelled down from London to Salisbury to take charge of his army. The trouble was, his former supporters were deserting him: generals, dukes, even his daughter Anne, the future queen, had disappeared into the night, abandoning her father. James simply didn't know whom he could rely on.

Now, in Salisbury, and probably under immense stress, having just held a crucial council of war, James started to have a nosebleed. It wasn't just a simple matter. It went on and on. Doctors were called, but in those days the only cure they could think of was to 'bleed' him even more. Nevertheless, James's nose refused to stop. Day after day it bled, and the doctors in their wisdom bled him themselves four more times. Eventually, poor James became quite disorientated.

One lucky result was that he didn't go to Warminster as he had planned, and so escaped an ambush which was being carefully prepared for him there. On the other hand, John Churchill, his trusted army commander, became so disgusted with the king's feeble dithering that he dramatically deserted him, switched sides and joined William's invading forces.

Eventually, James, with his nose still bleeding, fled back to London to make preparations for an escape to France.

Also on this day:
1600   Birth of the future King Charles I, second son of King James VI of Scotland and Anne of Denmark, in Dunfermline Palace, Scotland.

NOVEMBER 20   1947
THE LAST UNTELEVISED ROYAL WEDDING

Princess Elizabeth, heir to the throne, married her handsome young Viking, Philip, on this day in Westminster Abbey. It was two years after the ending of the Second World War, but in England many items, including clothes, were still rationed. Elizabeth wore a beautiful wedding gown designed by Norman Hartnell, and the occasion brought a touch of glamour and luxury into drab postwar Britain. However, it is strange to think that television cameras were not yet around for events like this and even the newsreels were in black and white.

One of the curious features about this marriage was the fact that Philip had only just been given his present name. True, he had been Prince of Greece, but he had renounced his Greek citizenship and had applied for British naturalisation after the end of the war. In fact this British citizenship was not made official until 18 March – just eight months before his marriage.

In renouncing his Greek title, Philip was left with his extraordinary and cumbersome family name of Schleswig-Holstein-Sonderburg-Glücksburg. Surely something more 'English' would now be appropriate? After some considerable official head-scratching, the College of Heralds, noticing that Philip's family tree included the Dukedom of Oldenburg, came up with the suggestion that he might adopt an anglicised version of this and become 'Mr Oldcastle'.

It was left to the Home Secretary, Chuter Ede, to come up with the final answer, and Philip took the name of his Uncle Dickie, becoming Philip Mountbatten.

Just one day before the royal wedding George VI elevated Philip to the style of Royal Highness, also giving him three other titles: Duke of Edinburgh, Earl of Merioneth and Baron Greenwich. The king was under the impression that he was also making him a prince, but in fact this was not the case, and it was not until ten years later, on February 22 1957, that Elizabeth, as queen, awarded him this title for his contribution to public life.

Also on this day:

1272   Proclamation of the succession to the throne of King Edward I, aged thirty-three, on the death of his father, King Henry III.

1737   Death of Caroline of Brandenburg-Ansbach, aged fifty-four, wife of King George II. She was buried in Westminster Abbey.

1925   Death of Queen Alexandra, aged eighty, widow of King Edward VII, at Sandringham. She was buried in St George's Chapel, Windsor.

NOVEMBER 21   1673
JAMES MEETS HIS WIFE FOR THE FIRST TIME
AND MARRIES HER AGAIN

James II was still Duke of York when the fifteen-year-old Mary of Modena arrived in England on this day in 1672 to meet him and become his wife again (see SEPTEMBER 30).

She arrived in Dover, where the castle was still a royal residence, and here their proxy marriage was confirmed and they spent a 'honeymoon' of three days here before travelling up to London.

James, of course, had already been married, to Anne Hyde, by whom he had two daughters, the future Queen Mary II and the future Queen Anne. Nevertheless, a son would be welcome, so he must have looked with happy anticipation at the Italian girl he had just met.

NOVEMBER 22   1682
MARRIAGE OF THE GREAT-GREAT-GRANDSON
OF MARY, QUEEN OF SCOTS

Such is the nature of life that we very rarely know our great-grandparents and never know our great-great-grandparents. In 1682 less than a century had elapsed since Mary, Queen of Scots, had been executed in 1587, and now her great-great-grandson was being married.

Life-styles change immeasurably in just a few generations, so that it sometimes requires an effort of imagination to associate ancestor with descendant even in so short a time. It may come as a surprise therefore that Mary's descendant being married on this day in 1672 was none other than our future George I. He was marrying the sixteen-year-old Princess Sophia Dorothea. The marriage was not to last, however (see NOVEMBER 2) and poor Dorothea was to spend thirty-two years of her life in prison. Royal life is seldom easy.

NOVEMBER 23   955
A USEFUL SUM TO BUY OFF THE DANES

On St Clement's Day 955 the Saxon King Edred died in Frome, Somerset, aged only about thirty. A grandson of Alfred the Great, he had reigned energetically for nine-and-a-half years, beating off the Danes as his grandfather had done. Although he is a shadowy and almost forgotten figure nowadays, he did valiant service to the kingdom by establishing dominance in Northumbria, when the ferocious Viking Eric Bloodaxe was killed.

In his will he continued to make provision for getting rid of the marauding Danes, leaving a sum of about £1,600 to be set aside specially for buying off any invading heathen army and also for famine relief.

Edred was taken for a ceremonial burial in Winchester's Old Minster, and his remains lie in an old box there still, among the oldest kingly bones in the country.

King Edwy, aged about fifteen, succeeded to the throne on the death of his uncle, King Edred, and was crowned in Kingston upon Thames.

NOVEMBER 24   1588
QUEEN ELIZABETH ATTENDS A THANKSGIVING SERVICE FOR THE DEFEAT OF THE ARMADA

Probably the most elaborate service to take place in Old St Paul's Cathedral was the great thanksgiving service held this day for England's deliverance from the Spanish Armada.

Queen Elizabeth I was carried in state through garlanded streets, seated in a triumphal car like a throne, with a canopy over it supported by four pillars. The canopy was in the form of an imperial crown. In front of the throne were two low pillars on which stood a lion and a dragon, and the whole chariot-throne was drawn by two milk-white steeds, attended by state footmen.

Following the queen came Robert Devereux, Earl of Essex, who had recently succeeded Leicester as her Master of Horse. He was leading her majesty's richly caparisoned horse of estate. Then came ladies of honour, and guards carrying halberds.

As she arrived at Temple Bar, the queen was presented with a jewel set in gold and was formally welcomed to the City of London by the lord mayor and aldermen, who then attended her on her way to St Paul's. Houses and shops were hung with banners, and the cathedral itself was decorated with trophies and banners taken from the conquered Armada.

Entering St Paul's, Elizabeth spent some minutes kneeling in silent prayer, and then under another rich canopy she was led up the aisle to her place. It was now thirty years since she had come to the throne, and she must have felt deep satisfaction as she heard John Piers, Bishop of Salisbury, preaching on the text: 'Thou didst blow with Thy winds and they were scattered.'

Also on this day:

1326 Hugh Despenser, favourite of King Edward II, having been captured by Edward's wife Isabelle, was hanged, drawn and quartered in Hereford.

NOVEMBER 25   1120
THE WHITE SHIP DISASTER

The 'White Ship' disaster was comparable in its day to the sinking of the *Titanic*, but with the added misfortune that three of King Henry I's children, including William, the heir to the throne, were drowned.

Like the *Titanic*, the White Ship was brand new. It was sailing to England from Barfleur, carrying about three hundred of Henry's courtiers as well as his children. The whole boatload of princes, passengers and sailors were in a rip-roaring mood, boozing and feasting, and jeering at the priests who had come on board to bless the ship as it set sail on its maiden voyage. Even the pilot was drunk. As it left port, it struck a rock and sank like a stone. Only one man lived to tell the tale: Berold, a butcher from Rouen.

Henry, of course, was devastated to hear the news. He had gone on ahead of his children, and was in Southampton when he learned about the accident a couple of days later. A famous phrase in nineteenth-century history books asserts that 'he never smiled again'. As a direct consequence of this accident, the Empress Matilda became Henry's heir, and this led to the pointless rivalry and civil war as her supporters fought Stephen for the throne for so many years after Henry's death.

Also on this day:

1487 Elizabeth of York, aged twenty-one, wife of King Henry VII and daughter of Edward IV, was crowned in Westminster Abbey.

1609 Henrietta Maria, daughter of King Henry IV of France, and future wife of King Charles I, was born in the Louvre, Paris.

NOVEMBER 26   1688
PRINCESS ANNE DESERTS HER FATHER

The last days of James II's reign were filled with tension and confusion. James returned to Whitehall from Salisbury having been deserted there by his military commander John Churchill (see NOVEMBER 19), only to find that his own daughter Anne had deserted him too. Princess Anne, later Queen Anne, was the closest of friends with Sarah Churchill, John Churchill's wife. Clearly, Anne was in a position of divided loyalties, especially as her sister Mary was married to William.

On November 26 she pretended she was not feeling well, and went to bed, asking not to be woken until she rang her bell. Then, in the middle of the night she stole out of her room at Whitehall with her ladies in waiting, and disappeared into the dark. Lord Dorset and Henry Compton, Bishop of London, were waiting for her with a coach and they swiftly drove to a special hideout in Epping Forest.

James had been shattered by the defection of John Churchill, but now, finding that his daughter Anne had also left him, he burst into tears. 'God help me!' he cried, 'my own children have forsaken me in my distress.'

Within less than a month he had fled to France.

NOVEMBER 27   1120
HENRY I LEARNS OF THE DEATH OF
HIS CHILDREN

On this day the dreadful news of the White Ship disaster reached Henry in Southampton: all his children were drowned (see NOVEMBER 25).

William, Henry's son and heir to the throne, was only seventeen, but already he had shown himself to be a strong and successful leader. He had fought with his father in France, and had recently married Alice, daughter of the Earl of Anjou. Indeed, the celebrations following this wedding seem have have been going on for months when King Henry decided to go back to England, leaving William to follow on after.

Fitz-Stephen, the captain of the brand new vessel *Blanche Nef* ('White Ship'), had particularly requested Henry to give him the honour of conveying the heir to the throne. He was proud of the fact that his father had been captain of the *Mora*, the very ship which had brought William the

Conqueror to England in 1066. Now he boasted that his new vessel, *Blanche Nef*, was the swiftest galley in the world.

Young Prince William was keen to overtake his father and beat him to England, so he encouraged Fitz-Stephen to do everything to prove how fast his ship could go. The prince had already ordered three casks of wine to be distributed to the crew and the ship was rushing at a crazy speed through the waters when it hit a rock and sank almost immediately.

At first, no one dared tell Henry the awful news. Finally, a little page was given the dreadful task, and when he knelt before the king and told him that the ship was lost and all those on board had drowned Henry is said to have fallen to the floor, fainting with shock.

William's body was never found.

NOVEMBER 28   1290
ELEANOR CROSSES MARK THE QUEEN'S LAST JOURNEY

Eleanor of Castile and Edward I formed a splendid royal team. Eleanor had been only ten and Edward fifteen when they were married, and they shared life to the full. They had been together on a crusade, during which Eleanor had saved Edward's life and nursed him back to health. Indeed while they were in Acre she bore him a daughter, one of their many children, sixteen in all, although not all survived.

She was only forty-six when she was suddenly taken ill at Harby in Nottingham, on her way to join Edward on one of his Scottish campaigns. Alas, she never reached him, and his response to her unexpected death gave England one of the most beautiful set of memorials ever built – the 'Eleanor Crosses'.

Obviously, Eleanor had to be taken for a ceremonial burial in Westminster Abbey. This was a considerable distance for her funeral cortège and in those days the journey took weeks. In a splendid romantic gesture Edward ordered that a memorial cross should be erected in each of the stopping-places. In all, there were twelve: Lincoln, Grantham, Stamford, Geddington, Northampton, Stony Stratford, Woburn, Dunstable, St Albans, Waltham, Cheapside, and – best known of all, the final village just before Westminster itself – Charing. Of course, the village became known by the name of the memorial, Charing Cross.

Today it is the name of a busy railway station, and in the forecourt, surrounded by parked cars and taxis there is a tall monument – a memorial to Eleanor, who died this day in 1290. It is a Victorian replacement of the one which originally stood at the top of Whitehall, on the site now occupied by a statue of Charles I on horseback.

Edward also ordered that wax candles should burn beside Eleanor's statue in Westminster Abbey for ever. They burned for two-and-a-half centuries, and were extinguished only in the reign of Henry VIII.

NOVEMBER 29   1530
DEATH OF THE 'OTHER KING' –
CARDINAL WOLSEY

Cardinal Wolsey, suffering from dysentery, died in Leicester Abbey, on his way to face punishment, possibly execution, at the hands of Henry VIII. He had already given his vast palace Hampton Court to the king in a vain attempt to buy back favour, but Henry had stripped him of all his power and dignity and in the previous month had required him to yield up the great seal of the office of Lord Chancellor. This had now passed to Sir Thomas More.

Wolsey had not only been Lord Chancellor but also cardinal and papal legate. During his period in power he had been successively Bishop of Bath and Wells, Abbot of St Albans, Bishop of Lincoln, Archbishop of York, Bishop of Durham and Bishop of Winchester. Incidentally, he was also Bishop of Tournai in France.

On his disgrace, Wolsey was allowed to retain the Archbishopric of York, so earlier in this month he made preparations to go there to be enthroned on November 7. (He had never actually bothered to take up the appointment previously, although he had been created archbishop sixteen years before: he had just pocketed the money.)

However, Wolsey never reached York, for he was arrested on November 4 and forced to turn south, probably in a desperate state of mind, towards London to meet his king. At Leicester, he died and was buried in the the Lady Chapel of Leicester Abbey. Nowadays visitors can see a memorial slab in Abbey Park, but it is debatable whether he lies beneath it. His remains are lost for ever.

In his time he had been known as *alter rex* ('the other king').

NOVEMBER 30   1016
EDMUND IRONSIDE IS STABBED
IN THE BOTTOM

Edmund II, son of Ethelred the Unready, was murdered on this day in 1016, according to the medieval chronicler Henry of Huntingdon.

If we believe the good scribe, King Edmund suffered an appalling fate – being stabbed in the bottom as he sat one night in a privy. His assassin, the son of Ealdorman Edric, was lurking in the smelly pit below, and mortally wounded the king in his bowels as the royal victim was about to relieve himself.

Edric was delighted, and brought the good news to Canute, who at that time was sharing the partitioned kingdom with Edmund. 'Hail! thou who art sole king of England!' he cried, and told him all the revolting details of Edmund's murder.

Canute is supposed to have replied: 'For this deed I will exalt you higher than all the nobles of England,' whereupon he ordered Edric's head to be chopped off and publicly displayed on a pole 'on the highest battlement of the Tower of London'.

It seems a little churlish to point out that the Tower of London was not yet built. But then, veracity is not always necessary in a good chronicler. It certainly makes a good story.

DECEMBER 1   1648
CHARLES I IS TAKEN FROM THE ISLE OF WIGHT
BACK TO THE MAINLAND

It was a long, slow, difficult matter to bring Charles to trial, but now came the beginning of his final journey to Whitehall.

Charles was taken from Carisbrooke Castle on the Isle of Wight and moved to mainland Hampshire. Hurst Castle was the place chosen for him. This was a tiny blockhouse built in 1544 on the orders of Henry VIII; it stood on a spit of land jutting out into the Solent. It would be virtually impossible for him to to escape from such an awkward spot. He was to stay imprisoned there for the next nineteen days.

The treatment he received was an odd mixture of firm authority and polite deference. Even now, months after his capture and weeks before his execution, he was accorded the treatment normally given to royalty at court. His dinner was given to him by servants on bended knee; the dishes were ceremonially uncovered and tasted, as a precaution against poison; and local people were occasionally admitted to watch the regal spectacle as poor Charles ate his lonely meals.

No one knew what the final outcome would be. But with hindsight we know that now he had just under two months to live. (See DECEMBER 19)

Also on this day:

1135 Death of King Henry I, aged sixty-seven, at Lyons-la-Forêt near Rouen, France. He was buried in Reading Abbey.

1844 Birth of the future Queen Alexandra, wife of King Edward VII, daughter of King Christian IX of Denmark.

DECEMBER 2   1849
DEATH OF QUEEN ADELAIDE

Queen Adelaide died at Bentley Priory, near Harrow in Middlesex. She was only fifty-seven and was deeply mourned by Victoria, who had appreciated Adelaide's kindness and common sense.

It was twelve years since her husband William IV had died, and Adelaide had lived quietly as 'Queen Dowager' – a rather more formidable title than 'Queen Mother'. She had managed to cope with an extraordinary situation, coming into the royal family after the grotesque final years of George IV and having to come to terms with her husband's ten grown-up bastards by Dorothea Jordan. But she had been a triumphant success, diplomatically covering up her husband's eccentricities.

She enjoyed her freedom after William's death, and one of her acts of generosity was to pay for the Anglican Cathedral in Valetta, after she had visited Malta in 1838–9. She also sent many of her books to Australia, to begin the library in a new city just being planned there. She was pleased to know that this city, founded in 1837, was given her own name, Adelaide. It is a pity she never had an opportunity to visit it.

DECEMBER 3   1987
'PRINCE CHARGES PLANNERS WITH RAPE OF BRITAIN' (*THE TIMES*)

This headline appeared in *The Times* on December 3 1987, referring to Prince Charles's speech to a gathering of architects the previous day. The subject was the proposed development of the area surrounding St Paul's Cathedral. There were architectural schemes competing for a complete modernization of Paternoster Square. The prince was indignant, and waxed eloquent:

> Why does St Paul's matter so much? Because it is our greatest national monument . . . On the terrible night of December 29 1940, when the surroundings of the cathedral were devastated and an incendiary bomb lodged in the outer dome, it was Mr Churchill himself who had dispatched the message to the Guildhall: 'St Paul's must be saved at all costs.'
>
> What, then, have we done to it since the bombing? In the space of a mere fifteen years, in the sixties and seventies, and in spite of all sorts of elaborate rules supposedly designed to protect that great view, your predecessors, as the planners, architects and developers of the City, wrecked the London skyline and desecrated the dome of St Paul's . . . You have, ladies and gentlemen, to give this much to the Luftwaffe: when it knocked down our buildings, it didn't replace them with anything more offensive than rubble. We did that.

Prince Charles's passionate intervention has, arguably, saved London just as his royal predecessor Charles II did, in a rather different manner, in 1666. (See SEPTEMBER 2.)

In a previous speech, Prince Charles had effectively prevented a 'monstrous carbuncle' being built 'on the face of a much loved and elegant friend,' i.e. the National Gallery.

DECEMBER 4   1745
BONNIE PRINCE CHARLIE REACHES DERBY

On this day in 1745 Charles Stuart and his Scottish army of 6,000 men arrived at Derby, the southernmost point of his invasion of England.

Communications then were dependant on the speed of the fastest horse, so there was no way that the prince and his companions could know that George II was in such a state of panic that he was getting ready to leave the country: he had already placed his valuables on board a ship in the Thames. As for the Prime Minister, the Duke of Newcastle, he spent an entire day seeing no one and trying to decide which side to support. It was a situation almost reminiscent of the days when William of Orange had marched on London from the West Country.

One of the most tantalising 'what-ifs' of history is the speculation surrounding the next few days. It is just possible that a swift and decisive march on London would have resulted in what Bonnie Prince Charlie so desperately longed for – a Jacobite victory. However, the prince's older, wiser and more prudent companions realised that the English forces gathering in several places in the country were far stronger and better organised. A council of war was held the following day at which it was decided to turn back to Scotland, and on December 6, 'Black Friday', the sad march homeward began. Prince Charles said he would rather be twenty feet underground.

Today, a beautiful modern statue of Bonnie Prince Charlie on horseback has been placed in Derby, near the cathedral, to mark this poignant moment in Jacobite history.

DECEMBER 5   1553
MARY I DISSOLVES HER FIRST PARLIAMENT, HAVING BECOME LEGITIMATE AGAIN

Four days after her coronation on October 1, Mary Tudor summoned her first Parliament: there was so much she had to do. Now, on December 5, she dissolved it, after a two-month session. She was probably pleased with the laws she had made and the laws she had repealed. Certainly she had now begun the long process of eradicating the Protestantism of her half-brother, Edward VI.

One of her first acts was to repeal her father's declaration that his marriage with her mother Catherine of Aragon was unlawful. Thus Mary ceased to be illegitimate. All mention of Anne Boleyn, however, was studiously avoided, so Elizabeth's legitimacy was still left in doubt, at least in theory.

Perhaps surprisingly, another set of laws that she repealed were those relating to life and property. Under Henry VIII the number of crimes incurring the death penalty had increased enormously: one could be put to death for stealing a hawk's egg, or for conjuring, or even misusing names and badges. Raphael Holinshed, a contemporary historian, reckoned that 72,000 people had been executed on the gibbet in the last few years of Henry's reign.

It must have been a great relief, then, to the members of Mary's first Parliament, that much of Henry VIII's paranoic legislation had now been swept away. They must have felt that a gentler, kinder reign would now ensue.

Also on this day:

1560 Death of King Francis II of France, aged sixteen. This meant that his wife, Mary, Queen of Scots, was no longer Queen of France and would return to her Scottish kingdom.

DECEMBER 6   1421
CATHERINE OF VALOIS DISOBEYS HER HUSBAND HENRY V

Henry V, the great victor of Agincourt, possessed a curious streak of superstition. Apparently he enjoyed dabbling in astrology and examining the position of planets in order to forecast people's horoscopes.

His wife, Catherine of Valois, was pregnant when he left her to continue his wars in France, and before he departed he gave her one important instruction: in no circumstances should the baby be born at Windsor Castle. He seemed to believe that this would result in dire consequences for the royal child.

However, the moment his back was turned Catherine moved into Windsor, and sure enough, on this day in 1421 she produced a fine healthy baby boy – the future Henry VI – in the very place which her husband had forbidden.

Why did she do it? What made Catherine so blatantly disregard Henry's explicit instructions? The old chroniclers tell how Henry's first question on hearing the news was 'Where was the boy born?' And of course they took great delight in recording how the king gave a great sigh, producing an impromptu prophecy:

> I, Henry, born at Monmouth,
> Shall small time reign, and much get;
> But Henry of Windsor shall long reign, and lose all of it,
> But as God will, so be it.

As he grew up, Prince Henry was pleased to note that he had been born on St Nicholas's Day, and he adopted Nicholas as his patron saint. Later on he named his famous 'King's College, Cambridge' as 'the College of Our Ladye and St Nicholas'.

DECEMBER 7   1870
SANDRINGHAM IS READY FOR THE
PRINCE OF WALES TO OCCUPY

The new Sandringham House, the 'Big House', was completed on this day for the Prince of Wales, the future Edward VII. As he came of age, his parents, Victoria and Albert, were anxious that he should find a house of his own, well away from London. They had already found Balmoral and Osborne for themselves, and they felt it was necessary for 'Bertie' to have his own establishment.

Albert had died before Sandringham was found, but Victoria continued searching, as she insisted that Albert's wishes should be carried out. Eventually in 1862 Bertie fell for Sandringham, a large estate about 8 miles from King's Lynn, with a much smaller dwelling, Sandringham Hall. He moved in immediately, and brought his bride Alexandra here the following year. Thereafter, as their family grew, he abandoned any idea of enlarging the old hall and ordered an entirely new house to be built, now known to everyone simply as 'Sandringham'. This day in 1870 the new royal residence was ready.

Over the years Edward entertained guests on a lavish scale here: the German Kaiser, Tsar Nicholas II of Russia and King Carlos of Portugal were among those who came to enjoy his hospitality, and, above all else, the shooting. When it was realised that more than thirty thousand game birds a year were being killed, Edward ordered the largest larder in the world to be built at Sandringham, in order to accommodate them.

Of course, the estate had to be restocked with game birds from time to time, and when one of Edward VII's tenants wrote a book entitled *Eighteen Years of the Sandringham Estate*, the king was furious to find that it contained complaints that these birds were gobbling up all the crops in the neighbourhood. He promptly ordered that the entire edition of the book should be bought up and burnt.

Also on this day:

1688   James Edward, the baby Prince of Wales, future 'Old Pretender', was hidden overnight in Guildford, on his way to be smuggled out of the country. Meanwhile the invading William, future King William III, arrived at an old coaching inn, *The Bear*, in Hungerford, on his way to London.

DECEMBER 8   1542
BIRTH OF A SCOTTISH PRINCESS,
SIX DAYS LATER TO BE QUEEN

The Scottish King James V seemed under a curse when his daughter, the future Mary, Queen of Scots, was born this day in the Palace of Linlithgow. The previous year his two sons, both infants, had died and he had just lost the Battle of Solway Moss.

It is said that the Scottish king had a dream before these infant deaths in which he was warned that he would soon lose both his arms and then his head, as a punishment for his sins. Rumour, of course, with hindsight, interpreted these deaths as the loss of his sons, and then, naturally enough, he fulfilled the prophecy by dying himself quite soon after, aged only thirty.

James lived to learn of the birth of his daughter, but he was a mortally sick man and died just six days later. He showed no great pleasure at the news that he had a daughter, merely making the prophetic observation: 'Adieu, fare well! It came with a lass, it will pass with a lass.' He was referring to the founding of the Stuart dynasty by the marriage of Marjorie Bruce and Walter Stewart.

The infant Mary, six days old, 'a very weak child, and not likely to live' according to the report sent to her great-uncle Henry VIII, thus became Queen of Scotland.

DECEMBER 9   1688
QUEEN MARY ESCAPES, DISGUISED AS AN ITALIAN WASHERWOMAN

James II and his queen, Mary of Modena, agreed to make their separate ways to France as they escaped the revolution which had burst around them.

The night was wet and stormy as Mary, disguised as an Italian washerwoman, arrived at Gravesend to make the Channel crossing with a small company of attendants. She was carrying her baby son, just six months old (see JUNE 10), wrapped up to look like a bundle of laundry. Luckily, the child did not cry or whimper, and the company managed to get on board the yacht without anyone becoming suspicious.

Ten days before James II had ordered Samuel Pepys, the famous diarist and Admiralty official, to get his two royal yachts ready. 'Order the Anne and Isabella yachts to fall down to Erith to-morrow,' he had written. It was his last command to Pepys. However, it was felt that the royal yachts would provoke too much suspicion, and so the vessel carrying Mary and her son was much smaller and less luxurious. Poor Mary, no great sailor at the best of times, was dreadfully sick during a particularly rough crossing.

'It was a very doleful voyage,' she said later, 'and I wonder still that I lived through it.'

DECEMBER 10   1936
EDWARD VIII FORMALLY ABDICATES

George V died in January 1936 having grave misgivings about the jazzy modern life-style of David, his eldest son and heir, who became Edward VIII. He even confided his fears to the Archbishop of Canterbury: 'After I'm gone,' he said, 'the boy will ruin himself in twelve months.' It was a shrewd prophecy. In actual fact, Edward VIII lasted just 335 days before he made his formal declaration of abdication on this day in 1936.

Stanley Baldwin, the Prime Minister, had desperately tried to persuade the king to abandon Wallis Simpson, but when the king dug his heels in, he told him it was either the throne or Wallis; he couldn't have both. Trying to be tactful, he told Edward: 'Whatever happens, my missus and I wish your happiness from the depths of our souls', at which the king burst into tears. But tears were useless: by then the whole affair had got completely out of hand.

Briefly, a 'King's Party' was vaguely formed and Winston Churchill was hissed out of the Commons for trying to support it. Meanwhile, as it was nearing Christmas, the cockney carol-singers were lustily roaring out: 'Hark! the herald angels sing, Missis Simpson's pinched our King!'

On this day, Edward signed the 'Instrument of Abdication', renouncing the throne for 'the woman I love'. And that night, for the first and only time in history, the guards at Buckingham Palace were issued with live ammunition.

DECEMBER 11   1936
THE ABDICATION BROADCAST

The day after his abdication, ex-King Edward spoke to his former subjects on the 'wireless' from Windsor Castle. The unthinkable had happened, and a brief farewell speech was needed.

Sir John Reith (later Lord Reith), the Director-General of the BBC, announced him as 'His Royal Highness Prince Edward' and left the duke (as he now had become) to speak:

> I have for twenty-five years tried to serve. But you must believe me when I tell you that I have found it impossible to carry the heavy burden of responsibility and to discharge my duties as king as I would wish to do without the help and support of the woman I love . . . God bless you all. God save the king.

The duke's friend Walter Monckton was present, and when the broadcast was over, Edward put his arm on Monckton's shoulder, saying, 'Walter, it is a far better thing I go to.'

DECEMBER 12   1911
KING GEORGE V'S 'CORONATION DURBAR'

George's 'Coronation Durbar' (an old Persian word meaning a prince's court) arguably represented the apotheosis of the British Empire. Six months after being crowned in Westminster Abbey, George V and Queen

Mary were enthroned at a magnificent ceremony in Delhi. The King-Emperor, a 'semi-divine figure', accepted homage from India's richest and most powerful princes under a golden domed pavilion. The scene was set in the centre of a huge amphitheatre, watched by thousands.

Everything was exotic. Attendants bore peacock fans, yak-tails and gilded maces. Turbaned sons of maharajas formed an impressive entourage as the king and queen moved towards the marble dais covered with cloth-of-gold, on which awaited gleaming solid silver thrones. A special crown was made for the occasion, costing £60,000. Emblematic lotus flowers, king cobras and Tudor crowns mixed with one another in an astonishingly opulent display of majesty.

In his speech, the newly crowned Emperor George decreed that India's capital city would transfer from Calcutta to Delhi – New Delhi – and to launch this new seat of government he laid its foundation stone. Sir Edwin Lutyens had designed the buildings which would soon be built there, worthy of the English Raj.

The ceremony was unique. No other king or queen enjoyed a Durbar: Victoria, the original Empress, was too old and still in perpetual mourning; Edward VII was too preoccupied with the delicacies of European alliances; Edward VIII was too busy with Mrs Simpson; George VI had wartime problems, and England relinquished its power in India in 1947 (see AUGUST 15).

After the Durbar, George relaxed, hunting in Nepal. He bagged four bears, eighteen rhinos and no fewer than thirty-nine tigers.

Also on this day:

1688 King James II was captured in Faversham as he tried to escape to France. He was held prisoner for three days before being escorted back to London. (See DECEMBER 18.)

DECEMBER 13   1918
KING GEORGE V VISITS SOLDIERS IN FRANCE

The *Daily Mirror* had four photographs of King George V on its front page today, showing him visiting graves and inspecting troops on the recent battlefields. It was just over a month since the Armistice had been signed and the king had visited his troops in France on several occasions during the war. Once his horse had reared up, startled when the men gave three cheers for their monarch, and George was thrown off, with the horse falling on top of him. He broke his pelvis.

The news was telephoned to Buckingham Palace by Frederick Ponsonby who records that he 'managed to make Stamfordham hear, which was truly wonderful at so great a distance'. The great fear was that the Germans would hear about the incident and bomb the villa where the king had been taken to recover. One senior officer, Sir John French, said it would be necessary to move him at once.

George V took umbrage at the very suggestion: 'You can tell French from me to go to hell and stay there. I don't intend to move for any bombs,' he declared.

DECEMBER 14   1861
VICTORIA IS DEVASTATED AT ALBERT'S DEATH

This was the day which changed the life of Victoria for ever. Her beloved Albert died.

About a fortnight before, he had gone to Cambridge to reprimand his son Bertie, who had just discovered the facts of life with the actress Nellie Clifton. 'You must not, you dare not be lost,' Albert had told him. 'The consequences for the country, for the world, would be too dreadful.'

But the weather was cold in Cambridge and Albert had caught a chill. Now, in mid-December, his condition had deteriorated so badly that he confessed to Victoria that he could hardly hold a pen. He was in fact suffering from typhoid fever. Victoria herself hardly realised just how ill he was until the very end. Then, as they held hands, she describes that worst moment in her life:

> Two or three long but perfectly gentle breaths were drawn, the hand clasping mine, & (oh! it turns me sick to write it) *all all* was over . . .
> I stood up, kissing his dear heavenly forehead & called out in a bitter agonising cry 'O! my dear Darling!' & then dropped on my knees in mute, distracted despair, unable to utter a word or shed a tear!

She wrote to her uncle Leopold: 'My life as a *happy* one is ended! The world has gone for *me*. . . . *His* wishes, *his* plans . . . about everything, his views about *every* thing are to be *my laws*! And no human *power* will make me swerve from what *he* decided and wished.'

1878
DEATH OF VICTORIA'S DAUGHTER

Seventeen years to the day after Albert's death, Victoria suffered another painful bereavement as her second daughter Alice, Grand Duchess of Hesse, died of diphtheria, aged thirty-four. Alice was the third child of Victoria and Albert, and the first to die. This date, therefore, December 14, became a day of double mourning for the royal household.

1895
BIRTH OF THE FUTURE GEORGE VI

Despite Victoria's feeling that this date was highly inappropriate, her great-grandson, the future George VI, was born at York Cottage, Sandringham, on this day.

She finally brought herself to make the comment that the new baby's birth had 'broken the spell of this most unholy date'.

Also on this day:
1541 Katherine Howard, fifth wife of King Henry VIII, aged about twenty-one, was arrested on the charge of adultery.

DECEMBER 15 1785
SECRET MARRIAGE OF PRINNY AND MARIA FITZHERBERT

Maria Fitzherbert had no desire whatever to become Prinny's mistress, but the more she said 'no', the more he wept and cursed and howled. The prince's frantic demands at last became so embarrassing that Maria, in November 1784, decided to leave the country and live abroad. When he heard of this, Prinny almost killed himself by drinking three pints of brandy.

Just as Maria was about to leave England, he sent word to her that he had stabbed himself, and only her presence would save his life. So, although she half-suspected some sort of trickery, Maria allowed herself to be taken to Carlton House. Here she found Prinny with an apparent wound in his side, blood oozing everywhere. Maria almost fainted. A garbled account was given that the prince had tried to shoot himself but had missed, whereupon he had grabbed a carving-knife and had plunged it into his side. The probable truth of the matter was that Prinny had had himself 'bled' and had spread a sticky mess over his shirt. In the circumstances, what could Maria do but agree to marry him?

However, she was still reluctant to marry, and did indeed leave the country, not returning until December the following year. Honouring this somewhat enforced betrothal, Maria finally gave in. Prinny found a young curate, the Revd Robert Burt, who was prepared to marry them for £500 down and the promise of future preferment.

With Maria's uncle and brother as witnesses, the pair were married in her house in Park Street, Mayfair, at about six o'clock in the evening on this day in 1785.

Also on this day:
1810   The Prime Minister, Spencer Percival, appointed a special committee of peers to inquire into the mental state of King George III.
1899   Queen Victoria, fulfilling the last public duty of her reign, opened the Royal Convalescent Home.

DECEMBER 16   1653
OLIVER CROMWELL IS INSTALLED AS LORD PROTECTOR

The solemn installation of Oliver Cromwell as Lord Protector was virtually a coronation, although of course he was not crowned nor anointed.

The ceremony was held in Westminster Hall. A procession of the Lord Mayor, sheriffs and aldermen accompanied Cromwell as he rode in state, using the king's state coach of crimson and gold, drawn by six white horses.

Dressed in purple velvet, edged and lined with ermine, Cromwell was led to the Coronation chair, which had been removed from Westminster Abbey for the occasion; in front of this was a table upon which had been placed a Bible, a sword and a sceptre. Then, sitting alone, he swore to rule 'upon such a basis and foundation as by the blessing of God might be lasting, secure property, and answer those great ends of religion and liberty so long contended for'.

A flourish of trumpets proclaimed that Cromwell had taken the oath and another fanfare outside Westminster Hall signified the same to the huge crowds thronging the streets. Afterwards there was no banquet. Instead, people were invited to the Banqueting Hall to hear an hour-long sermon delivered by Nicholas Lockwood, Cromwell's chaplain.

The French ambassador wrote that Cromwell had 'all the state and dignity of a sovereign, no difference, the same bowing and scraping, the same Ambassadors, the same decorations, the same trumpeting and magnificence – *comme s'il était roi*'.

However, a curious change which Cromwell did make was to alter the uniform of the Yeomen of the Guard from scarlet and gold to grey trimmed with silver. People complained that it was a dull colour.

Also on this day:

1431 Coronation of King Henry VI, aged ten, as King of France, in St Denis, Paris. (See OCTOBER 13 and NOVEMBER 6.)

1485 Birth of Catherine of Aragon, daughter of King Ferdinand II and Queen Isabella of Spain, future first wife of King Henry VIII.

DECEMBER 17   1290
BURIAL OF ELEANOR OF CASTILE

On this day Eleanor was buried in Westminster Abbey after her long journey south from Harby in Nottinghamshire. Her memorials, the 'Eleanor Crosses' are famous, but her gilt bronze effigy in Westminster Abbey is also well worth looking at: it is one of the finest in the abbey.

An odd rhyming epitaph, an English version of a former Latin inscription, used to hang near her tomb. Traditionally, this translation was made by Thomas Skelton in the reign of Henry VIII. Eleanor, the much-loved queen of Edward I, was thus described:

Queen Eleanora is here interred, a royal virtuous dame
Sister unto the Spanish king, of ancient blood and fame;
King Edward's wife, first of that name, and Prince of Wales by right,
Whose father Henry, just the third, was sure an English wight.
He craved her wife unto his son; the prince himself did goe
On that embassage luckily, himself with many moe,
This knot of linked marriage the king Alphonso liked
And with his sister and this prince the marriage up was striked.
A dowry rich and royal was, for such a prince most meet,
For Ponthieu was the marriage gift, a dowry rich and great;
A woman both in counsel wise, religious, fruitful, meek,
Who did increase her husband's friends, and 'larged his honour eke.

LEARN TO DIE!

DECEMBER 18 1688
JAMES II MAKES A SECOND ATTEMPT TO ESCAPE FROM ENGLAND

James had already made one unsuccessful attempt to get away, but unfortunately for him he had been waylaid by ruffians and held prisoner in Faversham. After a confused few days he had returned to Whitehall, and now, on December 18, he was ready to make a second bid to escape to join his wife in France (see DECEMBER 9).

The day was wet and stormy as James boarded the royal barge at Whitehall. Rain teemed down on the crowds who had gathered to watch him go, but the king had spent so long in embarking that the tide was lost, and he had to sit in the barge getting soaked for another hour before the signal was finally given for the rowers to move off.

In mid-December darkness came early, and he did not arrive at Gravesend till seven o'clock in the evening, and he simply had to spend the night there, before continuing on his way to Rochester. Some advisers were still urging him to raise an army and meet William's troops head-on, but James, rather sensibly, argued that though it might be done, it would cause a civil war, and he 'would not do so much mischief to the English nation, which he loved'.

Over and over he kept repeating 'God help me, whom can I trust? My own children have forsaken me.' It was a miserable day.

DECEMBER 19 1648
CHARLES I ARRIVES IN WINCHESTER ON HIS WAY TO HIS TRIAL

During the civil war, Winchester had been torn by divided loyalties. Cromwell himself had fired his cannon on the castle in 1645 in order to bring the city under parliamentarian authority. Even today, a housing area to the west of Winchester retains the name 'Oliver's Battery'. However, royal supporters still existed in Winchester when King Charles was brought here in December 1648 on his way from Hurst Castle to London (see DECEMBER 1).

Memories were still vivid of that time when Charles and Henrietta Maria had visited the city on their progress ten years before, in 1635, when they had been received with all the pomp and ceremony due to them. Now, in very different circumstances, the king was again arriving at the ancient capital of England, and it was felt by many that he should be given at least some degree of civic welcome.

So, as Charles arrived at the Westgate under parliamentarian escort, the Mayor of Winchester received him with courtesy and solemnly presented him with the keys of the city according to tradition. Immediately the poor mayor was rewarded for his loyalty by being beaten up by the Cromwellian soldiers.

Also on this day:
1154 Coronation of King Henry II, aged twenty-one, in Westminster Abbey.

DECEMBER 20   1192
KING RICHARD LIONHEART IS CAPTURED BY DUKE LEOPOLD OF AUSTRIA

Romantic legend tells how Richard, travelling back overland through Europe from the Holy Land, was hoping to disguise his true identity by acting as a kitchen turn-spit. Rather foolishly, he wore a fabulously valuable ring on his hand, and of course everyone drew the right conclusion as to who he was.

On this day Leopold of Austria captured the king, and quickly sent him to a good strong castle overlooking the Danube. Tourists travelling by boat along the Danube to Vienna can still see the remains of Durnstein Castle, and remember how Blondel, the king's favourite minstrel, came to sing beneath its windows. According to tradition Richard heard the first lines of the song which he and Blondel had composed together, and revealed his whereabouts by bursting into song himself.

No child is taught these stories nowadays. But at least they should know that Richard was indeed captured, and was released only after an enormous ransom had been collected in England. Richard was finally set free on February 4 1194.

On Richard's release, the King of France thoughtfully sent word to John, who was busy taking control of things behind Richard's back, with the warning: 'Look to yourself: the devil is loose!'

Also on this day:
1075 Burial of Edith, widow of King Edward the Confessor, in Westminster Abbey.

DECEMBER 21   1327
EMBALMED, EDWARD II IS BURIED AT GLOUCESTER

The homosexual Edward II was cruelly murdered in Berkeley Castle (see SEPTEMBER 21) after abdicating on January 20 1327 at Kenilworth, Warwickshire. On this day, just before Christmas, his embalmed body was buried in St Peter's Abbey, Gloucester (now the cathedral). Whatever his son and successor, Edward III, privately thought about his father, he was at least determined to give him a splendid funeral and a noble tomb.

The hearse, painted with the golden leopards of England, was accompanied by his widow, Queen Isabella, his fifteen-year-old son Edward III, and many of the lords and officers of the court. Special timber barriers had been sent up specially from London to restrain the expected crowds. After the ceremony King Edward III ordered a beautiful canopy to be built over his father's tomb, and he had an alabaster effigy made, to honour his saintly memory.

The royal burial was a godsend for the monks of Gloucester, for they had been deeply in debt and their abbey had suffered fire after fire, and everywhere there were cracks appearing in the masonry. Now, with the sacred body of the king buried in the centre of their abbey, they were soon welcoming thousands of pilgrims who came to venerate the murdered Edward II as a martyr and offer gifts at his shrine.

Edward III, Richard II and Henry V all came to Gloucester as pilgrims to pray at Edward's tomb.

DECEMBER 22   1715
'JAMES III' ARRIVES IN SCOTLAND TO SEIZE THE THRONE FROM GEORGE I

James Stuart, the 'warming-pan baby' who had been bundled out of Whitehall in a pile of laundry by his mother in 1688, landed today at Peterhead, just north of Aberdeen on the east coast of Scotland. He hoped his Jacobite supporters would rally to his cause.

History knows him as the 'Old Pretender', which perhaps gives him a slightly antiquated image. In actual fact he was aged just thirteen when his father, the exiled James II, died at Saint-Germain-en-Laye, near Versailles, in

1701. As a proud and ambitious youngster, he must have been excited when the French King Louis XIV had proclaimed him 'James III'.

Growing up with royal ambitions, he had already tried once before, in 1708, aged twenty, to land in Scotland, but he had caught measles at the crucial moment (see MARCH 14).

Now a more mature twenty-seven, he was trying his luck once more. But everything seemed against him. He disguised himself as an ordinary sailor and landed at Peterhead, but he was so seasick and ill that he had to be carried ashore. Worse still, he had no army, no guns, and no money: he had lost virtually everything in a shipwreck. Unfortunately, the support he had hoped for from Louis XIV failed to materialise: the old French monarch had died just four months before.

James simply could not get a proper army together and was forced to go back to France. Even here, fortune failed him, as the French refused to grant him any further asylum. He went on to Rome, where he continued to call himself James III until his death in 1766.

Oddly enough, if this had been a genuine reign, it would have been the longest in English history – sixty-four years.

Also on this day:

1135 King Stephen, aged about thirty-eight, seized the throne in defiance of King Henry I's will that he should be succeeded by his daughter, the Empress Matilda.

DECEMBER 23   1861
VICTORIA CANNOT BRING HERSELF TO GO TO ALBERT'S FUNERAL

The days following the Prince Consort's death were terrible. An old servant, Mrs Macdonald, described it: 'It was an awful time – an awful time. I shall never forget it. After the Prince was dead, the Queen ran through the ante-room where I was waiting. She seemed wild. She went straight up to the nursery and took Baby Beatrice out of bed, but she did not wake her. That's so like the Queen. Orders were given at once for the removal of the Court to Osborne. All the servants were sent off in haste. It was thought necessary to get the Queen away as soon as possible. It seemed as though her grief would kill her. She did not cry – and they said that when she once got into the Prince's room no one seemed able to persuade her to leave it. When the Queen did cry she cried for days. It was heart-breaking to hear her.'

Nine days after his death, Albert was buried in the royal vault at St George's Chapel, Windsor. But Victoria was already miles away: she had fled to Osborne House, where she could mourn him in solitude. Bertie, the Prince of Wales, represented his mother at his father's funeral. Crowds filled the streets of Windsor as soldiers of the Grenadier Guards lined the route leading from Windsor Castle, where he had died, to St George's.

Before retreating to Osborne, Victoria went to Frogmore, to choose a spot for the building of a special mausoleum where she and Albert would eventually lie together (see MARCH 15).

Also on this day:
1688 King James II finally left England for exile in France. He departed from Rochester.

DECEMBER 24   1167
THE FUTURE KING JOHN IS BORN IN OXFORD

It is hard to imagine Oxford without its university, but when Eleanor of Aquitaine gave birth to her tenth (and last) baby here on this day in 1167, the university was still far into the future. The earliest foundation, University College, was founded by William of Durham in 1249 (though enthusiasts celebrated its thousandth anniversary in 1872, claiming that it had been founded earlier, by King Alfred).

But although there was no university, there was a royal residence, known as Beaumont Palace, built by Henry I in about 1132. Although there is no trace of it today, it was used as a royal palace for about 150 years and is still remembered by the fact that Eleanor gave birth to two future kings here: Richard I, on September 8 1157, and King John, on Christmas Eve, 1167.

Today the memory of this palace lingers on in the name Beaumont Street, where the Ashmolean Museum stands.

DECEMBER 25   1066
WILLIAM THE CONQUEROR IS CROWNED

The year 1066 was a 'year of three kings' – that is, a year during which three kings successively sat on the throne. In 1066 Edward the Confessor, Harold II and now William the Conqueror each claimed royal authority over the land.

William had fought his way to victory at Hastings in October, but now, before the year was out, he was determined to take what he knew was his by right – the crown of England. He had been promised it by his uncle, Edward the Confessor, and in any case he claimed that he had blood right to the throne through Emma, daughter of Duke Richard I of Normandy and mother of Edward the Confessor.

Westminster Abbey, built by Edward the Confessor, was less than a year old, having been consecrated on December 28 1065, but this was already its second coronation. The actual ceremony almost turned into a riot. When those present in the abbey were asked to shout out their acclamation to acknowledge William as their rightful king, the noise they made was interpreted by the guards outside as being the beginnings of a rebellion. They promptly set fire to all the surrounding houses. Panic ensued, and some of the congregation, not knowing what was happening, fled into the neighbouring fields.

However, order was restored, and Duke William of Normandy finished the day as William I of England.

1932
KING GEORGE V MAKES THE FIRST CHRISTMAS BROADCAST

It is difficult for people today to imagine what a solemn and moving moment it was when George V, with his deep and slightly guttural voice, made the first royal Christmas broadcast today in 1932.

Radio was still in its infancy, but those who had a 'wireless set' sat with rapt attention as the king spoke from a specially arranged room in Sandringham. The table he used was covered with a thick cloth, to muffle any sounds he might make with rustling paper.

'I speak now from my home and from my heart to you all,' he said, '. . . to men and women so cut off by the snows, the desert, or the sea, that only voices out of the air can reach them.'

The words he spoke had been written by Rudyard Kipling.

Also on this day:

1141 King Stephen was recrowned in Canterbury Cathedral, after having been captured and temporarily deposed by the Empress Matilda earlier this year.

1950 The Coronation Stone was stolen from Westminster Abbey by Glasgow students.

DECEMBER 26   1292
THIRTEEN COMPETITORS FOR THE THRONE OF SCOTLAND

It seems an odd way to find a monarch, but as the throne of Scotland had been vacant for two years, King Edward I of England decided that he would choose the next. He had hoped to marry his son Edward to Alexander III's four-year-old daughter Margaret, but she had died from seasickness in Orkney on the voyage from Norway.

Thirteen candidates had presented themselves for the job of King of Scotland. Obviously the first thing Edward had to do was to make sure that in every case the winner would acknowledge Edward as overlord of Scotland. Then, having made quite clear to everybody that he was the ultimate boss, he announced his decision at Berwick Castle on December 17: it was to be John Balliol, great-grandson of David I.

John duly had himself crowned on the ancient 'Stone of Destiny' at Scone – the last Scottish monarch to use the stone for his coronation. Then, on December 26, King John, as Balliol had now become, dutifully came to Newcastle to pay homage to Edward I of England. His subservience did not last long, however, and John Balliol had to learn the hard way that the 'Hammer of the Scots' was not to be trifled with. Ex-King John spent time imprisoned in the Tower of London before dying in exile in Castle Galliard, Normandy.

Also on this day:
1135   King Stephen, aged about thirty-eight, was crowned in Westminster Abbey.

DECEMBER 27   1591
KING JAMES VI OF SCOTLAND ESCAPES MURDER

James VI of Scotland, and future James I of England, almost met his Maker on this day when he was roused from his bedchamber in his palace of Holyrood by a sudden commotion. When he opened his door, he found the evil Wizard Earl of Bothwell kneeling in front of him with a naked sword in his hand. Bothwell had already been imprisoned earlier in the year in Edinburgh Castle on charges of witchcraft against the king, and he was supposedly the leader of a coven of witches. Unfortunately for James, he had escaped, and was now seeking his revenge.

Poor James shouted 'Treason!', thinking his last moment had come. Then he faced the satanic Bothwell and told him he would prefer death to shame and captivity. Bothwell's bluff was called and he handed his sword over to James, daring him to strike.

Not surprisingly, after this incident James made it a habit to wear padded clothes as a precaution against sudden attacks.

DECEMBER 28 1665
CHARLES II FATHERS YET ANOTHER BASTARD

This had been the year of the great plague, with piles of corpses lying in the streets of London. Cries of 'Bring out your dead' echoed throughout the capital. Although Charles stayed in Whitehall longer perhaps than was prudent, eventually he decided to move his court to cities at a safe distance. He spent the months from October 1665 to January 1666 in Oxford – always a loyal haven for royalists.

Charles's long-term mistress Barbara Villiers, whom he created Countess of Castlemaine and Duchess of Cleveland, was staying at Merton College at this time, and caused much scandal on December 28 by giving birth to yet another baby boy. It was the third son she had produced for Charles.

The Dictionary of National Biography calls Lady Castlemaine 'a ravenous woman'. Charles gave her the most beautiful royal building in England, Nonsuch Palace, near Ewell in Surrey. It is to her everlasting shame that she promptly pulled it down and sold all the materials. Nothing remains.

Also on this day:
1065 Queen Edith, wife of King Edward the Confessor, attended the consecration of Westminster Abbey. King Edward was too ill to be present.
1694 Death of Queen Mary II, aged thirty-two, from smallpox, in Kensington Palace, London. She was buried in Westminster Abbey.

DECEMBER 29 1170
MURDER IN THE CATHEDRAL

Probably the most dramatic murder in English history took place on this day. Four knights – William de Tracy, Reginald Fitzurse, Hugh de Morville and Richard Brito – earned themselves lasting infamy by killing Archbishop

Thomas Becket in his own cathedral, believing that they were dutifully carrying out the orders of their master, King Henry II.

Their deed shocked Europe and shattered the king, and almost overnight Becket became the centre of a cult that lasted until the final destruction of his shrine by Henry VIII.

Arthur Stanley, the famous nineteenth-century Dean of Canterbury, wrote a blow-by-blow account of the murder, which can hardly be equalled in its detail. Here is part of his story, telling how Becket was protected by a monk named Grim:

Tracy . . . sprang forward, and struck a more decided blow. Grim, who up to this moment had his arm round Becket, threw it up, wrapped in a cloak, to intercept the blade, Becket exclaiming, 'Spare this defence.' The sword lighted on the arm on the monk, which fell wounded or broken; and he fled disabled to the nearest altar, probably that of St Benedict within the chapel.

The spent force of the stroke descended on Becket's head, brazed the crown, and finally rested on his left shoulder, cutting through the clothes and skin. The next blow, whether struck by Tracy or Fitzurse, was only with the flat of the sword, and again on the bleeding head, which Becket drew back as if stunned, and then raised his clasped hands above it. The blood from the first blow was trickling down his face in a thin streak; he wiped it with his arm, and when he saw the stain, he said – 'Into thy hands, O Lord, I commend my spirit.'

At the third blow, which was also from Tracy, he sank on his knees – his arms falling – but his hands still joined as if in prayer. With his face turned towards the altar of St Benedict, he murmured in a low voice, which might just have been caught by the wounded Grim, who was crouching close by, and who alone reports the words – 'For the name of Jesus, and the defence of the Church, I am willing to die.'

Without moving hand or foot, he fell flat on his face as he spoke, in front of the corner wall of the chapel, and with such dignity that his mantle, which extended from head to foot, was not disarranged. In this posture he received from Richard the Breton a tremendous blow, accompanied with the exclamation (in allusion to a quarrel of Becket with Prince William), 'Take this for love of my lord William, brother of the King.' The stroke was aimed with such violence that the scalp or crown of the head – which, it was remarked, was of unusual size – was severed from the skull, and the sword snapt in two on the marble pavement.

. . . Hugh of Horsea, the subdeacon who had joined them as they entered the church, taunted by the others with having taken no share in the deed, planted his foot on the neck of the corpse, thrust his sword into the ghastly wound, and scattered the brains over the pavements – 'Let us go, let us go,' he said in conclusion. 'The traitor is dead; he will rise no more.'

This was the final act. One only of the four knights had struck no blow. Hugh de Morville throughout retained the gentler disposition for which he was distinguished, and contented himself with holding back at the entrance of the transept the crowds who were pouring in through the nave.

Also this day:

1497 Sheen Palace was destroyed by fire. This palace had been partially demolished on the orders of Richard II after the death of his wife, Anne of Bohemia. However, it was rebuilt on the orders of Henry V. After this fire in 1497, King Henry VII rebuilt it again, and called it Richmond Palace.

DECEMBER 30   1745
THE DUKE OF CUMBERLAND FORCES THE JACOBITES IN CARLISLE TO SURRENDER

Leaving Derby, Bonnie Prince Charlie marched his troops through Carlisle, and insisted, against military advice, that a small garrison should be left there, waiting for his expected triumphant return. Over four hundred men were left behind, mostly Highlanders from the northern parts of Scotland.

On December 30, almost immediately after the prince had gone on his way to Scotland, George II's son, the Duke of Cumberland, appeared on the scene with his army and captured all these Jacobite supporters. They were herded into a dungeon in Carlisle Castle, where they were virtually starved to death. Even today there is a damp patch on the wall which, it is said, the poor prisoners licked in their agony of thirst.

Eventually they were brought to trial. The lucky ones were hanged. Those less fortunate were chained together, marched 300 miles to London, and then transported to America to work as slaves in the sugar plantations or tobacco fields.

But at least they avoided Butcher Cumberland's massacre at Culloden.

DECEMBER 31   1720
BIRTH OF 'BONNIE PRINCE CHARLIE'

On this last day of the year – Hogmanay, in fact – the Jacobite cause was given an enormous boost when the wife of the 'Old Pretender' gave birth to a son. The baby Stuart Prince was immediately christened with a mouthful of names: Charles Edward Louis John Casimir Silvester Maria. But for present-day tourists visiting the beautiful and melancholy places associated with him in Scotland, he is more readily recognised by the romantic name 'Bonnie Prince Charlie'. Historians know him as the 'Young Pretender', though his Jacobite supporters always referred to him as 'Charles III'.

His mother was a Polish princess, Maria Clementina Sobieska, and he was born in the old Palazzo Muti, in the square of the Holy Apostles in Rome – this was the place which the Pope had given to his father to use, when the French had refused to receive him back after the fiasco at Peterhead (see DECEMBER 22).

The birth was a moment of great rejoicing. Indeed a commemorative medal was struck with the inscription 'Charles, Prince of Wales, the Hope of Britain'. Little King Louis XV of France is said to have jumped for joy when he heard the news. After all, he was only ten at the time, and he must have been pleased to have a potential royal playmate.

However, sixty-eight years later, after a lifetime of disappointment, Charles Stuart returned to this same palace and died here on January 31 1788 in the arms of his illegitimate daughter Charlotte, born to his mistress Clementina Walkinshaw.

Also on this day:

1705   Death of Catherine of Braganza, widow of King Charles II, aged sixty-seven, in Portugal. She was buried in the church of Santa Maria de Belém, Lisbon.

MIDNIGHT 1999/2000
QUEEN ELIZABETH SINGS *AULD LANG SYNE* IN THE MILLENNIUM DOME AT GREENWICH

Defying police advice that it might be dangerous to take part in the celebrations, Queen Elizabeth II and Prince Philip, Duke of Edinburgh, went to the almost-finished Millennium Dome at Greenwich on this night to join the thousands of revellers who had gathered there to welcome in the twenty-first century.

Greenwich had witnessed many and varied royal occasions: the birth of Elizabeth I; the jealous rage of Henry VIII against Anne Boleyn; the arrival of George I and his German mistresses; Elizabeth II conferring knighthood upon Francis Chichester after his solo circumnavigation of the world. The opening of the Millennium Dome was to be the next royal moment of its history.

Queen Elizabeth did her duty and, linking hands with Prince Philip on one side and Tony Blair on the other, allowed the strains of *Auld Lang Syne* to echo around her. And then Elizabeth and Philip kissed. It was the first time in more than fifty years that they had permitted themselves such a public demonstration of affection.

***

Thirty-seven generations of English royalty had reigned since King Egbert of Wessex had been acknowledged as 'Bretwalda', or 'King of Britain' by the other Saxon rulers, almost twelve centuries before. But no one was in the mood to look to the past on that Millennium Night. It was the future that beckoned, with its brave new world of mobile phones, websites and digital wizardry.

What would a further thirty-seven generations bring? It's an intriguing speculation . . .

DATES OF SAXON AND DANISH KINGS BEFORE THE CONQUEST

MONARCH	REIGNED	DATE OF BIRTH	CROWNED	DATE OF DEATH	PLACE OF DEATH	BURIED
Egbert	802–839	c. 770/780		839		Winchester Cathedral
Ethelwulf	839–858	c. 800		858		Winchester Cathedral
Ethelbald	858–860	c. 834				Sherborne Abbey
Ethelbert	860–865	c. 836				Sherborne Abbey
Ethelred I	865–871	c. 840		871		Wimborne Minster Dorset
Alfred The Great	871–899	c. 849		26 Oct 899	Winchester	1 Winchester Old Minster 2 Hyde Abbey
Edward the Elder	899–924		8 Jun 900 at Kingston upon Thames	17 Jul 924	Farndon-on-Dee Cheshire	Winchester Cathedral
Athelstan	924–939	c. 895	4 Sept 925 at Kingston upon Thames	27 Oct 939	Malmesbury, Wilts	Malmesbury Abbey
Edmund I	939–946	921	900 at Kingston upon Thames	26 May 946	Pucklechurch, Gloucestershire	Glastonbury Abbey
Edred	946–955	923	16 Aug 946 at Kingston upon Thames	23 Nov 955	Frome, Somerset	Winchester Cathedral
Edwy	955–959	c. 940	Jan 956 at Kingston upon Thames	1 Oct 959	Gloucester	Winchester Cathedral
Edgar	959–975	943 or 944	11 May 973 in Bath Abbey	8 Jul 975		Glastonbury Abbey
Edward (Saint and Martyr)	975–978	c. 963	975 at Kingston upon Thames	18 Mar 978	Corfe Castle Dorset	1 Wareham 2 Shaftesbury 3 Brookwood
Ethelred II	978–1016	c. 968	14 Apr 979 at Kingston upon Thames	23 Apr 1016	London	Old St Paul's Cathedral

MONARCH	REIGNED	DATE OF BIRTH	CROWNED	DATE OF DEATH	PLACE OF DEATH	BURIED
Edmund II (Ironside)	1016 (seven months)	before 993		30 Nov 1016	Ross-on-Wye Hereford & Worcester	Glastonbury Abbey
Sweyn Forkbeard	1013–1014 (a few weeks only)			3 Feb 1014	Gainsborough Lincs	1 London 2 Denmark
Canute	1016–1035	c. 992	1018	12 Nov 1035	Shaftesbury	Winchester Cathedral
Harold I	1035–1040	1016		17 Mar 1040	Oxford	St Clement Dane's London
Hardecanute	1040–1042	1018 or 1019		8 Jun 1042	Lambeth, London	Winchester Cathedral
Edward the Confessor	1042–1066	c. 1003	3 Apr 1043 in Winchester Cathedral	5 Jan 1066	Westminster Palace	Westminster Abbey
Harold II	1066	c.1020	6 Jan 1066 in Westminster Abbey	14 Oct 1066	Senlac near Hastings	Waltham Abbey

DATES OF MONARCHS: WILLIAM THE CONQUEROR TO ELIZABETH II

MONARCH	REIGNED	DATE OF BIRTH	PLACE OF BIRTH	CROWNED	DATE OF DEATH	PLACE OF DEATH	BURIED
William I	1066–1087	1027/28	Falaise	25 Dec 1066	9 Sept 1087	Mantes	St Stephen's Abbey, Caen
William II	1087–1100	1058?	Normandy	26 Sept 1087	2 Aug 1100	New Forest, Hants	Winchester Cathedral
Henry I	1100–1135	1068	Selby, Yorks	5 Aug 1100	1 Dec 1135	near Rouen	Reading Abbey
Stephen	1135–1154	c.1097	Blois	26 Dec 1135	25 Oct 1154	Dover	Faversham Abbey
Matilda, 'Empress'	April to Nov 1141	Feb 1102	London	not crowned	10 Sept 1167	near Rouen	Fontevrault Abbey
Henry II	1154–1189	5 Mar 1133	Le Mans	19 Dec 1154	6 July 1189	Chinon	Fontevrault Abbey
Richard I	1189–1199	8 Sept 1157	Oxford	3 Sept 1189	6 Apr 1199	Chalus	Fontevrault Abbey
John	1199–1216	24 Dec 1167	Oxford	27 May 1199	18 Dec 1216	Newark	Worcester Cathedral
Henry III	1216–1272	1 Oct 1207	Winchester	28 Oct 1216 & 17 May 1220	16 Nov 1272	Westminster Palace	Westminster Abbey
Edward I	1272–1307	17 Jun 1239	Westminster Palace	18 Aug 1274	7 July 1307	Burgh-by-Sands near Carlisle	Westminster Abbey
Edward II	1307–1327	25 Apr 1284	Caernarvon Castle	25 Feb 1308	21 Sept 1327	Berkeley Castle	Gloucester Cathedral
Edward III	1327–1377	13 Nov 1312	Windsor Castle	29 Jan 1327	21 Jun 1377	Sheen Palace Surrey	Westminster Abbey
Richard II	1377–1399	6 Jan 1367	Bordeaux	16 July 1377	14 Feb 1400	Pontefract Castle	Westminster Abbey
Henry IV	1399–1413	April 1366	Bolingbroke Castle, Lincs	13 Oct 1399	20 Mar 1413	Westminster Palace	Canterbury Cathedral
Henry V	1413–1422	9 Aug or 16 Sept 1387	Monmouth	9 Apr 1413	31 Aug 1422	Château de Vincennes	Westminster Abbey
Henry VI	1422–1461 & 1470–1471	6 Dec 1421	Windsor Castle	6 Nov 1429 & 16 Dec 1431 & 13 Oct 1470	21 May 1471	Tower of London	St George's Chapel Windsor
Edward IV	1461–1483	28 Apr 1442	Rouen	28 Jun 1461	9 Apr 1483	Westminster Palace	St George's Windsor
Edward V	9 Apr–25 Jun 1483	2 Nov 1470	Abbot's House Westminster	not crowned	? Sept 1483	Tower of London	Possibly in Westminster Abbey
Richard III	1483–1485	2 Oct 1452	Fotheringhay Castle	6 July 1483	22 Aug 1485	Bosworth Field	Leicester (now lost)

MONARCH	REIGNED	DATE OF BIRTH	PLACE OF BIRTH	CROWNED	DATE OF DEATH	PLACE OF DEATH	BURIED
Henry VII	1485–1509	28 Jan 1457	Pembroke Castle	30 Oct 1485	21 Apr 1509	Richmond Palace	Westminster Abbey
Henry VIII	1509–1547	28 Jun 1491	Greenwich Palace	24 Jun 1509	28 Jan 1547	St James's Palace	St George's Windsor
Edward VI	1547–1553	12 Oct 1537	Hampton Court Palace	19 Feb 1547	6 Jul 1553	Greenwich Palace	Westminster Abbey
Lady Jane Grey	10 Jul–19 Jul 1553	?Sept 1537	Bradgate Park Leicester	not crowned	12 Feb 1554	Tower of London	Chapel of St Peter ad Vincula Tower
Mary I	1553–1558	8 Feb 1516	Greenwich Palace	1 Oct 1553	17 Nov 1558	St James's Palace	Westminster Abbey
Elizabeth I	1558–1603	7 Sept 1533	Greenwich Palace	15 Jan 1559	24 Mar 1603	Richmond Palace	Westminster Abbey
James I	1603–1625	19 Jun 1566	Edinburgh Castle	25 Jul 1603	27 Mar 1625	Theobalds Park, Herts	Westminster Abbey
Charles I	1625–1649	19 Nov 1600	Dunfermline Palace	2 Feb 1626	30 Jan 1649	Whitehall, London	St George's Windsor
INTERREGNUM							
Oliver Cromwell	1653–1658	25 Apr 1599	Huntingdon	Installed as Lord Protector 16 Dec 1653	3 Sept 1658	Whitehall Palace	Westminster Abbey (now lost)
Richard Cromwell	1658–1659	1626	Huntingdon	Installed as Lord Protector II	12 Jul 1712	Cheshunt, Herts	Hursley, Hants
MONARCHY RESTORED							
Charles II	1660–1685	29 May 1630	St James's Palace	23 Apr 1661	6 Feb 1685	Whitehall Palace	Westminster Abbey
James II	1685–1688	14 Oct 1633	St James's Palace	23 Apr 1685	6 Sept 1701	St Germain-en-Laye	St Germain-en-Laye, then Paris
William III	1689–1702	4 Nov 1650	The Hague	11 Apr 1689	8 Mar 1702	Kensington Palace	Westminster Abbey
Mary II	1689–1694	30 Apr 1662	St James's Palace	11 Apr 1689	28 Dec 1694	Kensington Palace	Westminster Abbey
Anne	1702–1714	6 Feb 1665	St James's Palace	23 Apr 1702	1 Aug 1714	Kensington Palace	Westminster Abbey

MONARCH	REIGNED	DATE OF BIRTH	PLACE OF BIRTH	CROWNED	DATE OF DEATH	PLACE OF DEATH	BURIED
George I	1714–1727	28 May 1660	Osnabrück, Hanover	20 Oct 1714	11 June 1727	Osnabrück	Herrenhausen Palace
George II	1727–1760	30 Oct 1683	Herrenhausen Palace, Hanover	11 Oct 1727	25 Oct 1760	Westminster Palace	Westminster Abbey
George III	1760–1820	4 Jun 1738	Norfolk House, St James's Square	22 Sept 1761	29 Jan 1820	Windsor Castle	St George's, Windsor
George IV	1820–1830	12 Aug 1762	St James's Palace	19 July 1821	26 Jun 1830	Windsor Castle	St George's, Windsor
William IV	1830–1837	21 Aug 1765	Buckingham Palace	8 Sept 1831	20 Jun 1837	Windsor Castle	St George's, Windsor
Victoria	1837–1901	24 May 1819	Kensington Palace	28 Jun 1838	22 Jan 1901	Osborne House	Frogmore, Windsor
Edward VII	1901–1910	9 Nov 1841	Buckingham Palace	9 Aug 1902	6 May 1910	Buckingham Palace	St George's, Windsor
George V	1910–1936	3 Jun 1865	Marlborough House, London	22 Jun 1911	20 Jan 1936	Sandringham House	St George's, Windsor
Edward VIII	20 Jan 1936 to 10 Dec 1936	23 Jun 1894	White Lodge Richmond Park	not crowned	28 May 1972	Paris	Frogmore House
George VI	1936–1952	14 Dec 1895	York House Sandringham	12 May 1937	6 Feb 1952	Sandringham House	St George's Windsor
Elizabeth II	1952–	21 Apr 1926	17 Bruton Street London	2 Jun 1953			

DATES OF QUEENS AND CONSORTS FROM WILLIAM THE CONQUEROR TO ELIZABETH II

MONARCH	CONSORT	BIRTH OF CONSORT	DEATH OF CONSORT	BURIED	DATE AND PLACE OF MARRIAGE	CONSORT'S AGE AT MARRIAGE
William I	Matilda of Flanders	c. 1032	9 Sept 1083	Abbaye aux Dames, Caen	c. 1053 Eu Cathedral Normandy	c. 18
William II	unmarried					
Henry I	1 Matilda of Scotland	1080	1 May 1118 Wesminster Palace	Westminster Abbey	11 Nov 1100 Westminster Abbey	20
	2 Adela of Louvain	c. 1103	c. 23 Mar 1151 Afflighem nunnery	Afflighem, Flanders	29 Jan 1121 Westminster Abbey	c. 18
Stephen	Matilda of Boulogne	c. 1103	3 May 1152 Heningham Castle, Essex	Faversham Abbey	1125	c. 22
Matilda	1 Emperor Henry V	1081	23 May 1125	Speyer, Germany	7 Jan 1114	12
	2 Geoffrey IV of Anjou	1113	7 Sept 1151	Le Mans Cathedral	2 Jun 1129	27
Henry II	Eleanor of Aquitaine	c. 1122	31 Mar 1204 France	Fontevrault Abbey	18 May 1152 Bordeaux Cathedral	c. 30
Richard I	Berengaria of Navarre	c. 1165	c. 1230	L'Epau Abbey near Le Mans	12 May 1191 Limassol, Cyprus	c. 26
John	Isabella of Angoulême	c. 1187	31 May 1246 Fontevrault	Fontevrault Abbey	26 Aug 1200 Angoulême	c. 13
Henry III	Eleanor of Provence	c. 1223	24 Jun 1291 Amesbury nunnery	Amesbury, Wilts	20 Jan 1236 Canterbury	c. 14
Edward I	1 Eleanor of Castile	c. 1244	28 Nov 1290 Harby, Notts	Westminster Abbey	October 1254 Las Huelgas monastery, Spain	c. 10

MONARCH	CONSORT	BIRTH OF CONSORT	DEATH OF CONSORT	BURIED	DATE AND PLACE OF MARRIAGE	CONSORT'S AGE AT MARRIAGE
	2 Marguerite of France	1282	14 Feb 1317 Marlborough Castle Savernake	Grey Friars Church London	10 Sept 1299 Canterbury	16
Edward II	Isabella of France	c. 1292	22 Aug 1358 Castle Rising Norfolk	Grey Friars Church London	25 Jan 1308 Boulogne	c. 16
Edward III	Philippa of Hainault	c. 1313	14 Aug 1369 Windsor Castle	Westminster Abbey	24 Jan 1328 York	c. 15
Richard II	1 Anne of Bohemia	1366	before 3 Jun 1394	Westminster Abbey	20 Jan 1382 St Stephen's Westminster	15
	2 Isabella of Valois	9 Nov 1389 The Louvre Palace, Paris	Sept 13 1409 Sheen Palace	Blois, then Church of the Célestines Paris	4 Nov 1396 St Nicholas Westminster	7
Henry IV	1 Mary de Bohun	c.1369	4 Jun or 4 Jul 1394	St Mary de Castro, Leicester	1380 or 1381 Rochford Essex	12
	2 Joan of Navarre	c.1370	9 July 1437 Havering-atte-Bower Essex	Canterbury Cathedral	7 Feb 1403 Winchester Cathedral	c. 32
Henry V	Katherine de Valois	27 Oct 1401 Hotel de St Pol Paris	3 Jan 1437 Bermondsey Abbey	Westminster Abbey	2 Jun 1420 St John's Church Troyes	18
Henry VI	Margaret of Anjou	23 Mar 1429 Pont-à-Mousson Château of Lorraine	25 Aug 1482 Château of Damprièrre	Angers Cathedral	23 Apr 1445 Tichfield Abbey, Hants	14
Edward IV	Elizabeth Woodville	c. 1437	8 Jun 1492 Bermondsey Abbey	St George's Chapel Windsor	1 May 1464 Grafton Church Northants	c. 27
Edward V	unmarried					
Richard III	Anne Neville	1456 Warwick Castle	16 Mar 1485 Westminster Palace	Westminster Abbey	12 Jul 1472 Westminster Abbey	16

MONARCH	CONSORT	BIRTH OF CONSORT	DEATH OF CONSORT	BURIED	DATE AND PLACE OF MARRIAGE	CONSORT'S AGE AT MARRIAGE
Henry VII	Elizabeth of York	11 Feb 1466 Westminster Palace	11 Feb 1503 Tower of London	Westminster Abbey	18 Jan 1486 Westminster Abbey	19
Henry VIII	1 Catherine of Aragon	16 Dec 1485 Alcala de Henares Spain	7 Jan 1536 Kimbolton Castle, Cambs.	Peterborough Cathedral	11 Jun 1509 Chapel of the Observant Friars	24
	2 Anne Boleyn	c. 1500	19 May 1536 Tower of London	Chapel of St Peter ad Vincula Tower of London	25 Jan 1533 Whitehall Palace	c. 32
	3 Jane Seymour	c.1507	24 Oct 1537 Hampton Court Palace	St George's Chapel Windsor	30 May 1536 Whitehall Palace	c. 29
	4 Anne of Cleves	22 Sept 1515	16 Jul 1557 Chelsea Manor	Westminster Abbey	6 Jan 1540 Greenwich	24
	5 Katherine Howard	c.1525	13 Feb 1542 Tower of London	Chapel of St Peter ad Vincula Tower of London	28 Jul 1540 Oatlands, Surrey	c. 15
	6 Catherine Parr	1512	5 Sept 1548 Sudeley Castle Glos.	Chapel at Sudeley Castle	12 Jul 1543 Hampton Court Palace	31
Edward VI	unmarried					
Jane Grey	Lord Guilford Dudley	1536	12 Feb 1553 Tower of London	Chapel of St Peter ad Vincula Tower of London	21 May 1553 Durham House, London	16
Mary I	Philip of Spain	1527	13 Sept 1598 El Escorial	El Escorial	25 Jul 1554 Winchester Cathedral	27
Elizabeth I	unmarried					
James I	Anne of Denmark	1574 Scanderburg	4 Mar 1619 Hampton Court	Westminster Abbey	20 Aug 1590 Oslo	14

MONARCH	CONSORT	BIRTH OF CONSORT	DEATH OF CONSORT	BURIED	DATE AND PLACE OF MARRIAGE	CONSORT'S AGE AT MARRIAGE
Charles I	Henrietta Maria	25 Nov 1609 The Louvre The Louvre	1670 Château de Colombe Paris near Paris	St Denis Paris	1 May 1625, by proxy in Notre Dame, Paris 13 Jun 1625 in person in Canterbury Cathedral	14
INTERREGNUM						
Oliver Cromwell	Elizabeth Cromwell (née Bourchier)	1598 London or Essex			22 Aug 1620 St Giles, Cripplegate London	22
Richard Cromwell	Dorothy Cromwell	1627	5 Jan 1675 Hursley, Hants	Hursley Parish Church		
MONARCHY RESTORED						
Charles II	Catherine of Braganza	Nov 25 1638 Palace of Villa Vicosa, Portugal	31 Dec 1705 Bemposta Palace Portugal	Royal monastery of Santa Maria de Belém, Portugal	21 May 1662 Portsmouth	23
James II	1 Anne Hyde	1637	31 Mar 1671	Westminster Abbey	3 Sept 1673 Worcester House The Strand, London	21
	2 Mary of Modena	5 Oct 1658 Este, Modena	7 May 1718 St Germain-en Laye	Convent of the Visitation of St Marie, Chaillot	30 Sept 1673 by proxy at Modena 21 Nov 1673 in person at Dover	14
William III	Mary II	30 Apr 1662 St James's Palace	28 Dec 1694 Kensington Palace	Westminster Abbey	4 Nov 1677 St James's Palace	15
Anne	Prince George of Denmark	1653	28 Oct 1708 Kensington Palace	Westminster Abbey	28 Jul 1683	30
George I	Sophia Dorothea of Celle (never considered to be queen)	1666	2 Nov 1726	Celle	21 Nov 1682 (divorced 1694)	16

MONARCH	CONSORT	BIRTH OF CONSORT	DEATH OF CONSORT	BURIED	DATE AND PLACE OF MARRIAGE	CONSORT'S AGE AT MARRIAGE
George II	Caroline of Ansbach	1683	20 Nov 1737 St James's Palace	Westminster Abbey	22 Aug 1705 Hanover	17
George III	Charlotte of Mecklenburg-Strelitz	1744	17 Nov 1818 Kew, Surrey	St George's Chapel	8 Sept 1761 St James's Palace	17
George IV	1 Mrs Maria Fitzherbert (married in secret and later annulled)	Jul 26 1756	1837		15 Dec 1785 Park St Mayfair	29
	2 Caroline of Brunswick	1768	7 Aug 1821 Hammersmith	Brunswick	8 Apr 1795	26
William IV	Adelaide of Saxe-Meiningen	1792	2 Dec 1849 Bentley Priory Middlesex	St George's Chapel Windsor	13 Jul 1818 Kew, Surrey	25
Victoria	Prince Albert of Saxe-Coburg-Gotha	1819 Schloss Rosenau, near Coburg	14 Dec 1861 Windsor Castle	Royal Mausoleum, Frogmore, Windsor	10 Feb 1840 St James's Palace	20
Edward VII	Princess Alexandra of Denmark	1844 Denmark	20 Nov 1925 Sandringham, Norfolk	St George's Chapel Windsor	10 Mar 1863 St George's Chapel Windsor	18
George V	Princess Mary of Teck	1867 Kensington Palace	24 Mar 1953 Marlborough House London	St George's Chapel Windsor	6 Jul 1893 St James's Palace	25
Edward VIII	Mrs Wallis Simpson	1896 USA	24 Apr 1986 Paris	Royal Burial Ground Frogmore, Windsor	3 June 1937 Château de Candé near Tours	40
George VI	Lady Elizabeth Bowes-Lyon	4 Aug 1900 St Paul's, Waldenbury, Herts.	30 March 2002 Royal Lodge, Windsor	St George's Chapel, Windsor	26 Apr 1923 Westminster Abbey	22
Elizabeth II	Prince Philip of Greece	10 Jun 1921 Corfu			20 Nov 1947 Westminster Abbey	26

Genealogical Chart of the English Monarchs

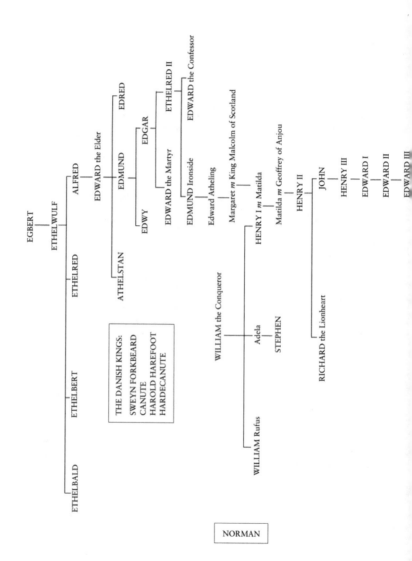

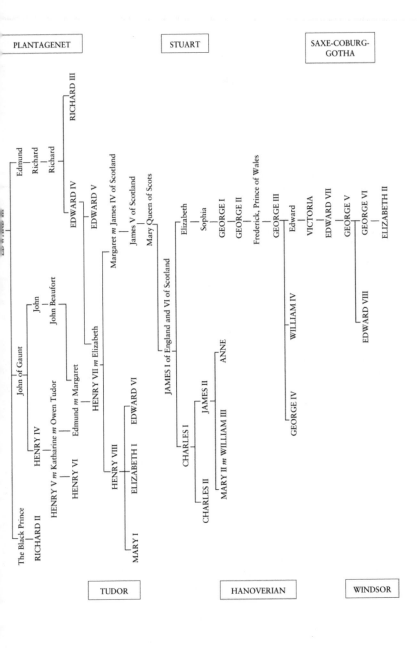

PLANTAGENET

STUART

SAXE-COBURG-GOTHA

TUDOR

HANOVERIAN

WINDSOR

SOURCES

❦ ❦

Ashdown, Dulcie M., *Princess of Wales*, John Murray, 1979

Bates, David, *William the Conqueror*, George Philip Ltd, 1989

Brendon, Piers and Phillip Whitehead, *The Windsors, A Dynasty Revealed*, Hodder Headline, 1994

Brewer, Clifford, TD, FRCS, *The Death of Kings*, Abson Books, London, 2000

Bryant, Arthur, *King Charles II*, Longmans, Green & Co., 1931

Bussby, Frederick, *Winchester Cathedral 1079–1979*, Paul Cave Publications Ltd, 1979

Chapman, Hester W., *Lady Jane Grey*, Pan Books, 1972

Cheetham, Erika, *The Final Prophecies of Nostradamus*, Futura Publications, 1990

Churchill, Winston S., *Marlborough*, Macmillan 1933–38

Compton, Piers, *Harold the King*, Robert Hale, 1961

Cumming, Alex A., *Sir Francis Drake & The Golden Hind*, Jarrold Publishing, 1987

Davey, R., *The Pageant of London*, Methuen, 1906

Dimbleby, Jonathan, *The Prince of Wales: A Biography*, Little, Brown & Co., 1994

Farmer, David Hugh, *The Oxford Dictionary of Saints*, Oxford University Press, 1978

Fisher, Graham and Heather, *Monarchy and the Royal Family*, Robert Hale, 1979

Forman, Joan, *Haunted Royal Homes*, Harrap Ltd, 1987

Fraser, Antonia, *Mary, Queen of Scots*, Weidenfeld & Nicolson, 1969

Fraser, Antonia, *The Six Wives of Henry VIII*, Weidenfeld & Nicolson, 1992

Green, David, *Blenheim*, William Collins & Co., 1974

Green, Margaret, *Winchester Cavalcade*, Winton Publications, 1965

Harris, Kenneth, *The Queen*, Weidenfeld & Nicolson, 1994

Heald, Henrietta (ed.), *Chronicle of Britain and Ireland*, Chronicle Communications Ltd 1992

Hole, Christina, *Witchcraft in England*, Batsford, 1977

Kenyon, J.P., *The Stuarts*, Fontana, 1966

Kinross, John, *Discovering Battlefields of England and Scotland*, Shire Publications, 1998

Lacey, Robert, *Majesty*, Hutchinson Publishing Group, 1977

Levine, E., *Oliver Cromwell*, Macdonald, 1966

Lindsay, Philip, *The Loves of Florizel*, Hutchinson, 1951

Mackie, J.D., *The Earlier Tudors*, 1485–1558, Oxford University Press, 1994

Mercer, Derrik (ed.), *Chronicle of the Royal Family*, Chronicle Communications Ltd, 1991

Middlemas, Keith, *The Life and Times of Edward VII*, Weidenfeld & Nicolson, 1972

Milton, Roger, *The English Ceremonial Book*, David & Charles, 1972

Moncreiffe of that Ilk, Sir Iain, *Royal Highness, Ancestry of the Royal Child*, Hamish Hamilton, 1982

Lindsay, Philip, *Crowned King of England*, Ivor Nicholson & Watson, 1937

Longford, Elizabeth (ed.), *The Oxford Book of Royal Anecdotes*, Oxford University Press, 1991

Palmer, Alan and Veronica, *Royal England*, Methuen, 1983

Plumb, J.H., *The First Four Georges*, Fontana, 1966

Potts, D.M. & Potts W.T.W., *Queen Victoria's Gene*, Alan Sutton, 1995

Rowse, A.L., *Windsor Castle in the History of the Nation*, Weidenfeld & Nicolson, 1974

Stanley, Arthur P., *Historical Memorials of Canterbury*, John Murray, 1854

Street, Sean, *Tales of Old Dorset*, Countryside Books, 1985

Strickland, Agnes, *Lives of the Queens of England*, G. Bell & Sons, 1911

Talbot, Godfrey, *The Country Life Book of Queen Elizabeth the Queen Mother*, Country Life Books, 1978

Tayler, Henrietta, *Bonnie Prince Charlie*, Thomas Nelson, 1945

Tisdall, E.E.P., *Queen Victoria's Private Life*, Jarrolds, 1961

Trench, Charles Chenevix, *The Western Rising*, Longmans, Green & Co. Ltd, 1969

Wedgwood, C.V., *The Trial of Charles I*, William Collins, 1964

Weinreb, Ben and Hibbert, Christopher (eds), *The London Encyclopaedia*, Macmillan, 1983

Weir, Alison, *Elizabeth the Queen*, Jonathan Cape, 1998

——, *Eleanor of Aquitaine, By the Wrath of God, Queen of England*, Jonathan Cape, London, 1999

——, *Britain's Royal Families: The Complete Genealogy*, Pimlico, 2002

Williams, Neville, *The Life and Times of Elizabeth I*, Weidenfeld & Nicolson, 1972

Windsor, HRH the Duke of, *A King's Story*, Cassell, 1951

INDEX

❦ ❧

INDEX

Browne, Christopher 264
Bruce, Lord 170
Bruce, Marjorie 285
Brunel, Isambard Kingdom 140
Buckingham, Duke of ('Steenie') 32, 247–8
Buckingham Palace
  George III 122, 200
  Queen Victoria 39, 53, 167–8, 264
  George IV 46, 51, 111, 218–19, 287
  Elizabeth II 182, 208, 267
Buckland Abbey, Devon 82
Burgh-by-Sands, near Carlisle 162
Burghley, Lord (William Cecil) 31, 60
Burke, Edmund 158
Burley, Simon 171
Burney, Fanny 161
Burt, the Revd Robert 291
Butler, R.A. ('Rab', former Home Secretary) 72

Caen, Normandy 144, 216, 259
Caernarvon Castle, Wales 99, 156, 168
Callaghan, James, former Prime Minister 82
Cambridge University 100
  Christ's College 26, 153
  King's College 17, 121, 159, 178, 284
  St John's College 26, 153
  Sidney Sussex College 72
Campbell, Archibald, Marquis of Argyll 1
Canterbury 128, 172, 217
Canterbury Cathedral 14, 135, 141, 190, 298 see also Becket, Archbishop Thomas
Canute, King (or Cnut) 6, 33, 57, 58, 65, 107, 136, 197, 221, 247, 266, 279
Cardiff, Wales 33
Carey, Sir Robert 73
Carisbrooke Castle, Isle of Wight 280
Carlisle 302
Carlos I, King of Portugal 284
Carlos, Major, companion of Charles II 213–14
Carlton House, London 29, 290
Carmarthen, Wales 76
Carnwath, Earl of 141

Caroline of Ansbach, queen of George II 55, 183, 202, 272
Caroline of Brunswick, queen of George IV 9, 30, 84–5, 118, 173–4, 183, 198–9, 262
Carteret, Margaret de 239
Castle Carey, Somerset 237
Castlemaine, Lady see Palmer, Barbara
Catherine of Aragon, first queen of Henry VIII 8–9, 41, 46–7, 49, 61, 69, 80, 123, 139, 148–9, 150, 153, 174, 233–4, 263, 270–1, 283, 292
Catherine of Braganza, queen of Charles II 115, 138, 238–9, 268, 303
Catherine of Valois, queen of Henry V 20, 25, 32, 50, 132, 210, 283–4
Caxton, William 26, 80, 154
Cecil, Robert 71
Cecil, William see Burghley, Lord
Cecily, daughter of William the Conqueror 144–5
Chaillot, monastery at 110
Châlus, France 83
Chamberlain, Joseph 52
Chamberlain, Neville 229
Chapuys, Eustace, Spanish Ambassador 129
Charing Cross, London 277–8
Charles I 31–2, 37, 74, 105, 132, 140, 143, 145, 244, 260, 262, 271, 275, 278
  civil war and execution 2–3, 4–5, 25, 28, 39, 61, 65, 108–9, 141, 157, 179, 201–2, 225, 226–7, 250, 280, 293–4
Charles II 1, 12, 34–5, 36, 37, 72, 74–5, 77, 96–8, 115, 127–8, 146, 160, 161, 169, 192, 210–11, 212, 213–14, 221, 227, 236–8, 246, 268, 281, 303
  mistresses of 32, 86, 139, 239, 266–7, 300
Charles V, Holy Roman Emperor and King of Spain 16, 177
Charles VI ('The Mad'), King of France 9, 132, 220, 260
Charles VII, King of France 269
Charles, Duke of Orleans, 2nd husband of Isabella of France 10
Charles, Prince of Wales 24, 35, 37, 85-6, 127, 128, 146, 147, 156, 165, 172, 182, 208, 221, 267–8, 281–2

322

INDEX

INDEX

INDEX